THE GREAT
GHOST
HUNTER

THE GREAT
GHOST
HUNTER

Elliott O'Donnell

Edited by

HARRY LUDLAM

foulsham

LONDON · NEW YORK · TORONTO · SYDNEY

foulsham

Yeovil Road, Slough, Berkshire SL1 4JH.

ISBN 0-572-01613-1
Copyright © Elliott O'Donnell. This compilation 1990.

Printed in England at St. Edmundsbury Press, Bury St. Edmunds.

CONTENTS

THE BRIDGE AT MIDNIGHT

The Royal Aquarium is a mere name in history books of London now, but in my youth it was still a very lively place, one where you could go in the afternoon or evening and always be sure of an interesting entertainment. There was always something on : a play, a pantomime, or a concert in the Imperial Theatre, and numerous sideshows in other parts of the building. Its demise, due to certain kill-joys, was deplored by thousands.

Basil N. Hill, an elderly actor whom I used to meet occasionally in the Old Lounge in Maiden Lane, once had a curious experience in the Royal Aquarium.

His story begins one night many years ago when, very down on his luck and pushed to the limits of endurance, he wandered on to the Thames Embankment with the grim thought of suicide uppermost in his mind. He was peering over the wall into the murky, moonlit water beneath, when someone touched him on the shoulder. It was a brother actor named Bert, who was equally down on his luck. He, too, had wandered on to the Embankment with the same dark thoughts in mind. Such was the extreme poverty and desperation of those years.

While they were morbidly thinking the matter over, wondering whether death by drowning was very painful and if the Powers on the Other Side—providing there was another side—would punish them for taking their own lives, a policeman who had been standing a little way off, watching them for some time, came up to them.

" Here's a tanner for you, boys," he said. " It's all I can afford, but better than the river." And he slipped a sixpence into Basil Hill's hand.

"How did you know we were thinking of jumping in?" Hill asked him.

"By your appearance," the constable replied. "Anyone like me, who is used to the Embankment, can always tell the real down and out. There are plenty of sham ones, but you two have the genuine desperate look, which usually means the river. Since I've been on this beat I've seen several suicides, and saved probably a dozen or more from jumping in. Get a bit of grub and something warm to drink with that money, and maybe your luck will turn in the morning."

Much touched by the policeman's kindness, both men promised to do as he suggested; though while on their way to a coffee stall to get some much needed food, they solemnly agreed to meet on Waterloo Bridge at midnight the next day—and if they had had no luck during the day, to jump into the river together. After devouring some sandwiches and coffee (sixpence went a long way then) they parted company, renewing their pledge to meet one another on the bridge in twenty-four hours' time. What remained of the night Hill spent under the Covent Garden arches.

He was wandering in the direction of Poverty Corner in the morning, when he ran into another actor friend, who happened to have just got a part with a touring company.

"They're still looking for someone to play a parson's part, Basil," he said, "and you're just the man for it. Come along to the rehearsal room at eleven sharp, and I'll introduce you—but get a shave and a tidy up first."

With the good nature that is so characteristic of actors who have been through it themselves, he lent Hill a shilling or two, and Hill, taking his advice, made himself look a little more presentable, and got the part. His friend offered him a bed, and he was having a merry time of it that evening, when he suddenly remembered his promise to Bert. Telling his friend he had an urgent appointment but would soon be back, he hurried as fast as he could to Waterloo Bridge.

When he arrived there it was a quarter-past twelve, and being a wet night the bridge was deserted. He waited there in the rain for some time, and then, concluding that something had prevented Bert from coming—perhaps he, too, had had a stroke of luck—he came away.

The next morning Hill went to the Royal Aquarium to meet another friend he had run into on his way to the rehearsal room and a job. Hill was walking about, waiting for this man, when to his surprise he suddenly saw Bert, standing in an entrance to one of the sideshows, looking fixedly at him. He walked towards Bert with the intention of asking how he came to be there and what had happened to him the previous night, and was within a few paces of him, when he suddenly and very mysteriously, disappeared.

A few minutes later Hill again saw Bert, this time in another part of the hall, and as before, Bert was gazing fixedly at him. Then, as their eyes met, Bert beckoned him. Determined he should not elude him again, Hill made for him at once, and was close to him, when again, to his utter amazement, Bert disappeared.

Much puzzled, Hill was wondering whether he was the victim of a hallucination or an illusion of some kind or another, when the friend he had come to meet finally arrived, and for the next hour or two he thought no more of the incident. But as he was leaving the building with his friend, Bert passed him in the street, and, turning round, again looked at him with the same strange fixed expression.

" Excuse me a minute," Hill said to his friend, " but I must speak to that fellow."

He hurried after Bert and had almost overtaken him, when for the third time, he disappeared. There was no crowd now with which he might possibly have mingled, nor any doorway through which he might have slipped, there was only the pavement, deserted on account of the heavy rain. Hill had seen him on the pavement one moment, and the next moment he had seen nothing. Bert had inexplicably and unquestionably vanished.

A feeling of intense eeriness now came over Basil Hill, and when he rejoined his friend he was shaking all over, so much so that the friend jokingly asked if he had seen a ghost. Hill replied huskily, " Yes, undoubtedly it was a ghost."

The next morning, with a nagging fear at the back of his mind, he went to a public library and scanned the papers. One of the first headlines that caught his eye was " Man's body found in the Thames ", and under it he read that the body of a man who had been seen to jump from Waterloo Bridge at midnight on Monday— it was at that hour and night he had arranged to meet Bert—had been found on the mud at low water, and subsequently identified as that of an out-of-work actor.

I shall never forget Basil Hill's eyes as he told me this story, for the ghastly incident left a very deep impression on him to the end of his days.

THE MUMMY OF AMEN-RA

MANY WEIRD stories have been told about Egyptian mummies, and the sudden deaths and disasters that have followed on the opening and desecration of their tombs. A well-known case is the series of misfortunes which attended the discovery of the great tomb of Tutankhamen, on which a curse had been placed by the priests of long ago. Many odd and mysterious accidents and deaths followed the opening of this royal resting place.

An earlier case of this nature, and the one which, for me, remains unsurpassed for its incredible ghostly aspects, concerns another of these Egyptian antiquities which found its way over to Britain and into the quiet precincts of the British Museum; and even there produced a further succession of alarming disturbances. This was the ghostly mummy of Amen-Ra. I sought evidence of some of the strange events and later spoke to some of the people who had been involved in this curious case. Some shortened accounts of it have appeared from time to time, though the complete story has never been told. It really all began long before the acquisition of the ancient relic, on an ordinary day in London in the 1880s.

In those late Victorian years many people, including the famous and even princes and other royalty, were being attracted to the consulting rooms of the noted palmist and mystic, Cheiro (Count Louis Hamon), whose readings proved uncannily accurate (in fact this brilliant man went on to predict in exact terms the deaths of Lord Kitchener, King Edward VII, and the evil monk Rasputin). On the day to which we refer, one of Cheiro's visitors happened to be a young man named Douglas Murray.

Cheiro had not the slightest idea as to his visitor's identity, but this was not uncommon as there were many "men about town" who came to consult him out of curiosity or for some mild amusement. Mr. Murray did indeed fall easily into this category for he then had no particular interest or pursuit in life, and like so many other wealthy men of the period went about "killing time" as pleasantly as possible.

Mr. Murray, approaching the palmist in a very lighthearted mood, sat opposite him and, putting his hands on the small table between them, said jokingly, "Which of my hands are you going to take?" For Cheiro, a professional man of much experience, and therefore well used to masking his emotions from his clients, what happened next was a very great shock. As he took his visitor's right hand in his own, an unaccountable feeling of dread and horror seemed to creep from it, and as quickly as he took the hand, he dropped it back on the cushion.

Mr. Murray laughed, and asked what was wrong, but Cheiro found himself unable to reply. "The hand," as he later described, "*seemed to speak to me*. It was not that I attempted to read it, there was no need for me to make such an effort. It was as if I was taken possession of by some occult force of which I cannot give any explanation. Without any regard to the effect my words might have, and with the feeling of listening to myself speaking without the power of preventing the words coming, I blurted out rapidly, 'I feel this right hand of yours will not be yours for long. A picture forms in my mind of a gun of some kind bursting and shattering it to pieces. This is followed by terrible suffering and finally the entire arm will have to be amputated,' and I added quickly, 'Your hand, sir, seems to be calling to me to try and save it from this impending disaster.'"

Mr. Murray laughed again, not a bit convinced, but Cheiro continued. "Your hand shows me another picture. It draws a number out of a lottery, the number gives you a prize that you do not want to have. Out of obstinacy and fatalism you take it, and from that moment on commences a series of misfortunes, beginning with the loss of your right arm."

The amused reply from his client was, "I've never won a thing in a lottery yet, and I don't believe I ever shall! But does this wonderful hand of mine tell you what this extraordinary prize is likely to be?"

Another picture formed clearly and distinctly in Cheiro's mind. At first it took only the shape of an oblong object, then strange hieroglyphics appeared, and it stood out as an Egyptian sarcophagus with a carved figure on the lid. He found himself saying to Murray, "I beg of you don't touch it. If you do it will bring misfortune to you and all others who have anything to do with it."

This was too much for Mr. Murray. "My dear Cheiro," he declared,

" if you work yourself up into a state like this with all your clients, it is I who must predict that before long, it is you who will be in an oblong box with your name on a brass plate—in good English lettering!" And with that he ended the interview, after cheerfully handing over his card " so that you will remember my name."

As it transpired, it was a name that Cheiro, and quite a few other people, too, were not likely to forget.

A year or two later Douglas Murray went out to Egypt, being possessed of a sudden whim to do some shooting with two friends who were going up the Nile. Before they left Cairo, however, his dragoman told him of a mummy case of rare beauty, and in an unusually good state of preservation, which could be bought from an Arab. This being a time when the new science of egyptology, with its multitude of discoveries, had reached a peak of fascination for visitors to Egypt, Murray of course showed immediate interest. He went along to see the case, and was informed that the hieroglyphics on it described its ancient occupant, a woman, to have been a priestess of the famous Temple of Amen-Ra. She had died in Thebes about 1600 B.C. The lid of the case bore her image worked out in superb colouring, though the mummy itself was missing; this was believed to have been burned by superstitious Arabs.

Although so interested, Mr. Murray was not particularly enamoured of the mummy case. In fact as he later admitted, he felt an extraordinary aversion to having anything to do with it. Yet there was no denying its great beauty and he could not resist the temptation to buy it, so a bargain was struck with the Arab owner, and Murray had the case despatched to his hotel.

That night his two friends were loud in their admiration of his wonderful find and openly expressed their envy of it, so much so that he generously suggested they should draw lots for it. They did so, and he drew the winning number. Someone then suggested that, as there were three in the party, it should really be drawn for three times, and the man who drew it twice should be declared the owner. Mr. Murray was quite amenable to this, and so the draw was made all over again. To everyone's surprise, not the least his own, he drew the winning number for the first, second and third time. That settled the matter, and he gave orders for the mummy case to be packed up and sent off to his address in London. Some other antiquities which he had bought, and which he regarded as being far more interesting and valuable, he retained to take back to England in his personal luggage aboard ship.

A few days later, when shooting up the Nile, the gun Mr. Murray was carrying exploded in his right hand. Suffering the most intense agony, he ordered the dahabieh to head back for Cairo, but a head-wind of unusual force prevented the boat making much headway, and it was some ten days from the time of the accident before he finally reached medical aid. By this time gangrene had set in. The hospital doctors did their utmost to prevent it spreading, but in spite of everything they could do, after weeks of suffering his right arm had to be amputated above the elbow.

Further shocks came on the voyage back to England, when both his companions suddenly took ill and died, and were buried at sea. Also, by a singular stroke of fate, two trunks containing the valuable scarabs and curiosities which he had bought besides the mummy case were stolen on the ship's arrival at Tilbury, and in spite of the very large reward which he immediately offered, were never recovered or heard of again.

Feeling extremely ill, and in a very depressed state of mind, Mr. Murray reached home to find that the mummy case had already been unpacked and was waiting for him in the hall. As he later confessed his feelings at the time, " If such a thing could be, as I looked at the carved face of the priestess on the outside of the mummy case her eyes seemed to come to life, and I saw such a look of hate in them that my very blood seemed to turn to ice."

The following day a well-known literary woman called to talk to Mr. Murray on his return. She listened to his amazing story of the catastrophes which he now directly attributed to the mummy case, expressed her stout disbelief, and gave as her considered opinion that it was all nothing more than a mere string of coincidences. Anyway, she averred, nothing occult could affect *her,* and she persuaded him to let her take the mummy case to her house on the outskirts of London, so that she might study it.

However, from the moment the case passed inside her door, misfortune after misfortune followed. Her mother, coming down the stairs to welcome her, fell and broke her thigh, and died shortly afterwards. Then her fiancé, for no apparent reason, backed out of their engagement; and within a short time every pet animal she owned, including three or four prize dogs, mysteriously took ill and had to be destroyed. Finally, she became ill herself with a peculiar wasting disease that could not be explained, and at last, becoming terrified with the many misfortunes that had so suddenly appeared, she telephoned her solicitor to come and prepare her will. He was a practical man and on learning of the probable cause of her distress, acted swiftly; without even seeking her permission he had the mummy case returned to Douglas Murray that very day.

Mr. Murray now decided he would have to get rid of the thing, and to this end had it taken away to a photographic studio in Baker Street to be photographed for sale purposes. Within a week the photographer called, very much bewildered and troubled, to say that although he could guarantee that no one but himself had handled his camera, something quite extraordinary had occurred; one photograph of the case which he had taken distinctly showed the face of a *living* Egyptian woman staring out of the plate with an expression of malevolence. Not long afterwards this photographer died suddenly and without physical cause. The spoiled plate was never found, and presumably he had destroyed it.

Douglas Murray now decided against offering the mummy case for sale, feeling that the risk of its malignant influence being brought to bear on an innocent purchaser was too great (for this same reason he had already refused to dispose of it to friends). He came to the conclusion that his best plan was to offer it to the Egyptian Section of the British Museum, where it might be studied to scholarly advantage and at the same time hurt no one. Feeling too ill to see about the necessary formalities himself, he enlisted the help of an old friend to make the arrangements and donate the case to the museum. This man, being an ardent egyptologist, was only too glad of an opportunity to examine thoroughly the hieroglyphics on the case, and while waiting for the decision of the Council of the British Museum, he had it removed to his own house. A few weeks later his friends were startled by the news that he was found dead in bed one morning. At the inquest that followed, his valet testified that from the night the mummy case had reached the house, his master had become troubled with insomnia. An empty bottle of chloral was found by his bedside and the verdict was " death by misadventure ".

Finally the mummy case was accepted by the British Museum, the trustees declaring it to be one of the most perfect of its kind and a fine example of coffin decoration under the XVIIIth dynasty. But even its simple removal to the museum brought more fatalities. The carrier who carted it there was dead within a week, while of the two porters who carried the case up the museum stairs, one fell on the steps and broke his leg, and the other died suddenly the following day while apparently in good health.

After a while some extraordinary reports began to reach the ears of the authorities of strange happenings that took place in the Egyptian Section. For example, it was rumoured that some unaccountable thing happened to anyone who attempted to make any drawing or sketch of the beautiful mummy case. One well-known artist attempted to draw it on no less than four occasions. Each time he met with a bad accident, the last time being run over by a horse and cab as he left the gates of the museum, and the sketch he was carrying was completely destroyed.

As time went on, the number of strange occurrences mounted. Instance after instance was vouched for by people who had made disparaging remarks about " superstition " in front of the mummy case, and afterwards met with serious trouble. A visitor who, after gazing at the case, remarked " What an ugly old hag !" fell from his bicycle as he left and broke an arm. A lady who made a similar criticism of the exhibit set herself on fire by accident the same evening, and was badly disfigured. A photographer who tried to take a picture of the mummy case afterwards slipped and broke his nose, and on arriving home found that his child had met with a serious accident.

If anything, though, it was the museum staff who suffered the most. At night, as they testified, a " something " which seemed to emerge from the mummy case rambled through the various rooms, breathing heavily down the nightwatchman's neck and " meddling with the exhibits ". Occasionally a disturbing hammering and sobbing was heard coming from the case. Doctor E. A. Wallis Budge, the keeper of Assyrian and Egyptian antiquities at the museum, when these nightly incidents were reported to him treated the matter with aplomb. The case, he said, was the home of a rather important and evidently beautiful princess, and perhaps she was not satisfied with her present position. He directed that she be given a more prominent position, " and a very large ticket with a laudatory notice." After this was done all was quiet, but not for very long.

Soon, some responsible psychic investigators claimed to have seen a spirit lurking near the mummy case, and sought permission to hold a seance near it, in an attempt to solve the mystery. But Doctor Budge declined. He did, however, allow a press photographer to take a photograph of the now famous exhibit. Next day the photographer returned in a great state of excitement and showed a print to the Doctor. " Look at the face in the print, sir," he said—" it's not the same one that is painted on the case, it's the face of a modern young woman . . . !" After leaving the museum the photographer went home, destroyed the print, mysteriously locked himself in his bedroom and shot himself.

With this, what had at first seemed a harmless " sensation " of the type much loved by the newspapers now took on a more sinister aspect, and the museum authorities became both alarmed and annoyed at the curiosity which the " demon mummy case " had aroused. Be it coincidence or not, no fewer than thirteen people linked with the case had now died, and the museum staff continued to be highly troubled. Most of the male cleaners employed there were scared of the mummy's ghost, which they were convinced exerted a harmful influence, and they would incline their heads or make some other discreet salutation when passing the case. One man who flicked a duster derisively in the priestess's carved face had one of his children die of a slight attack of measles soon afterwards.

Then came a frightening manifestation of the ghost. The door-keeper of the mummy room was making his rounds one winter evening when he saw a figure suddenly sit up in the bottom half of the case of the priestess (the lid had been temporarily removed for examination) and glide smoothly towards him. It had, he said, a horrible yellowish-green face wrinkled like a sheep bladder, and gave off a kind of glow. The figure leapt towards him and he thought it was going to dash him fifty feet down an open trapdoor. He lunged forward to thrust the thing away from him, and knew no more until he felt his forehead bump on a stone figure, and his hands touch the ground, for the ghost vanished even as it came within his clutches.

The museum authorities now decided that the troublesome mummy case would have to be withdrawn from exhibition, and so it was removed and taken down to the vaults. This operation was performed by two reluctant attendants assisted by the chief messenger (others of the staff having judiciously made themselves scarce at the time). In the move, one of the men suffered a severely sprained ankle, while a few days later the chief messenger was found dead beside his desk.

The withdrawal of the mummy case led to all sorts of rumours, and it was widely believed that it was eventually sold to the New York Museum, and was actually in passage on the *Titanic* when she went to her doom on her maiden voyage in 1912. But in fact after a long absence, and when it was judged all the fuss had died down, the mummy case, or at least its ornate yellow-green lid, bearing the carved face and hands of the priestess, was returned to exhibition. Soon, once again, some queer things began to be noticed by staff and public alike. One member of the staff kept a detailed written " log " of the various disturbances, all of which followed more or less the same pattern as before, though at less frequent intervals and without any more fatalities.

This was the situation when, on January 2nd, 1921, two very ordinary-looking men of middle-age entered the British Museum. Their names were Mr. Wyeth and Mr. Neal, and they had formed an unusual partnership brought about by the acute psychic powers which each of them demonstrably possessed. They knew absolutely nothing about the " demon mummy ", or its chequered history, and were simply acting on a curious spirit message which they had received, and which had instructed them to " go to a place on earth which you call the British Museum, and destroy the elemental whose time has come."

Never having heard of an evil spirit at the museum, the two men entered the place and cautiously asked an attendant if he had ever known of such a thing existing in the place. " Oh yes," replied the attendant at once, " you must mean the priestess's mummy—everyone still asks for that." Leading them to the mummy case lid, he then produced the long list of recent strange incidents for the two men to see. What happened shortly afterwards is best described in the words of Mr. Neal.

" I saw the troublesome spirit almost at once. It appeared on the breast of the lid, above the hands. It was like a mop, with a flat face in it, flat as a jellyfish. I called to Wyeth, ' Look out, there it is !' Wyeth didn't see it, but I felt, rather than saw, a flame-like substance passing from Wyeth towards the mummy case, and a minute afterwards everything was clear and natural." The " flame " from Wyeth marked the transmission of a destructive or cleansing power which was his particular psychic ability.

Mr. Wyeth and Mr. Neal afterwards described what they had learned psychically about the unknown priestess. She was, they said, named Amen-Otu, and lived in the Temple of Amen-Ra. " She was what was called a ' Looking Maid '. That is to say, she looked into a silver cup, and could then see anything that was happening at a distance. She was a clairvoyant, and very useful to her priest, who had the same name as the god. This was a period of vile black magic, and ghastly rites in which dead bodies played a part were celebrated in the temple and elsewhere. When the priest Amen-Ra died, he, and this ' Looking Maid ' and an assistant priest, were protected by very strong curses, so that their bodies should not be used in these horrible rites. This protection was attached to the lid of the mummy case, and took the form of an elemental, or disembodied spirit. When a ' black ' magician wished to protect anything, he would enslave the departing spirit of a dying person—often a tortured slave—and hypnotized it to perform a certain task, binding it to a certain place. When any violation of this place was threatened, the ' Thing ' would strike, blindly, as it had been bidden."

Whatever substance we may find in this extremely interesting information, the certain thing is that the curious type of exorcism performed by Mr. Wyeth and Mr. Neal had an immediate effect. From that day onwards nothing else strange occurred, not a single incident to add to the previously long list, and the mummy case was rendered as calm and quiet as all the rest of the objects in the Egyptian Section.

As to Mr. Douglas Murray, after the loss of his arm and his other uncanny experiences with the mummy case, he was never the same gay man again. Ever since getting rid of the mummy case he had kept well clear of it and the many excitements it aroused. However, as fate would have it, he died in almost the same year as its malevolent spirit was finally put to rest.

THE RECTORY HORRORS

IT MIGHT be thought that the least surprising setting for a haunting would be a church or church-house; and, being the son of a parson, I would quite agree. A minister spends his life tending to spiritual needs, and it is only to be expected that some reluctant departed spirits will attempt to linger in their earthly sanctuary, or to revisit it.

Church hauntings are really quite common, though of course the circumstances of them vary considerably. I have investigated quite a number. As an example of the more usual type of haunting I am reminded of the case of the parish church at Leyton, Essex, in 1934. Let the vicar there, the Reverend R. Bren, describe his experience.

"I entered the church one night by the South door, with the object of switching off the lights. The main switch was at that time situated at the far end of the church, and I had to grope my way towards it, aided only by the feeble light given out by two dim lamps under the West gallery. On turning towards the front pew, I noticed two women, dressed in grey, kneeling as though in prayer. I took no notice at first, then I realized that they could not have followed me into church, and certainly could not have been in the church before me. When I looked again a moment later they had vanished."

The eerie appearance of the praying apparitions did not alarm the vicar, whose church was already well known to be haunted by the ghost of a young man clad in Elizabethan clothes, who periodically glided through the pews and vanished into a wall. It did, however, upset some nervous members of the church and was responsible for many absentees at evening services. For some time even the church officials would not venture into the building after dark.

Most church hauntings are, like this one, quite harmless and un-remarkable. But there do occur others of a very different nature, and one that remains unique in its horror is a case from many years past. This is the haunting of the old parsonage at Warblington, a village about a mile from Havant, in Hampshire. The events at Warblington have since tended to be elaborated into near fiction, so it is well to go back to the original, well authenticated eye-witness story of the haunting, which occurred as long ago as the year 1695. This was some twenty years after the death of a previous rector at Warblington, the Reverend Sebastian Pitfield.

In 1695 the rector at Warblington was the Reverend Mr. Brereton. Because of events late that year he was a very disturbed and worried man. The tenant of his parsonage house had abruptly fled, and he was totally unable to get another tenant, even though he had offered to reduce the rent by ten pounds a year—a considerable sum. Mr. Brereton was strongly against disclosing the strange reasons for the tenant's hasty departure. However, his curate, the young Reverend Thomas Wilkins, being of an independent mind, decided to tell all. On December 15th, 1695 Mr. Wilkins made the following deposition.

"At Warblington, near Havant, Hampshire, within six miles of Portsmouth, in the parsonage house, dwelt Thomas Perce, the tenant, with his wife and child, a manservant Thomas, and a maid-servant. About the beginning of August 1695, on a Monday, about nine or ten at night, all being gone to bed except the maid with the child, she being in the kitchen, and having raked up the fire, took a candle in one hand and the child in the other arm, and turning about, saw some-one in a black gown walking through the room and thence out of the door into the orchard. Upon this the maid, hasting upstairs, having recovered but two steps, cried out; on which the master and mistress ran down, found the candle in her hand, she grasping the child about its neck with the other arm. She told them the reason of her crying out, and would not that night tarry in the house, but removed to another belonging to one Henry Salter, farmer, where she cried out all the night from the terror she was in, and could not be persuaded to go to the parsonage house upon any terms.

"On the morrow, Tuesday, the tenant's wife came to me, lodging then at Havant, to desire my advice, and have consultation with some friends about it. I told her I thought it was a flam, and that they had a mind to abuse Mr. Brereton, the rector, whose house it was. She desired me to come up. I told her I would come up and sit up, or lie there, as she pleased, for then, as to all stories of ghosts or apparitions, I was an infidel.

"I went thither and sat up on the Tuesday night with the tenant and his manservant. About twelve o'clock I searched all the rooms in the house, to see if anybody were hid there to impose on me. At last we came into a lumber-room; there I smilingly told the tenant that was with me, that I would call for the apparition, if there was any, and oblige him to come. The tenant then seemed to be afraid, but I told him I would defend him from harm, and then I repeated *Barbara celarent Darii,* etc., jestingly. On this the tenant's countenance` changed, so that he was ready to drop down with fear. Then I told him I perceived he was afraid, and I would prevent its coming, and repeated *Baralipton,* etc. He then recovered his spirits pretty well, and we left the room and went down into the kitchen, whence we were before, and sat up there the remaining part of the night, and had no manner of disturbance.

"Thursday night the tenant and I lay together in one room and he saw something walk along in a black gown and place itself against a window, and there stood for some time, and then walked off. Friday morning, the man relating this, I asked him why he did not call me, and I told him I thought that it was a trick or flam. He told me the reason why he did not call me was that he was not able to speak or move.

"Friday night we lay as before, and Saturday night, and had no disturbance either of the nights.

"Sunday I lay by myself in one room (not that where the man saw the apparition), and the tenant and his man in one bed in another room, and betwixt twelve and two the man heard something walk in their room at the bed's foot, and whistling very well, and at last it came to the bed's side, drew the curtain and looked on them. After some time it moved off, then the man called to me, desired me to come, for that there was something in the room went about whistling. I asked him whether he had any light or could strike one; he told me no. Then I leapt out of bed, and not staying to put on my clothes, went out of my room and along a gallery to the door, which I found locked or bolted. I desired him to unlock the door for that I could not get in, then he got out of bed and opened the door, which was near, and went immediately to bed again. I went in three or four steps, and it being a moonlight night, I saw the apparition move from the bedside and stop up against the wall that divided their room and mine. I went and stood directly against it, within my arm's length of it, and asked it, in the name of God, what it was that made it come disturbing us? I stood some time expecting an answer, and receiving none, and thinking it might be some fellow hid in the room to fright me, I put out my arm to feel it, and my hand seemingly went through the body of it, and felt no manner of substance till it came to the wall. Then I drew back my hand, and still it was in the same place.

" Till now," continued Mr. Wilkins, " I had not the least fear, and even now had very little. Then I adjured it to tell me what it was. When I said those words it, keeping its back against the wall, moved gently along towards the door. I followed it, and it, going out at the door, turned its back towards me. It went a little along the gallery. I followed it a little into the gallery and it disappeared, where there was no corner for it to turn, and before it came to the end of the gallery, where were the stairs. Then I found myself very cold from my feet as high as my middle, though I was not in great fear.

" I went into the bed twixt the tenant and his man, and they complained of my being exceedingly cold. The tenant's man leaned over his master in the bed, and saw me stretch out my hand towards the apparition, and heard me speak the words; the tenant also heard the words. The apparition seemed to have a morning gown of a darkish colour, no hat nor cap, short black hair, a thin, meagre visage of a pale swarthy colour, seemed to be of about forty-five or fifty years old, the eyes half-shut, the arms hanging down, the hands visible beneath the sleeves, of a middle stature.

" I related this description to Mr. John Lardner, rector of Havant, and to Major Battin of Langstone, in Havant parish. They both said the description agreed very well to Mr Pitfield, a former rector of the place, who has been dead above twenty years. Upon this the tenant and his wife left the house, which has remained empty since.

" The Monday after last Michaelmas," Mr. Wilkins went on, " a man of Chodson, in Warwickshire, having been at Havant fair, passed by the foresaid parsonage house about nine or ten at night, and saw a light in most of the rooms of the house. His pathway being close by the house, he, wondering at the light, looked into the kitchen window, and saw only a light, but turning himself to go away, he saw the appearance of a man in a long gown. He made haste away; the apparition followed him over a piece of glebe-land of several acres to a lane, which he crossed, and over a little meadow, and then over another lane to some pales which belong to farmer Henry Salter, my landlord, near a barn, in which were some of the farmer's men and some others. This man went into the barn, told them how he was frightened and followed from the parsonage by an apparition, which they might see standing against the pales if they went out.

" They went out, and saw it scratch against the pales and make a hideous noise. It stood there some time, and then disappeared. Their description agreed with what I saw. This last account I had from the man himself whom it followed, and also the farmer's men."

Such was the curate's weird statement, and of its authenticity there is no doubt, for the document was sent to the learned Dr. Bentley, then living at the home of the Bishop of Worcester, by

Caswell, the mathematician, to whose ghost-hunting efforts we owe these records. In a covering letter to Dr. Bentley, Caswell explained:

" I have sent you enclosed a relation of an apparition. The story I had from two persons, who each had it from the author, and yet their accounts somewhat varied, and passing through more mouths has varied much more. Therefore I got a friend to bring me the author, at a chamber, where I wrote it down from the author's mouth, and which, when I read it to him, and gave him another copy, he said he could swear to the truth of it as far as he was concerned. He is the curate of Warblington, Bachelor of Arts in Trinity College, Oxford, about six years standing in the university. I hear no ill report of his behaviour here. He is now gone to his curacy. He has promised to send up the hands of the tenant and his man, and the farmer's men, as far as they are concerned.

" Mr. Brereton, the rector, would have him say nothing of the story, for that he can get no tenant, though he has offered ten pounds a year less.

" Mr. Pitfield, the former incumbent, whom the apparition represented, was a man of very ill report, supposed to have got children of his maid, and to have murdered them; but I advised the curate to say nothing himself of this last part of Mr. Pitfield, but to leave that to the parishioners who knew him."

Whether the spectre of the ungodly Mr. Pitfield ever appeared again, we do not know; nor whether poor Mr. Brereton finally managed to re-let his troubled house.

Moving on to more modern times, a remarkable haunting is that of the old rectory at Rattlesden, a village in Suffolk. This case is of special interest not only for its chilling aspects but also for the example it gives of the truth lying behind a village superstition. It also shows how the more determined and patient ghost-hunter can ultimately get at the underlying truth, and few were more determined than the late Robert Thurston Hopkins. Mr. Hopkins, like myself, did not settle for inconclusive evidence and hearsay but was always ready to jump on his bicycle and investigate; and so he unearthed the full story of Rattlesden.

His first intimation of the haunting came by pure chance, one winter's evening of 1908. He had arrived at Ipswich, and put up for the night at an inn. There he had supper with another resident for the night, a cyclist passing through on his travels, and after their meal they were joined by the landlord, a tall, powerful man who carried his seventy years very lightly. The conversation took an antiquarian turn, and the landlord spoke of a rambling, red-brick rectory house that stood on an ancient mound overlooking a long dried-up quayside at Rattlesden; which, he said, Hopkins really ought to see, as the rectory was about five hundred years old. Then, taking his listeners into a sudden confidence, the landlord told them how he had once stood face to face with a ghost. He emphasized that they could think what they liked of his story, but he would tell them truly and conscientiously what had occurred.

When he was about twenty, said the landlord, he worked for a carpenter at Stowmarket. He was handy with tools, and so was often in request to repair hot water tanks, wells, pumps and so on at country houses. One afternoon he was told to go over to Rattlesden and repair some panelling which had rotted away in the old rectory.

" I was delayed in starting by a deluge of rain, so when I did make a start it was almost twilight. I was working on some oak panelling near the pantry. Within the house were many small, ancient chambers, a regular rabbit warren of a place it was. There was some of the original panelling and many zigzagging passages. According to local gossip one of these passages near the pantry was called the ' Ghost Walk ', because a ghost was often heard at night walking along it.

" As I worked away at the panelling I noticed a sour, musty smell, which made me feel depressed. Rats suggested themselves to me as an explanation, for I was told the old woodwork was full of rats. But all the same, I felt there was something wrong with the house. It seemed hostile, aloof and secretive. I had a silly impression of being watched, so that I kept looking over at the pantry door in case there might be someone peeping out of it and keeping an eye on me. The door was partly open, and I had thrown over it a large dust sheet which I always carried in my bag in order to cover any article of furniture or carpet while working.

" Suddenly I heard a rustling and shaking inside the pantry—surely, I thought, more than a rat could cause. It happened many years back now, but you gentlemen will hardly realize how uncanny it was for me to see two hands suddenly come over the top of the door and pull my dust sheet into the pantry. Somehow the idea of walking over to that door and pulling it open seemed intolerable to me—I couldn't bear the idea that those two hands might suddenly clutch me . . . A moment later there was a whistle, low and eerie, the door opened wide, and I got a horrible shock as there came out my white dust sheet with a head lolling on top of it.

" For some seconds it remained silent and motionless, just outside the pantry door. Then it whistled again, the same low whistle. Believe me, I was a perfectly sane lad, not given to fancies, and I was as strong as an ox. I was almost instantly seized with the idea that the vicar's coachman was playing a trick on me to give me a scare. So I picked up my heavy hammer and bounded at the figure, yelling ' Stop fooling and come out of that sheet !' But with a sudden smooth motion the thing rushed passed me and took up a position in a corner near the well staircase. As it made this rush it dropped the sheet, and I was horrified to see that it was naked—a thing with pale, blotchy skin the colour of old parchment.

" For a few seconds I watched this apparition in a state of benumbed perplexity, and as I watched it my brain seemed to begin to go muzzy. I felt that some force was passing from the thing in the corner to me : it seemed to be some foul influence which was thrusting itself upon my brain and sapping all the powers of my mind and body. I felt that my consciousness was gradually being smothered by a thick black mist. As I stood there half dazed the thing began to move again—in a kind of crouching posture. I have said it was naked and shaped like a man, but I could not see its face distinctly—only a kind of phosphorescent glow. I remember I wondered if the thing had eyes—I couldn't see them. Anyway, it appeared to be blind, for it came towards me with arms outstretched, just as a man would advance if he was feeling his way in the darkness. I had a sickening, overwhelming feeling of evil and was conscious again of that sour, musty smell.

" Up to that time I had laughed at ghost stories, but when I saw that thing coming towards me, with nodding head and arms held out gropingly, I was certain it wasn't human, and I'll admit to you that the terror and suspense which I endured at that moment almost caused me to lose my mind. I can tell you, gentlemen, that for many a year afterwards I was what you might call a haunted man; yes, even ten years later the very memory of that encounter was enough to put me off balance for days.

" As I saw the thing come groping its way towards me I remember trying to throw off the feeling of paralysis which had seized me, and I suppose I must have roused myself out of it, for with an effort of power I found myself wrestling with the ghost. I was again conscious of that horrible smell, and felt a cold, sightless face pressed close to mine. I think that was the final shock, for the place spun round and I believe I fainted."

When he came to, said the landlord, the thing had vanished, but the " horrible, fusty smell of churchyard mould was terrible."

Then, seeing the look of inquiry on the faces of his two listeners, the landlord became a little nettled. " If ever a man saw a ghost in the world," he said defiantly, " I did that day, and that's as sure as the stars look down on us and the sun shines on us. It all happened years ago, but all the old people at Rattlesden know of it. Some of them saw it, just as I did."

Asked if he could describe the face of the apparition, no matter how vaguely, the landlord said it couldn't be called a face at all, but it was intensely horrible to look at. " It looked like a wizened pig's bladder, and a dried-up, blue-looking tongue dangled from its mouth. It was rather dark in that hall—I couldn't see very clearly and was only about half-conscious at the time."

Was the old rectory still standing? He did not know, he had not been over that way for years. Why did he think the ghost haunted the place? He did not *think*, said the landlord, he was absolutely certain : the ghost haunted the rectory because his body had been buried under one of the corridors. "Most people in Rattlesden know that one vicar who died in that old rectory never came out in a coffin. It may have been a hundred years ago that it all happened, but the story goes that something very devilish was on foot at the rectory in those days. I could tell you a lot more about Rattlesden old rectory but I should only be echoing village gossip. How when the servants tried to open the pantry door there was often a quick and powerful pressure on the other side and it sometimes shut with a crash. How no dog would ever stay in the house. How one of the vicars had the pantry door nailed up, after which the most extraordinary sounds came from the other side of it—bumping and thumping, accompanied by the crash and rattling of iron pots and pans . . . I can't tell you if these tales are true or just village tittle-tattle, but my account of the affair is perfectly true."

And that was how it was left, on that night of 1908. Not for more than thirty years was Mr. Hopkins able to follow up the landlord's strange story. Then, in November 1941, finding himself in the vicinity of Rattlesden, he called at the rectory. It was something of an anti-climax, for no rambling, ghostly old building met his gaze but one comparatively new. From the vicar he learned that the old rectory had been pulled down in 1892, and not a vestige of it remained. However, the vicar was able to produce some very valuable evidence in the form of a collection of holograph notes and photographs made by a past vicar, the Reverend Olorenshaw. And here, Hopkins found the solution to the haunting.

Among the faded photographs was one, a view of the hall near the haunted pantry, which pictured age-blotched floors, a sooty low ceiling, damp-stained and time-blotched walls, and a dreary well staircase with ancient dumpy balusters; a very gloomy, suggestive scene. No wonder a former vicar who had lived in the place described it as a "rat infested nest of dark rooms and twisting corridors entirely given over to the Powers of Darkness." There were many well vouched for facts about the ghost in the pantry. The Reverend Mr. Olorenshaw, while he did not enter into any discussion about these in his notes, made meticulous record of the fact that village people and his own servants found there was some "presence" in the old rectory that made solitude at times almost impossible. The haunted pantry, he

said, was tiled with ancient red bricks, and exactly in the centre of it
was a depression in bricks of a darker colour—and the depression was
shaped like a coffin.

In 1892, when the old rectory was demolished, Mr. Olorenshaw
made sure to be present when the floor of the pantry was removed.
In the course of the digging the workmen found a skeleton and some
rotten wooden planks. On examination the skeleton was found to be
that of Robert Bumpstead, who died in 1780. Inquiries brought to
light that the unhappy man had died in debt, and the creditors were
waiting to seize his body. It was not clear whether he was a vicar or
a churchwarden, but evidently he was in some way connected with
the rectory, and his friends thought that once he was buried in the
pantry his remains would be safe from the body-snatchers.

Mr. Olorenshaw had the bones carefully collected and buried in the
churchyard, near the grave of several churchwardens. But even that
was not the end of it. Apparently Robert Bumpstead " walked " the
churchyard after he was buried, till at length the Archdeacon had to
be called in, and clergy assembled, in order that his still troubled spirit
might be " laid ". After this service he seemed to find peace at last.

THE HAUNTED HUSBAND

SOMETIMES THE spirit of an intimate member of the family will make a single appearance after death; other times the haunting will go on, at intervals, for years.

I am reminded, as I write, of the Dowager Countess whose dead husband has followed her around her home, the family seat, for years. She sees him for split seconds at a time, and he has spoken to her. She thinks he wants to tell her that he now believes in something she told him during their married lives, and which he did not believe at the time. However, he is never quite able to get the message across to her.

The Countess has had the local vicar offer prayers in every room of her eighteenth-century residence, but still the shade of her husband follows her about. Happily this does not distress her, though the same continual haunting by a dead spouse often can, and does, cause much anguish and terror.

In the 1930s I visited a half-derelict cemetery at Milehouse, Plymouth, in which was a grave reinforced with iron bars by a husband driven to desperation by the constant visits of the ghost of his dead wife. The grave, which was overgrown with brambles, was brought to light when the caretaker of the graveyard had a large tree cut down. Built up with bricks and stones, it was held together by powerful iron bolts, and on the old and decayed headstone was inscribed : " Sacred to the memory of Mary Ann, wife of John Blowey, who died July 14, 1880, aged 57 years ".

Inquiries produced the history of this strange resting place. Soon after Mary Ann was buried in 1880, on the windswept hillock in the then new cemetery, her husband, a Devonport dockyardsman, complained that she was haunting him. Determined to lay the ghost he obtained a number of thick iron bolts, bricks, tiles, stones and other materials, which he used to carry in small loads to the cemetery on Saturday afternoons. And there, while other bereaved relatives were setting flowers on adjoining graves, John Blowey worked hard at the task of " sealing up " his wife's spirit. He piled his bricks on the grave, cementing them over with care, and set the steel bars in position, swearing that her ghost would never get past them.

What happened when he had done all this, no one knew, though it is a safe conclusion that Mr. Blowey discovered that no bricks and bolts can hold a ghost.

My files contain the particulars of several cases of haunting by deliberately spiteful spirits, and among those known to have returned with the apparent object of wreaking revenge on their spouses, or gaining retribution for a deed done, few, I think, offer as compelling a story as the return of the ghost of murdered Mrs. Julia Sheward.

This wife of a tailor in Norwich, in 1851, was a plain-featured, taciturn, over-houseproud and ultra-respectable woman in her middle-forties, whose cold, domineering manners, and excessive scrubbing and polishing and dusting of corners reputedly drove her husband to distraction. William Sheward was some years younger than his wife, and completely opposite in character, being a bit of a dreamer, and how the two came to matrimony in the first place is one of those small mysteries of life. From all accounts, the upshot of their unlikely partnership seems to be that, in consequence of being heavily dominated by his wife, William Sheward took more and more to drowning his sorrows in drink. As for the gloomy, acid Julia, she was said to hate children and dogs and have a special love of attending funerals. Ultimately, and prematurely, she attended her own, for in a moment of black despair, William took up his cutting scissors and stabbed her to death.

No one knew of his action, that day in 1851. Julia Sheward simply disappeared. What in fact happened, and what transpired afterwards, was reconstructed much later from the evidence given at his trial and his own confessions.

After stabbing his wife in what is nowadays described as a " mental blackout ", William sat and stared helplessly at her corpse for some hours. Not until close to dawn was he able to pull himself together, when with extraordinary callousness for a man of such a placid nature, he dismembered the body, took the parts and buried them in various places in Deepdene Lane, on the outskirts of Norwich.

He explained to neighbours that his wife had left him, a fact which caused little surprise, for Julia had told many people that she intended to leave her husband, as she could not put up with his drunken, idle ways. So it was thought she had gone back to London, as threatened, to find a new life there. Everyone knew that the couple had first met in London.

A very precipitous and clumsy murder, therefore, turned out to have all the elements of the "perfect crime", and William Sheward might have lived safely with his secret to the end of his days. But he had not reckoned with the vengeful spirit of his wife.

William could not keep away from the lane in which he had buried his wife's body. Some strong compulsion forced him frequently to the spot. Sometimes, even when busy in his shop, he would feel the urgent call to revisit Deepdene Lane, and be forced to drop everything and go there. His dead wife seemed to gain control of his thoughts and movements.

Eventually a young policeman noticed how Sheward seemed drawn to the spot, and his suspicions were aroused. Why was Sheward always poking around in the ditches and undergrowth with his walking stick? he wondered. Had the man hidden something there? After watching the tailor's movements a few times in the lane, the constable began to put two and two together. Suppose the missing Mrs. Sheward had been killed by her husband, and buried there? The constable took a bloodhound and searched the undergrowth where he had seen William Sheward poking about. His search was soon rewarded when the hound found a human hand in a ditch. Now a full-scale search was made and the police also found a foot, and many other parts of a woman's body—but no head. A surgeon who examined the remains described the woman as being of medium build, with a good figure. She took size $4\frac{1}{2}$ shoes. She had clean, well-trimmed fingernails, and both hands and feet belonged to a person "who was not accustomed to toil." The woman's age, he reported, was between twenty-six and thirty; and she probably had light brown hair, and weighed about eight stone.

But Julia Sheward was 56 at the time of her disappearance. And her hair was black, and her weight nearly ten stone.

The misleading medical report, for which we have no good explanation, saved Sheward, and people who had been ready to condemn him now rushed to befriend him. His shop drew more customers and he doubled his profits. In time he became well prosperous, acquiring other shops, houses and land. But he never lost a feeling of unease, and was convinced that the vengeful shade of his wife still haunted him, seeking to control his thoughts, and drawing him back to the place where he had buried her. He also lived in constant fear of the police, whom he was certain knew the truth, that he had really killed Julia.

He felt his time was up when, one day, a stranger entered his shop and announced himself as a detective inspector from Scotland Yard. Sheward's exact feelings then we will never know, for he never explained them, but even at such a moment he showed a certain cleverness, suggesting, rather as a joke, that perhaps his trade tab had been found in some clothing connected with a crime? No, said the inspector, he wanted Mrs. Sheward's address, and William was the only man likely to know of it. Why, what was the matter? asked Sheward, masking his worst fears. The inspector explained that a sum of money—three hundred pounds—had been left to Mrs. Sheward, but she could not be traced. If she wanted the money, she had to appear before a magistrate and claim it. Sheward laughed with relief. No, he said, his runaway wife had certainly not told him where she was going, nor had he heard from her since.

In 1861, ten years after the murder, William Sheward married for a second time. As he confessed later, he did so simply to gain company. The ghost of Julia haunted him so persistently that he could stand it no longer; he wanted to feel there was a real, solid human being touching him, talking to him, and just being with him. The second Mrs. Sheward, however, did not take kindly to his habit of waking her in the middle of the night just to talk to her and ease his fears. She also complained of the " imaginary voices " he heard, and of his peculiar habit of walking in Deepdene Lane and thrashing the undergrowth with his walking stick. The couple were overheard to have many quarrels.

Near Christmas in 1868, Mrs. Sheward suggested it would do them both good to have a change, and William agreed. So his wife went ahead and made arrangements for them to spend a few days in London.

When they arrived at the hotel which his wife had booked, William was suddenly uneasy. He complained to his wife that there was " something wholly funny about the place." What he did not tell her was that by some awful coincidence, they were staying in the very same London square where, some thirty years previously, he had first met Julia.

It was too much; from this moment, William Sheward was a doomed man. His somewhat garbled descriptions give us his thoughts at that time, all very confused, bizarre and horrifying. The shade of his late wife was everywhere, even staring at him out of mirrors, and from panes of glass in the windows. She was too strong for him. Even after *eighteen years* she was hounding him, hounding him . . .

Suddenly the distraught Sheward ran downstairs and out into the street to a policeman, to whom he made the full, astonishing confession of his crime.

He was tried and executed. Julia had won.

I cannot leave the question of the haunted spouse without a comment regarding other cases of the type, which, although much less dramatic in content, hold great nervous stress for those concerned. It is perfectly understandable that a surviving partner of a loving marriage should wish to see the image of the other, out of a need for reassurance. However, such desires, it would seem, are best left alone. I quote the following case told to me by a doctor's wife, who often used to sit with the patient described.

" My husband attended a certain old man and his wife who were very devoted to one another. They were quite elderly people, but sound and sane—not at all fanciful or inclined to be foolish. When the old man died, his wife felt his loss most dreadfully. She never quite got over it, and, when she took to her bed with illness, she was constantly saying that she wished she could see her husband again. Her nurses told her that she ought not to say such a thing, but the wish grew upon her until one day, being alone, she spoke to him and begged him to come back.

" Immediately, he appeared, sitting in a chair by her bedside. But, though her wish was gratified, she was terrified. ' Go away, go away !' she cried, ' I don't want you !' The vision vanished. Some days later she died."

HOUSES OF TERROR

WHEN I was a young man there was a house in Birmingham, near the Roman Catholic Cathedral, that was once very badly haunted. A family who went to live there complained of hearing all sorts of uncanny sounds, such as screams and sighs, coming from a room behind the kitchen.

Once the tenant's wife, on entering the sitting-room, was almost terrified out of her senses at seeing, standing before the fireplace, the figure of a tall, stout man with a large grey dog at his side. What was so alarming about the man was his face—apparently a mere blob of flesh devoid of any features.

The wife screamed out, at which there was a tremendous crash, as if all the crockery in the house had been suddenly dashed down on the stone floor. A friend of hers who, on hearing the noise, rushed to the spot, arrived in time to see two clouds of vapour, one resembling a man and the other a dog, hovering over the hearth for several seconds, before they finally dispersed.

A gasfitter, when working in the house, saw the same figures no fewer than nine times, and so distinctly that he was able to give a detailed description of both the dog and the faceless man—" He had no eyes, nor nose, nor mouth, only ears and long hair."

The spectres were not confined to the night or morning, they appeared at any time, and always when least expected. Frequently, ghastly sounds—shrieks, groans, sobs and desperate struggling, as if someone was fighting for their life—were heard coming from the ground floor and basement.

Inquiries established that the house was occupied in 1829 by a man who supplied medical students with human bodies, and it was said to have been noticed at the time how some people who were seen to enter the house in the company of the owner were never seen to leave it again.

This was such a well-known and authenticated haunting that a Chief Constable of Warwickshire wrote about it in his memoirs.

The fact is, although haunted houses may be popular in fiction, in real life they are generally far from pleasant, especially for the innocent people living in them who have to endure the unnatural and frightening disturbances that take place. Some examples of the cases I have recorded during the course of the years will show the infinite variety of such hauntings.

A house well known to me near the Crystal Palace, London, suffered periodic hauntings. My first note of it concerned an innocuous, though highly curious experience of the then tenant.

He was sitting in the drawing-room one evening with a woman friend, when both suddenly saw a picture on the wall sway to and fro in the most remarkable fashion. As soon as the lady got up and walked towards the picture, it became still. But the moment she sat down it began rocking and swaying again. This went on for some minutes. No vehicles were passing at the time to cause any vibration in the room. Everything in the road, a very quiet turning off Gipsy Hill, was still, and there was nothing to account for the phenomenon.

The incident had very nearly been forgotten when a visitor to the house, being aroused from a nap one day by the sensation that she was no longer alone in the room, looked up to see a tall, shadowy, hooded figure in long black robes bending over her. She was so fearful of what might happen next that she shut her eyes again, and when she ventured to open them the figure had gone.

A few years later another girl staying in the house had a similar experience in the adjoining room. She awoke one moonlight night to see the same tall, hooded figure, which she thought was a man in clerical robes, bending over her. On neither occasion was the face of the figure seen.

Then occurred another gap of many months, until the house was taken for a brief period by an actress friend of mine. Returning home late one night she was surprised to see a bedroom window aglow with light. Wondering how this could be, for there was no one at home, she entered the house, and on approaching the room, saw a light under the door. But on opening the door she found the room to be in complete darkness. She could discover no natural explanation.

One night shortly afterwards she dreamed vividly that this particular room was occupied by a very grotesque figure, and waking from her dream in panic, she was conscious of something entering her own room and standing by her side. She got the impression, for the thing did not actually show itself, that it was exactly similar to the grotesque figure she had seen so strongly in her sleep.

After another long silence and change of tenancies, the house came to my notice once again when, immediately before the death of a relative of the owner of the house , inexplicable knockings were heard. Also, the servants complained of heavy footsteps following them about from room to room.

The case is typical of the more usual kind of haunted house, in which the disturbances occur with no apparent motive, except perhaps to alarm, and with no apparent cause.

My introduction to a strange haunting at a house in Chelsea was curious to say the least. For many years the house was occupied by a Scottish gentleman with a large circle of friends and acquaintances. The incident I refer to happened when I and others were having tea with him, a few years prior to his death. He and I were talking together apart from the rest of the company, when he abruptly left me, and walking to the far side of the room addressed himself to some-one else. Later on he returned and explained his odd conduct.

" When I was talking to you just now," he said, " I suddenly saw the phantom figure of a woman lying on the Chesterfield, near us. Her head was lolling helplessly on one side, and there was an ugly gash in her throat, which appeared to have been slashed from ear to ear. I was so shocked that I had to move away from it and you, to the other side of the room. Did you see it?"

I told him I had not seen the apparition, but that I had seen some-thing else peculiar, though it may have been only an optical illusion. I had naturally gazed after him when he abruptly left me, and while he was talking to a woman guest on the far side of the room, I had seen a figure standing behind him which was the exact counterpart of himself.

" That's very interesting," he said, " because my projection, or phantom, or whatever you may like to call it, has been seen here by someone else, too."

He then went on to tell me that one day, when in his garden, he had looked up at the house and seen an exact duplicate of himself leaning out of one of the windows. A friend who was with him in the garden also saw the figure. As if this were not enough, another phantom seen in the house, he told me, was that of a bear, which invariably rose from the floorboards and disappeared near the fire-place.

The bear, at least, might be easily explained, for I subsequently learned that the house stood on ground that was once part of an estate owned by Anne Boleyn's father, and as bear-baiting was much in vogue at that period, the ghost could have been one of the dead animals. But the cases of "projection" are without explanation.

I found quite a number of haunted houses in the Chelsea district at this time, and even a studio in the King's Road which was claimed to be haunted by the ghost of a little old man seen peering over the balustrade of the gallery.

Another haunting was in Glebe Place, and of this I had personal experience. One summer evening my wife and I both heard sounds as of someone choking in the room adjoining ours. In seconds the sounds appeared to move and come from just outside our room. We opened our door immediately and went on to the landing, but could see no one. However, as we stood at the head of the stairs listening, we heard the sounds again, first on the staircase and then on the first floor landing, which was immediately below ours. The same disturbing sounds travelled on down the next flight of stairs and into the hall, where they finally stopped.

There was no one in the house at the time but ourselves, and no animal, and any explanation of the phenomena on physical grounds seemed impossible. On making inquiries I found that several other people had experienced inexplicable happenings in the house.

Another house in the same street was said to be haunted by the phantom of a man on horseback, but I was unable to investigate this.

Two other hauntings, though of an indecisive nature, occurred at houses in Wellington Square and Poulton Square, in both of which a notorious murder had been committed.

A case of haunting by the believed phantom of a murderer, or murderers, was told me by Miss Dalrymple, aunt of T. C. Dalrymple, the noted singer. Her experiences began the night of her arrival at The Lichens, the house her nephew was then renting, near Felixstowe.

On going up to bed she found the servants had made a very big fire in her room, and growing somewhat apprehensive about it, she got out of bed and took some of the coal off. Then, thinking that her alarm was rather foolish, and that as there was a large fender no danger could possibly arise, she put the coal on again and got back into bed. A few minutes afterwards the bedroom was invaded by a current of icy cold air which blew over the bed and rustled through her hair. The next moment she felt a cold, heavy hand laid on one of her shoulders, and she was steadily pressed down and down.

Miss Dalrymple's terror was now so intense that she could neither move nor make a sound. After what seemed to her an eternity, but which was in reality only a few seconds, the hand was removed, and she then heard seven loud thumps on the table at the foot of the bed, after which there was silence.

But Miss Dalrymple was now too upset to sleep, and she lay awake all night in a great agony of mind, lest there should be any further disturbances. In the morning she took one of the older servants into her confidence and asked if the house was haunted.

"Well, madam," was the maid's reluctant response, "people do say there's a house in the village which is haunted by the ghost of a murdered lady, but I'm not quite sure which house it is." It was an answer which implied much.

Miss Dalrymple did not have any further experiences there herself, but some time afterwards one of her great-nieces remarked to her— "Did you know, auntie, The Lichens was haunted?" The girl went on to say that once, when going upstairs, she had seen the figure of a woman in a grey dress bending over the basin in the bathroom as if to rinse her hands. Thinking it was the nurse, she went on her way unconcernedly, until she suddenly saw the nurse coming towards her from quite a different part of the house. Greatly surprised, she questioned the nurse, who assured her that she had not been in the bathroom for at least an hour. It transpired that the figure in grey was repeatedly seen, always in or near the bathroom, and always appearing as if rinsing her hands. Once, when one of the children was alone in a downstairs room which opened on to the lawn, a rather peculiar old man carrying a sack approached the window, and after peeping in at the child with an evil smile, placed his fingers knowingly alongside his nose and glided noiselessly away into the shrubbery. The child ran out at once and asked the gardener to look for the man, but despite a vigorous search, no such person could be found.

Another woman staying at the house, on going one day to her bedroom, heard something behind her, and turning round, saw to her horror the luminous trunk of a man, which had apparently been dismembered. The body, which was bobbing up and down in mid-air, approached her rapidly, and moving aside to let it pass, she saw it vanish through the door of the room Mrs. Dalrymple had occupied. After this ghastly manifestation Mr. Dalrymple, fearing for the sake of his family to remain any longer in such a place, left The Lichens, part of which was later pulled down and rebuilt.

To the end of her days, Miss Dalrymple's heart was never sound since feeling the ghostly hand on her shoulder, the horror of which, as any of her friends could testify, turned her hair white.

It may be asked if there was any connection between the figures of the woman in grey, the tramp, the mutilated body, and the hand. Maybe they were closely allied. One theory was that an old man had been murdered there by his mistress, who, after cutting up his body, had bribed a tramp to dispose of it, in which case the house would, of course, be haunted by the earthbound spirits of both the victim and agents of the crime. But it is also quite possible that the tragedy did not take place in the house at all but was enacted in some faraway spot, one or more of the principals being in some way connected with The Lichens. However, it is one of those cases that must, by reason of the uncertain history of the house, always remain a mystery.

A haunting of a similar nature occurred at a house near Leeds. The house, which had stood empty for a very long time, was eventually taken on a lease by my informants, Mr. and Mrs. Urquhart. They were a strong-minded couple who scoffed at the very idea of ghosts, but they had not been long in the house before they were caused to change their minds.

One evening shortly after their arrival Mrs. Urquhart was alone in the study, when on looking up from her needlework she saw what at first sight appeared to be a luminous disc—but which speedily developed into a head—emerge from the wall opposite, and, bobbing up and down in mid-air, slowly approach her. It was a woman's head, the woman having obviously been decapitated, the expression in the wide-open, staring eyes showing every indication of a cruel ending. The hair was long and matted, and the skin startlingly white. Mrs. Urquhart was at first too terrified to move, but as the ghastly object floated right up to her, the revulsion she experienced was so great that the spell was broken and she fled from the room.

When she told her husband what had happened he said laughingly, " Why, my dear, I never knew you had such a vivid imagination— you'll be asking me next to believe in hobgoblins and pixies!" At this rebuff Mrs. Urquhart dropped the subject. However, after dinner, hearing a great commotion in the study, she ran to see what was happening, and discovered her husband and his friend, both looking very white, thrashing about in the air with walking-sticks. On catching sight of her Mr. Urquhart cried out, " We've seen the head—the horrible thing came out of the wall, just as you said, and floated towards us."

Mrs. Urquhart recoiled in horror, nor could she be persuaded to enter the room ever again. Her husband, being also very shaken, agreed that they should leave the house as soon as possible, and soon after their removal they learned that the place had been pulled down. On making inquiries they discovered that some years previously an old woman had been murdered, and both were convinced it was her ghost they had seen.

At a house in the West Brompton Road, London, the tenants and servants were disturbed not only by mysterious footsteps, knocking, and the ringing of bells in the night, but by an apparently male figure, enveloped in grey drapery, which used to appear in all parts of the premises. Its hands were usually clasped in front of it, and it gave all who saw it the impression that it was altogether good and in no degree evil. It was shadowy and unsubstantial, but readily spotted by the luminous glow which seemed to emanate from all over it. It never moved its head or hands, or spoke, or made any noise, except on one occasion, when seemingly it let a parcel it held fall to the ground with a thud. It moved with a gliding motion, and when stationary, gazed at people fixedly. It usually vanished abruptly.

For seven years, at intervals, this curious haunting by the inoffensive apparition continued, as did the various noises, until the family left the house and moved to another in the same neighbourhood. But their troubles were far from over, for strange to say, the same phenomena occurred. But in addition to seeing in their new house the same tall, shadowy figure in grey and hearing the same noises, they also experienced other noises, much more disturbing. Doors were now heard banging at night where no doors existed, or where doors were closed; and sounds like metal trays being dashed down periodically awoke and startled everyone. Also, they heard in certain of the rooms, noises like furniture being moved about, constant tramping up and down the stairs and about the passages, windows being opened and slammed to, loud sighings and heavy breathing, and on one occasion at least, a sound like a match being struck.

Christmas Day saw no relief from the disturbances, the grey figure being seen by one of the daughters of the family in the morning, standing on the staircase, and later on in the day at the foot of her bed.

After hearing some of the manifestations, one of the children, a boy who was ill at the time, became much worse through fright and died two or three weeks later. For some days prior to his death the noises were very pronounced.

The noises and the figure also badly frightened one of the other children and a nursemaid, before the haunting eventually subsided.

There was nothing that anyone could discover about either of the houses which offered an explanation of the phenomena.

The story of events at a large country house not far from London came to me through Miss V. Vincent, a society beauty, who had the case reported to her by an old servant woman of the name of Garth, who was taken on in service there.

Miss Garth, who had no idea at the time that the house was haunted, was taking a short nap on her bed one afternoon when she heard the door slowly open, and on looking up, saw to her astonishment a small, sinister old man, who tiptoed up to her bed and, leaning over her placed his finger on his lips as if to caution her to silence —an unnecessary move as she was far too terrified to utter a sound. On seeing her fright, a smile of satisfaction stole over the man's face, which Miss Garth later described as " yellow and wizened ". He left the bed and turning round, glided surreptitiously through the open doorway. Greatly nervous, Miss Garth mentioned the affair to the other servants, who instead of laughing at her at once explained, " Why, you've seen old Simon. He committed a murder just outside the door of your room, many years ago, and is frequently seen about the house and grounds. If you examine the boarding in the passage carefully, you will see the bloodstains." As Miss Garth refused to sleep in the room again, a valet of one of the visitors was put there, and he experienced precisely the same phenomenon.

But that was not the end of it for Miss Garth. She constantly saw the phantom of " old Simon " in various parts of the house. Sometimes she would meet him face to face on a staircase; sometimes he would creep stealthily after her, down one of the numerous, gloomy corridors. Indeed, she never seemed to be free of him, and in the end her nerves became so upset that, although the job was an excellent one, she was obliged to give in her notice. To cap it all she encountered other ghosts outside the house. On several occasions, in the orchard, she heard the sound of galloping horses and saw the misty figures of two people engaged in earnest conversation. On her approaching them, however, they always melted away into thin air.

Miss Vincent, after questioning Miss Garth thoroughly, made discreet inquiries and eventually got into communication with other people who had witnessed exactly the same phenomena. No one, however, could offer any explanation for the hauntings, which remain a mystery.

Now a case from Edinburgh. Widowed Mrs. R. O. Douglas, an independent woman with three growing daughters, took a flat in a big house. Although it was a big building it was neither very old—not more than seventy years—nor, being in the city, was it very isolated. The ground floor and first floor were used as chambers and offices, and the Douglas's flat was on the second storey. The flat above them was untenanted, and used for the storage of furniture.

Mrs. Douglas and her daughters, with their two servants, had not been in their new quarters more than a week before Mrs. Douglas was driven to asking the night porter who it was that made such a noise racing up the stairs between two and three o'clock in the morning. It had wakened her every night, she told him, and she would be glad if something could be done about it. The porter was apologetic but said he could not understand it, as no one used the rooms above the Douglas flat, nor were any of the offices used after normal daytime hours. He suggested it might be a noise carried over from the building adjoining, sounds being deceptive on still nights.

But Mrs. Douglas was not at all convinced, and made up her mind to complain to the landlord should the noise occur again. That night nothing happened, but on the next night she was roused from her sleep at two o'clock by a feeling that something dreadful was going to happen. Being a woman who ridiculed the idea of ghosts she tried to find a rational explanation for the noise that still alarmed her— the rushing up the stairs. Yet, argue with herself as she would, it could not have been the wind, on a still night, nor rats. Rats did not wear heavy boots, and it was a heavy tread, rather than a clatter, that she had heard.

Mrs. Douglas longed to strike a light and awaken her eldest daughter, who was almost without nerves. She made a start, and loosing the bedclothes, thrust out a foot. The next moment she drew it back with a horrified gasp; the darkness had suggested to her a great, horny hand lying in wait to seize her. Very slowly she recovered and, holding her breath, sidled to the far edge of the bed and made a quick jab at the bell-push on the wall. But her finger missed the target and hit the wall, causing her to wring her hand in pain. Her consciousness of an unknown presence in the room increased, and she instinctively felt the thing pass through the closed door down on to the landing outside, and dash upstairs with a heavy tread, entering the storage flat immediately overhead, after which it began bounding backwards and forwards across the floor. After continuing for fully half an hour the noises stopped and the house became still again.

At breakfast Mrs. Douglas asked her daughters if they had heard anything in the night. They had not, and neither had the servants.

No further disturbances occurred for about a month. Then, the older daughter was sleeping in her mother's room, Mrs. Douglas being away on a brief visit. One evening, as Diana was going into her bedroom just before dinner, she saw the door suddenly swing open and something, she could not tell what, it was so blurred and indistinct, came out with a bound. It vanished past her on to the landing and rushed upstairs so noisily that the girl imagined, though she could see nothing, that it wore heavy boots. Greatly curious in spite of her alarm, she ran after it, and on reaching the upper storey heard a " great noise " in the room above her mother's. Finding the door unlocked she boldly flung it wide open, and in a room stacked with old furniture saw a filmy outline standing before an antique eight-day clock, which it was apparently in the act of winding.

Fear now struck Diana for the first time. What was the shadowy thing, and what would happen should it suddenly turn round and face her? She shut her eyes momentarily, but when she opened them it was still there, engrossed in what it was doing. Frozen to the spot now, and frightened of attracting the thing's attention to her, Diana suffered agonies through a sudden desire to sneeze. At last the shadowy figure began to veer round, but the faint echo of a voice below, calling her name, broke the spell that bound her to the floor and she turned and ran fast down the stairs, not stopping till she reached the dining-room. There she told her two sisters, who had each been aroused by a noise, all that had transpired.

That night she shared her sisters' bedroom, though none of them found sleep.

Nothing more happened until Mrs. Douglas's return. Then, one night as she was preparing to get into bed, the door of her room unexpectedly opened and she saw standing there the unmistakable figure of a man, short and broad, with a great width of shoulders and very long arms. He was clad in a peajacket, blue serge trousers and jackboots. He had a big, round, brutal head covered with a tangled mass of light coloured hair, but where his face ought to have been there was only a hazy blotch.

In spite of the man's frightening appearance Mrs. Douglas's attention was drawn to two objects which he carried in his hands. One looked like a bizarre bundle of red and white rags, and the other a small bladder of lard. While she was staring at these objects he swung round, hitched them under his armpits, rushed across the landing and with a series of bounds sprang up the staircase, his ghostly figure fading at some point before he actually touched the stairs.

This was the climax. Mrs. Douglas felt that another such encounter would be too much for her heart, besides there being the worry of the effect on her daughters. So, in spite of the fact that she had taken the flat for a year, and had only just commenced her tenancy, she ordered her goods packed, and both family and servants left the premises the next day.

The report that the building was haunted spread rapidly, and Mrs. Douglas, who took up residence in a new flat not far away, received several indignant letters from the landlord, who finally threatened to prosecute her for slander of title if she did not halt the rumours. Fortunately the matter did not in fact reach the courts, and when things had quietened, Mrs. Douglas persisted with inquiries into the history of the house. Of the many tales she listened to, only one seemed to provide a clue to the haunting. This said that a retired sea captain, many years previously, had rented the rooms she occupied. He was an extraordinary individual who would never wear anything but nautical clothes, including blue jersey and jackboots. His love of the bottle eventually brought on delirium tremens, and his excessive irritability in the intervals between each attack was a source of anxiety to all who came in contact with him.

At that time, it was said, there happened to be a baby in the rooms overhead, whose crying so annoyed him that he threatened its mother that if she did not keep it quiet, he would not be answerable for the consequences. His warnings having no effect, he flew upstairs one day when the mother was temporarily absent, and decapitated the infant with a breadknife. He then stuffed both head and body into a grandfather's clock which stood in one corner of the room, and retiring to his own quarters drank till he was insensible.

All this came out at his trial for murder, when he was found guilty but insane, and committed to a lunatic asylum. There the demented man committed suicide by opening an artery in his leg with a fingernail.

As the details of this tragedy filled in so well with the phenomena they had witnessed, Mrs. Douglas could not help regarding the story as a very probable explanation of the hauntings, but in view of the landlord's still simmering hostility she abandoned any deeper investigation.

For another Edinburgh haunting we must go further back in years. Letty Doyle was an old nurse with little time for what she termed "fanciful stories", yet one story she had to tell could have been judged more fanciful than most, were it not verified absolutely by other people involved. It was an episode that happened in Letty's young life, in the old house in Edinburgh where she first went on entering domestic service as a housemaid. It was called Peeble's Mansion, and was occupied at the time by an Admiral and his family, with their servants including a cook and a butler.

The two-storeyed house, which dated probably from the sixteenth-century, had no garden, only a large yard, covered with faded yellow paving stones, and containing a well with an old-fashioned roller and bucket. There was no basement, but there were three very roomy cellars.

On the ground floor were four reception rooms, all oak panelled, together with numerous kitchen offices and a cosy housekeeper's room. In the spacious entrance hall a broad oak staircase led up to the first floor, where eight bedrooms opened on to a gallery overlooking the hall.

The top storey, where the servants slept, consisted of attics connected with one another by narrow passages. One of these attics was claimed to be haunted, though in fact the ghost had also been seen in other parts of the house.

When Letty entered the Admiral's service she was a very young girl with no thought of ghosts, nor did the other servants enlighten her regarding the particular troubles of the house—the Admiral was very strict about this.

Letty's own home, humble though it was, had been very bright and cheerful and she did not much care for the dark precincts of the mansion, and was anything but pleased at the prospect of sleeping alone in an attic. Still, nothing occurred to alarm her till about a month after her arrival. It was early evening, soon after twilight, and she had gone down into one of the cellars to look for a bootjack, which the Admiral had sworn by all that was holy must be found before supper. Placing the light she had brought with her on a packing case, she was groping about among the boxes when she noticed that the flame of the candle had suddenly turned blue. She then felt icy cold and was startled to hear a loud clatter, as if some metal instrument had hit the stone floor in a corner of the cellar. Glancing in the direction of the noise, she saw looking at her two very bright eyes. Sick with terror she stood absolutely still. The clatter was repeated, and a shadowy form began to crawl towards her. . . . Then the Admiral's loud voice sounded as he came down the stairs, at which the phantom vanished. But the shock had been too much for Letty, who fainted. The Admiral, carrying her upstairs as carefully as if she had been his own daughter, gave orders that she should never again be allowed to go into the cellar alone.

But now that Letty herself had seen the ghost the other servants no longer felt bound to secrecy, and told her about the earlier hauntings. Everyone, they said, except the boy of the house and the butler, had seen one of the ghosts, and the cellar apparition was quite familiar to them all (that is, the Admiral, his wife and daughter, and the servants). They also said there were other parts of the house quite as badly haunted as the cellar.

As a result of these stories Letty always felt scared when crossing the passages leading to the attics. One morning as she was hurrying down one of them she heard someone running after her. Thinking it was one of the other servants, she turned round, pleased to think someone else was up early too, and saw to her horror a dreadful object that seemed to be partly human and partly animal. The body was small, and its face bloated and covered with yellow spots. It had an enormous animal mouth, the lips of which moved quickly, but without giving any sound. The moment Letty screamed for help the thing vanished.

But her worst experience was to come. The spare attic, which she was told was so badly haunted that no one would sleep in it, was the room next to hers. It was a gloomy room, the ceiling was low and sloping, and it was furnished with an old bed, a black oak chest, and a wardrobe which used to creak and groan every time Letty walked along the passage. Once she heard a low chuckle which she fancied came from the chest, and another time, when the door of the room was open, she caught the glitter of a pair of eyes—the same eyes that had so frightened her in the cellar.

From her earliest childhood Letty had been periodically given to sleep-walking, and one night, about a year after she went into service at the mansion, she got out of bed and walked in her sleep into the haunted room. She awoke to find herself standing shivering in the middle of the floor, with the room bathed in moonlight. The night was absolutely still, no breath of wind, yet the door suddenly swung back on its hinges and slammed shut. Fully expecting that the noise had awakened the cook, who was a light sleeper, Letty listened to hear her get out of bed and call out. But there was no sound. Then a sudden rustling made Letty glance at the bed, and she saw the valance swaying violently to and fro. There was a slight movement on the mattress, the white dust cover appeared to rise, and under it Letty saw the outlines of what she took to be a human figure gradually take shape. Praying that she was mistaken and that it was only a trick of her imagination, she was aware of a church clock striking two. The unmistakable sound of breathing now issued from the bed, and the dust cover began to slip aside. First, Letty saw a few wisps of dark hair, then a thick cluster, then a protruding forehead, two eyelids, yellow and swollen, and fortunately tightly closed, then an indistinct purple mass. The thing turned over in its sleep and a leprous white hand came groping out. Letty grasped for something to smash it with —the idea that she had to kill it was uppermost in her mind. A glimpse of the moonlight on her naked toes brought her to her senses and she crossed herself. There was a noise in the passage, the door of the room began to open, and a shadowy something slipped through and began to wriggle over the floor. Letty tried to move, but could not. The object crawled into the wardrobe. Then the wardrobe door opened and the eyes appeared, to gaze at the thing lying on the bed. There were not only eyes this time but a form, misty and irregular, but still with sufficient shape to enable Letty to identify it as that of a tall woman with a total absence of hair. There was a slither towards the bed, the bolster was snatched from under the sleeping head and pressed down on it. Then everything faded.

Letty, chilled to the bone but thoroughly alert, dashed back to her own room, where she spent the remaining night hours wide-awake, determining never to go to bed again without fastening one of her arms to the iron staples. She never saw another manifestation, though others did, and the Admiral's family finally had to leave.

All that Letty could discover about the house after she had left was that long ago, an idiot child was supposed to have been murdered there, but by whom tradition did not say. After the Admiral and his family cleared out no one else would stay in the house, presumably on account of the hauntings, and it was eventually demolished and a modern building erected in its place.

It is commonly supposed, probably from all the tales of fiction, that hauntings occur mainly in the dark of winter, and usually with thunder and lightning accompaniment. But in real life this is not so. Ghosts are not bound by the clock or the seasons. They can occur in the full light of the day, and in high summer.

It was during one wet summer that my friend Mrs. Christine Lockwood encountered the ghost of a house in Well Walk, Hampstead. Mrs. Lockwood had heard from her friends who were renting the house, that it was alleged to be haunted by something that was sometimes seen on the staircase, but as none of them had ever encountered it, they did not believe that the house was haunted at all. Some weeks after they had moved in Mrs. Lockwood went to stay there for a few days.

" I'm sure you won't mind sleeping in the 'haunted room '," her friend, the lady of the house laughingly remarked on her arrival— " only all the other rooms are occupied."

" The haunted room?" said Mrs. Lockwood. " I thought it was your staircase that was supposed to be haunted?"

" Well, yes," said her friend, " but the room is, too. You needn't worry, though—none of us has ever seen anything unusual in it !"

It was obvious that everyone treated the whole thing as a huge joke, so Mrs. Lockwood certainly had no qualms about using the room. Being very tired after a long journey she fell asleep almost as soon as her head touched the pillow and enjoyed a perfectly quiet, untroubled sleep.

The following night she was not so fortunate. Hardly had she got into bed than she heard loud knockings in different parts of the room, accompanied by light, stealthy footsteps and whispering. Thinking someone was in the room, probably to try and scare her—taking the joke much too far—she got up and lit a candle, but could see no one. She was about to put out the light and get back into bed when there was a gentle puff and the candle flame was blown out. This broke down her fortitude and she ran out of the room in a panic. She spent the rest of the night on a couch in the drawing-room, and the next day was transferred to an attic room, where a bed was improvised for her.

Several days later, arriving back at the house in a veritable downpour, she was going upstairs to this room to change her clothes when she saw a woman in a very smart, though somewhat old-fashioned blue tailormade costume, going up the stairs in front of her. The woman also appeared to have been out, for she wore a hat and carried a sunshade, but rather puzzlingly neither her hat nor dress, nor the sunshade were at all wet. Wondering who the stranger could be, but supposing her to be some friend of the family, Mrs. Lockwood followed her upstairs. On reaching the first floor, the woman walked quickly to the "haunted room" and entering it, closed the door with a loud bang.

Mrs. Lockwood thought no more of the incident, but continued up to the attic room to change her wet clothes.

On the following day, which proved to be very hot and fine, Mrs. Lockwood returned to the house at about the same time and again saw the woman in blue going up the staircase. This time, despite the dryness of the weather, the woman's dress and umbrella (which she now carried instead of the sunshade) appeared to be saturated. As before, she entered the "haunted room" slamming the door behind her.

Now considerably puzzled, Mrs. Lockwood determined to solve the mystery. She decided not to mention the matter to her friends, the people of the house, as they might think her rudely inquisitive. Instead, she found some excuse to remain indoors the next day, and sure enough, at exactly the same time, she saw the same woman in blue walking upstairs as before. Mrs. Lockwood immediately ran after her, and followed her into the "haunted room". The woman walked straight to the large mirror on the dressing table and threw back the the dark veil which had hitherto screened her face. The room was full of sunlight, so that Mrs. Lockwood, who was close behind the woman, could see her reflection in the mirror absolutely clearly. And what she saw was not the face of a living woman, but that of a ghastly, grinning skeleton.

Mrs. Lockwood did not faint, she was not given that way. She simply fled from the room, and that very afternoon packed and left the house, which she never visited again. Her friends shortly afterwards vacated the premises, the ghost at last having been seen by them, too.

Another summer haunting occurred in a house in Courtfield Gardens, South Kensington. Miss Evelyn Wakefield had not long taken up residence there before there was a very alarming incident.

A cousin was spending the evening with her, and as the weather was very hot, the two women sat in one of the as yet unoccupied rooms with the window open. At about ten o'clock Miss Wakefield remarked, "You won't mind my leaving you for a few minutes? I must just go upstairs and see to a few things."

Her cousin replied, quite pleasantly, "Of course not." When, however, Miss Wakefield returned a few minutes later, her cousin appeared to be very upset, and saying that it was time for her to be going, hurriedly quit the house.

Miss Wakefield did not see her cousin again until some months later, when they met in the street. The cousin seemed quite herself again, and on Miss Wakefield asking why she had not been to see her for so long, she said, " Well, perhaps it's better you should know what happened the last night I was in your house. After you left me alone in the room I saw something so dreadful that nothing will ever persuade me to enter it again."

She then told Miss Wakefield that directly she had gone upstairs a man suddenly appeared in the room. He did not enter by the door or window, but was simply there. He was dressed in white, with a death-like face, and a long beard. After walking three or four times round the room he disappeared through the wall near the fireplace. Immediately afterwards, waves of something white came out from the spot where he had vanished.

" It was awful to see," said the cousin. " I could not cry out, I could do nothing, only sit there and watch."

Miss Wakefield would have thought her cousin's story highly incredible had not a servant just left her after having a similar unnerving experience. The servant had described seeing the same bearded man lying on the floor, with his arms folded on his breast, and his face and eyes looking like those of a dead person, although the eyes were wide open and staring. She was so frightened that after telling what she had seen she left the house immediately, without serving notice.

Some weeks after this meeting with her cousin Miss Wakefield began to experience the hauntings herself. She was awakened at all hours of the night by the most extraordinary noises. First she would hear a rushing noise, then things would seemingly be thrown down in the kitchen with great violence, though it was always found in the morning that nothing had been disturbed.

Her new servant also was subjected to the phenomena. The girl was awakened one night by hearing footsteps on the stairs and then a tremendous crash, as if numbers of trays had been dashed down on the tiled floor.

The room in which the ghost was seen was in the basement, and even in the hottest weather there was always a strange chilliness in its atmosphere. Miss Wakefield did not stay on to see what happened in the winter.

According to a rumour in the neighbourhood a butler had committed suicide in the room.

An actor named Robinson, whom I used to meet occasionally at the Actor's Association in Regent Street, once told me of a curious experience he and his wife had in a flat which he rented in a house in Whitehead's Grove, Sloane Square. Besides hearing unaccountable sounds such as footsteps crossing the floor at all hours of the night, they would wake up suddenly to find that all the bedclothes had been taken off them and carried some little distance away. Also, on arriving home rather later than usual one night, they heard, to their astonishment, someone playing an old-world tune on, so it seemed to them, their piano. They went into the sitting-room fully expecting to find someone there, but the room was empty and the piano closed.

One evening when alone in the flat Mrs. Robinson heard sounds of laughter just behind her. Thinking it was her husband who had returned earlier than usual from the theatre, she turned round quickly to speak to him, and was considerably shaken to find no one there.

Perhaps the most remarkable of their experiences was a dual dream. Mr. and Mrs. Robinson both dreamed, on the same night, that on returning to the flat one day they met a tall, cadaverous looking man in black, with a hare-lip. He was just leaving the flat with a yard measure in his hand. They said to him, " Who are you? What do you want?" and he replied, " Don't worry, I've just been measuring her and she won't need one more than five feet long." The man then bade them a polite good morning, and was about to pass them by, when they awoke.

Struck by the singularity of the fact that they had each had precisely the same dream, the Robinsons made a careful note of the occurrence.

About a month later they went on a visit to one of Mrs. Robinson's aunts. Soon after their arrival the aunt caught a severe chill and died, and when the undertaker came to the house to see about the coffin, Mr. and Mrs. Robinson identified him at once. Tall, thin and hare-lipped, he was the man they had both dreamed about. He did not say, " Don't worry, I've just been measuring her and she won't need one more than five feet long," but what his double in the dream had said about the coffin was nevertheless true, for as Mrs. Robinson's aunt was a very small woman, only about four feet ten inches in height, the coffin made for her was consequently five feet in length.

Finally, back at the Whitehead's Grove flat, the ghostly disturbances got on the Robinsons' nerves to such an extent that they left before their lease was up.

A story that must be included here is that of the hauntings at an old house in Cheshunt, Hertfordshire. This is known to us through an account which Mr. and Mrs. Charles Kean, the famous stage stars, gave to two independent inquirers. The story concerns the experiences of Mr. Kean's sister and her husband, Mr. Chapman, during their tenancy of the house, which was a long, low, rambling structure standing in grounds that were once very extensive.

The Chapmans bought the seven years' lease of the house at so low a figure that one wonders why their suspicions were not immediately aroused, but I expect that, being young, they had very little experience of houses. For some time after they moved in all went well, and they were congratulating themselves on their bargain purchase when the totally unexpected happened. One evening Mrs. Chapman, going into a room they had named the Oak Room, saw a young girl, a complete stranger to her, leaning against the window and gazing anxiously out, as if expecting someone to arrive. The girl had dark hair hanging loosely about her neck and shoulders, and appeared to be only partly dressed, as she was wearing a short white bodice and silk petticoat. Wondering if she was " seeing things " Mrs. Chapman closed her eyes, and when she opened them again the strange girl had vanished.

Shortly after this incident the nurserymaid, a dependable girl, when passing by the lobby that led to an enclosed courtyard, saw a " hideous white face " peering in at her. The owner of the face was an old woman, and she was clad in the fashion of a bygone period. The maid was so frightened that she ran at once to Mrs. Chapman to tell her what had happened. Mrs. Chapman went into the courtyard, the outer gate of which was locked, and searched everywhere, but there was no trace of the old woman.

Then began unaccountable noises at night. Sometimes the household would be aroused from their sleep by the mysterious sound of pumping in the courtyard, while other times, in the dead of night, they would hear crashes and footsteps. In the daytime, too, ghostly footsteps once followed a maid to the fireplace in the Oak Room. Thinking at first they were those of a fellow servant, the maid looked round, and on seeing no one there was almost frightened out of her wits. The same footsteps approached Mrs. Chapman's bedroom one night, and as they stopped outside it, she summoned up all her courage, flung open the door and looked out, but no one was there. Again, when the Chapmans were seated in the drawing-room with the door shut, it frequently happened that they would hear the door handle turned and see the door open, and although they never saw anyone enter, they always felt on these occasions that something did come in, and that it stood by, watching them.

Mrs. Chapman became so nervous that when her husband was temporarily absent from home she had the servant girl, the one who had been followed by the footsteps, share her bedroom with her. And one night this girl had a strange dream. She dreamt she was in the Oak Room, and that suddenly she saw there a girl with long, dark hair, standing opposite a dreadful-looking old hag. The old woman, after gazing intently at the girl, exclaimed, " What have you done with the child, Emily? What have you done with the child?" To which the girl replied, " Oh, I didn't kill it. He was preserved, and grew up, and joined the Regiment, and went to India." Then, turning to the dreamer, the girl said, " I have never spoken to a mortal before, but I will tell you all. My name is Miss Black and this old woman is Nurse Black. Black is not her name, but we call her Black because she has been so long in the family." After a short pause the girl was about to continue speaking when the old hag came up to the dreamer and, placing a hand on her shoulder, said something the dreamer could not catch. Moreover, the impact of the hand produced such a sharp pain in the dreamer's shoulder that she awoke.

In the morning the servant described her dream to Mrs. Chapman, who at once recognized the girl as the apparition she herself had seen in the Oak Room, and the old hag as the hideous woman the nurserymaid had seen peering in at the lobby. Mrs. Chapman came to the conclusion that the dream was no ordinary dream, but one due to some psychic agency. Consequently she made inquiries in the neighbourhood and learned that, about seventy or eighty years previously, a Mrs. Ravenhall and her niece, Miss Black, had lived in the house. From this, Mrs. Chapman deduced that Miss Black and the phantom girl with the long, dark hair were one and the same. However, this was the only morsel of information she could get.

Some time after the affair of the dream, Mrs. Chapman again saw the ghost girl in the Oak Room. This time the apparition was staring into one corner of it with an agonized expression, and wringing her hands. Mrs. Chapman afterwards had the floorboards in that corner of the room taken up, but nothing was found.

The last thing that occurred while the Chapmans were in the house seemed to have no connection with any of the earlier hauntings. They were preparing to quit the place, even though their lease had only run for three years, when Mrs. Chapman awoke one morning to see a dark-complexioned man in a corduroy coat standing at the foot of her bed. He vanished as mysteriously and inexplicably as he had come. A few days afterwards Mrs. Chapman asked her husband to order some coal, as their supply had almost run out. This he promised to do. In due course the coal arrived, whereupon Mr. Chapman expressed astonishment, as he had quite forgotten to order any. This seemed remarkable, and Mrs. Chapman asked the servants if they had given the order, but all denied having done so, nor had any of them even seen the coal delivered. Mrs. Chapman, getting more and more mystified, now inquired of the person from whom they usually had coal, and he told her it had been ordered by a dark-complexioned man in a corduroy jacket and red comforter—a description which exactly fitted the man who had appeared mysteriously at the foot of her bed.

After this strange incident the Chapmans were by no means sorry to leave the house. Subsequent tenants, they learned, experienced similar disturbances, but could not account for them any more than the Chapmans. This case, which rests on the corroborative evidence of several people, affords yet another example of what so many bona-fide hauntings are, just a series of phenomena without any apparent reason.

It was at an old country house in recent years that my informant Mrs. R. Craven had an unsettling experience. While staying at the house, Mrs. Craven often used to look into the library for a few minutes' quiet reading, when she invariably found a priest sitting there, in a peculiarly pensive attitude. Wondering who he was, as she never saw him in any other part of the house, but not liking to disturb him, Mrs. Craven used to sit and steal furtive glances at him from over her book, until she felt she could no longer stand being in his presence, when she made her escape as silently as possible from the room.

This went on for some days, until one morning she determined to brave it out. She stayed in her seat till the priest somewhat electrified her by suddenly pointing in a very agitated manner to the book-shelves. Thinking him stranger than ever, but attributing his action to some possible disablement, Mrs. Craven went to the shelves and after some trouble discovered the book he apparently wanted. But on her bringing it across to him, he motioned to her to turn over the leaves, and to her astonishment the book seemed to open at the place he indicated, where she saw a loose sheet of paper covered with writings. Obeying his tacit instructions she threw the paper into the fire, where-upon the priest at once vanished.

Much startled, Mrs. Craven rushed to tell her hostess what had occurred, only to be coolly informed that, yes, the library was well-known to be haunted by just such an apparition, though it only appeared periodically and was never mentioned to visitors in case it should alarm them!

Sometimes hauntings occur in the presence of people making only a fleeting visit to a house, much less actually living in it. One striking case in point, concerning a house in Blackfriars, London, was des-cribed to me by Mrs. Michaelson. One summer, she and her husband set out to look for a cheap house to rent. What then transpired is best told in Mrs. Michaelson's own words.

" As our funds were very low we were much in need of a cheap place in which to live for the next year or two. So we went to an estate agent in the Blackfriars district. He had a large number of 'empties' on his list, but one close to the Blackfriars Road struck us as being absurdly cheap, considering its accommodation. It was a twelve-roomed house, not including the basement, which the agent told us consisted of a large kitchen and other domestic offices. He ex-plained that the street where it stood had at one time been fairly fashionable, but of late had deteriorated, and it was because of the run-down nature of the neighbourhood that the price was so low.

"Well, as my husband said, 'Beggars can't always be choosers', so we decided to have a look at the property. Being extremely busy, the agent could not spare anyone to show us over the house, so we took the key on its label and went there alone.

"It was a corner house, the outside of it blackened with the smoke and dirt of ages, and its sombre appearance was made all the worse by its general state of decay. Grass grew in the high, steep steps, broken as they were in many places, the rusty iron palings surrounding the house had become loose in their stone settings and several windows on the ground floor and in the basement were cracked and broken. We nearly turned away there and then, but having come so far we decided to go inside.

"When we opened the front door a gaunt-looking cat dashed past us into the street, and to my horror I saw cockroaches on the grimy hall floor. And there was that damp, musty smell peculiar to places that have been long shut up.

"'We could never live here,' I told my husband, as we viewed, one after another, the large, bare reception rooms, all oak-panelled —'I'd be terrified to be left here alone.'

"'We'd have to let out some of the rooms,' he replied. 'I rather like the place, it's so quaint and old-world.' But he had not then seen the basement. It was the largest and gloomiest basement I have ever been in, a big, stone-flagged kitchen with a big scullery beyond, both dank and dark.

"We got out of the basement as quickly as possible, and were think-ing of leaving the house without bothering to see upstairs—at least I certainly was—when we heard what sounded like the plaintive notes of a spinet coming from one of the upper rooms. Out of curiosity we went upstairs in the direction of the sounds, which apparently came from a room on the second floor. We had just reached the second floor landing when we heard a door on the landing above us open. The music then stopped, there were sounds of a struggle, a piercing scream, a heavy thud and a noise like someone being choked to death. We were both too shaken at first to do anything but just stare at each other in horror.

"My husband was the first to recover. He ran towards the stairs and was about to go up them and investigate when a woman came run-ning down. She was very solid-looking, not a bit ghostly, except for a strange air about her. She was tall, thin and very pale, with red hair, and wore a quaintly fashioned black dress with a white kerchief folded round her shoulders and across her bosom. On her head was a mob cap, as worn by servants in bygone years, and in one hand she held a piece of cord. There was something so startling about her that my husband shrank aside to let her pass. On reaching the head of the stairs leading to the ground floor she paused, turned round and leered, shaking her hand menacingly. Then she ran swiftly down the stairs.

"When she disappeared my husband seemed to recover the use of his limbs and was about to tear down after her when a loud, chuckling laugh prevented him. We both stood still to listen, but after that there was absolute silence. Though we were both now very frightened we forced ourselves to go upstairs, fully expecting to find evidence of some dreadful tragedy, but there was nothing. We went into every room, but they were all absolutely empty. No sign anywhere of a spinet or a body—just bare, dusty oak floors.

"Convinced now that what we had heard and seen was something supernatural we hurriedly left the premises and returned rather angrily to the estate agent (a reaction in our fright, I suppose) to tell him what had happened. He was full of apologies, and on our pressing him admitted that it was not the first time people who had visited or stayed in the house had complained to him of similar happenings. There was a tradition in the neighbourhood, he said, that a murder was committed in the house, but whether or not this was so, there was undoubtedly something strange about it and we were well out of it."

I would end this chapter on haunted houses with another experience of my own. Years ago there was a house I used occasionally to go to in Whitechapel, a rendezvous of itinerant freelance writers like myself, where, although I never actually saw any ghostly phenomena, I always had very strong impressions. The moment I crossed the threshold I felt I was in a big funeral procession following a hearse. It was a dull winter's day, I thought; there were inches of slush on the ground and the cold was intense. I could not see the faces of the people walking beside me, but I instinctively knew that they wore an expression of extreme relief, and that some even were laughing. We tramped on till we came to a steep hill, then there was a loud report, and at once everything became chaotic. After this my mind cleared and the impressions, which actually lasted only a matter of seconds, abruptly ceased.

There was no variation in these impressions, they always began and ended in precisely the same way. Moreover, I invariably received them whenever I entered the house.

One day I mentioned my experience to another regular visitor to the place, and he quite casually told me that several men who went there had had a similar experience, and he thought the landlord, if approached tactfully, might offer some sort of explanation. I spoke to the landlord and learned from him that half a century or more ago the house was owned by a wealthy tradesman, who, it was generally supposed, had made his money by sweating his employees. When he died, all the hands had to attend his funeral, but far from looking sad as they followed the coffin, they had shown every appearance of joy. Just as the procession reached the summit of a steep hill, a half-witted man fired a gun from a cottage window, and the horses drawing the hearse, taking fright, dashed down the incline and into a wall at the foot of it. Strange to say, no one was injured, but the coffin was thrown out and broken to pieces.

The landlord told me that I was by no means the only person who, upon entering the house so many years afterwards, had received a vivid mental picture of the scene.

THE TREES OF FEAR

BEFORE WORLD WAR I, when the police regulations were not enforced as strictly as they were in later years, I spent many night hours in Hyde Park, London, fraternizing with the flotsam and jetsam of humanity who knew no other home, and no other refuge from the rain and snow, than the park. It is, happily, a scene now very far removed, that depressing stream of homeless unfortunates, yet it is one I can never forget, for in my early days as a ghost-hunter I learned much from them.

The tricksters apart (and one could soon spot these) they lived close to the earth and believed in straight talk, and from them I gathered innumerable accounts of weird happenings. About tree ghosts, especially.

Many of these stories would centre around a particular tree, as instanced by the following story told me one summer evening by a down-and-out whom I sat beside on one of the benches skirting the path that runs parallel with the Bayswater Road.

" I was strolling across the grass close to here one night," said my informant, who had once been in the Church, " when I suddenly became conscious of someone walking in front of me, and on raising my head—I'd been walking with head bent in deep thought—I saw a woman a few yards ahead. She was going along in the same direction as I was, and the moonlight was so strong on her that I could see every item of her dress. It was a shabby 'turnout', a grey worsted shawl, a rusty black skirt, very bedraggled and frayed, an old battered bonnet and a pair of boots with slits in the back, through which I could see her bare skin. She looked so poor and solitary that a wave of pity went through me, and I quickened my steps to give her a penny for a night's lodging, which she needed more than me. But as fast as I walked, the distance between us still remained the same, though she never seemed to make an alteration in her pace. We continued on in this way, she moving along automatically, her head bent, and her bare heels glistening in the moonbeams, and I pounding away, straining every muscle in my legs to catch her up, until we came to a spot where several paths met.

" I then saw, some little way off to my right, a huge solitary tree with curiously shaped branches, one of which in particular took my attention. It stretched out from the trunk about six or seven feet from the ground—like a great arm—and at its end were what looked exactly like long, bony fingers, slightly curved, as if about to clutch hold of somebody. The woman ahead now turned sharply and made straight towards the tree. She was entirely in the open, the ground on either side of her being quite bare, and, as I gazed, I noticed an indistinctness, a something shadowy about her I hadn't noticed before. Again I quickened my steps in an attempt to overtake her, but still the distance between us remained the same. Then, the moment she came under the shadow of the tree, she turned round. As she did so, a ray of light fell on her face and made every feature of it stand out. It was horrible, for the thing that looked at me was not living, it was dead—long, long dead. I got the wind-up so badly I ran out of the park into the Bayswater Road, and spent the rest of the night wandering about the streets. Anywhere rather than go back to the park.

" By the next evening, however, I'd got over my fright and came here again. I looked everywhere for the tree, but couldn't find it. At last, after questioning several men who had been here for years, and getting nowhere, I asked a very old man, who I was told must know every inch of the park, if he could direct me to the tree I wanted to find. And he, at least, knew immediately what I was talking about. He took me to a broad open space which I seemed to recognize, and pointing to a certain spot, said, ' That's where the tree you're looking for stood, about twenty years ago. I remember it very well, it had a branch exactly like a human arm and hand. It fascinated people so much that they used to like to sleep under it, and quite a number who tried to were found dead in the morning. One or two, I believe, hanged themselves on its branches. It was cut down eventually, partly because of these suicides, and partly because it was said queer things had been seen and heard near it at night.'

" That is what the old fellow told me, and I believe it was true."

So the down-and-out ended his odd story, and moved on.

During my evening rambles in Hyde Park I noticed that the seat beneath a certain tree, midway between the Marble Arch and

Lancaster Gate, was rarely occupied, whereas all the other seats in that vicinity were invaded by couples. One evening, the weather being warm and sultry, I went and sat on the seat. I dozed off, and eventually fell into a deep sleep.

I dreamed that an old man and a young girl stood under the tree, whispering, and that as I watched them they raised their eyes, and looked in a horribly guilty manner, not at me, but at the space beside me, which I saw for the first time was occupied by a tiny child. Moving stealthily forward and holding in their hands an outspread cloth, they crept up behind the child, the cloth descended, and all three vanished.

Then something made me gaze up into the branches of the tree, and I saw a large, light, colourless heavily-lidded eye peering down at me with an expression of the utmost malevolence. It was altogether so baneful, so full of malice and hate, that I could only stare back at it in mute astonishment. The whole shape of the tree seemed to alter, and to become like an enormous dark hand, which, swaying violently to and fro, suddenly dived down and closed over me. I awoke at once, but was so afraid of seeing the eye, that for a short time I kept my own eyes tightly shut. When I opened them I saw bending over me a very white face, and to my intense relief a voice, unmistakably human, croaked, " No wonder you're scared, sitting here at this time of night by yourself ! "

The speaker was merely one of the scores of tramps for whom the park was reception and bedroom combined. His hat was little more than a rim, and his trousers cried shame on the ladies I saw every day with their skirts plastered all over with buttons. His cheeks were hollow, his eyes unnaturally bright, and his breath full of hunger. Still, he was alive, and anything alive just then was very welcome.

" I never sleep here," he said. " None of us do."

" Why?" I said.

" Because it's haunted," he replied. " You may laugh—so did I, years ago, afore I took to this sort of thing. But sleeping out of doors all night has taught me more than any politicians, bishops or school-masters know, or any of those fine ladies that swell about in their carriages know. I've seen sights that would make an angel afraid, I've seen ghosts of all sorts. They're not all like us, neither. Some of them ain't human at all, they're devils. You may laugh when you read about them in them library books, but it's no laughing matter when you see them, as I've seen them, all alone and cold, in some wayside ditch.

" This tree, I tell you, is haunted, and it's a devil that haunts it. Ask my mates, any of them that you'll find sleeping in the parks. There's many of them have experienced it. They've seen something hiding in the branches, and when they've seen it, they've felt they must either kill themselves or someone else. There's a devil in the tree that tempts you to do all kind of wicked things, and if you take my advice young man, you'll sit somewhere else."

"I think I will," I said, "and here's something for your warning." I gave him threepence, and, overwhelming me with thanks, he shuffled away.

Actually I heard almost my very first story of a tree-ghost not in Hyde Park, but on Clapham Common, from an old tramp who came and sat beside me on a seat.

"Do I ever see anything strange here at night?" he repeated in answer to my question. "Yes, I do at times, but what gives me the worst fright is a tree that I sometimes see close to the spot where that man was murdered some ten or twelve years ago. I never saw it before the murder, but a few nights afterwards, as I was passing the spot, I saw a peculiar glimmer of white, and on getting a bit closer I found, to my astonishment, that it was a tall, slender white thing with branches just like a tree, only it was not behaving like a tree. Though there wasn't a breath of wind, it kept lurching with a strange creaking noise, and I felt it was watching me—watching me furtively, just as if it had eyes—and was bent on doing me all the harm it possibly could. I was so scared I turned tail and never stopped running till I'd reached home."

"Home?" I said.

"Yes, a clump of bushes near the ditch, where I always turn in of nights. It isn't much of a home, to be sure, but it's the only one I've got, and I can generally count on lying there undisturbed till the morning."

Another kind of tree-ghost story came to me on Tooting Common, where I met a Northumberland miner who had come to London for the first time on a holiday, and, having had his pocket picked, was obliged to spend the night out-of-doors.

"Ghosts?" he said, when I asked if he had had any experience with the supernatural while working underground. "Yes, but not the kind of ghosts you read about in books. Me and my mates, when working in a drift at night, have heard the blowing of the wind and a mighty rustling of leaves, and have found ourselves surrounded on all sides by numerous trees and ferns that have suddenly risen from the ground and formed a regular forest. They haven't been like any trees you see nowadays, but what you might fancy existed thousands of years ago. There's been no colour to them, only a uniform whiteness, and they've shone like phosphorus. We've heard, too, all the noises such as go on daily in forests above ground—the humming and buzzing of insects, and the chirping of birds; and shafts and galleries have echoed and re-echoed with the sounds till you'd have thought that those away above us must have heard them, too."

To return to Hyde Park, and another story told me one evening by a very earnest tramp. This concerns 'Black Sally', a woman tramp of partly gipsy origin and of rather more than middle-age. Her usual beat was the West of England, between Bristol and Penzance, but occasionally she extended it and came to London. She was tall and slim, and that she had once been handsome was self-evident, as she still showed signs of more than ordinary good looks. She owed her nickname of Black Sally to the fact that her face was never clean. In fact, said my informant, it was her boast that she had not washed it for ten years—not since the eventful night when she and her husband had parted. He turned her out of doors having found someone he liked better, and so it was that she became a wanderer on the broad highway, with all interest in life gone. She seemed to labour under a constant fear that one day she and her husband would meet again, and that he would murder her. She often used to plague tramps in the park at night with talk of what he would do to her.

Like many other wayfarers, she had a real love for trees. They were, she said, her best and truest friends, and there was one tree in particular in Hyde Park that seemed to attract her more than any of the others. It was an old elm, a tree that everyone else avoided and would never sleep under, as they believed it to be haunted by something evil. Knowing its reputation Black Sally, it seems, resisted her desire to sleep under it for some time, but so great was her fascination that one night she succumbed to her desire, with the result that in the early hours of the morning she was found lying at the foot of it, cold, stiff and dead.

At that time such discoveries were by no means uncommon, they evoked little excitement or comment among the officials of the park and the general public, and the finding of Black Sally's body proved no exception to the rule. There being no visible marks of violence on her body, it was said by those in authority that death was due to natural causes. Some of the tramp fraternity, however, were of a different opinion. They had seen a dark, sinister-looking man, a complete stranger to them, loitering in the neighbourhood of the elm with the evil reputation, and remembering Black Sally's horror of her husband with regard to her death they could not help coming to a conclusion of their own.

The tramp who told me this story assured me that for several nights after this tragedy had taken place, sighings and moanings were heard coming from the spot where Black Sally's body had been found, and that at night a footprint swimming in what looked like blood was always to be seen there, the blood vanishing suddenly and mysteriously with the coming of the sun.

My informant took me to the tree, styled, he said, by him and his mates of the road 'Black Sally's tree', and pointed to the ground under it. The night being light, with a great silvery moon overhead, I was able to see very distinctly a mark, certainly not unlike the imprint of a long, narrow, human foot, but it was dry. When I commented on this, the tramp said " The blood hasn't been there lately, only the footprint, but those who knew Sally declare it to be hers."

As we moved away from the tree, I heard a sort of shuddering moan coming from it. I swung round, but no one was there; only Black Sally's tree, its slightly nodding branches darkly outlined on the moonlit soil.

THE MILLER'S HOUSE

IT IS not often that thoroughly reliable witnesses to a haunting come by the score, yet such was the case with the strange affair of the troubled mill house at Willington, in Northumberland. The full evidence of this persistent haunting was first brought to the notice of a wider public by W. T. Stead, the editor, author and ghost hunter, some forty years after its occurrence. Few were better qualified for the task, for he had spent his boyhood within a mile of the mill; he grew up hearing stories of the recent hauntings, and knew some of the people intimately involved.

This, together with the reports, letters and sworn testimony which existed, enabled Stead to present a complete and accurate account of the weird events, which has been added to here by further quotations from various testimonies.

In the 1830s the small hamlet of Willington, lying in a deep valley between Newcastle upon Tyne and North Shields, consisted of a parsonage, a few cottages, a large steam flour mill, and the miller's house. The mill, a four-storey building looking rather like a factory, stood on what was known locally as Willington Gut, a sluggish tidal stream which emptied itself into the Tyne between Willington Quay and Wallsend. The valley was crossed by a lofty railway viaduct, and the frequent engines from the coal mines as they passed overhead looked down on the tiny community of Willington, which no stretch of the imagination could make out to be more than a very commonplace scene.

The mill itself was said to have been built upon the site of a cottage occupied a century before by a witch, but this was a rather hazy local tradition. As for the mill house, a detached building of three floors, this was comparatively new, having been built about 1800, and there certainly was nothing the least spectral about its appearance.

This was the setting when Mr. Unthank and Mr. Procter, two businessmen who had acquired the mill as joint proprietors, successively took up domestic residence in the mill house. For some time previously there had been rumours that the mill house was haunted; that on several occasions, noises had been heard there which baffled and startled the hearers. Whether these rumours had any bearing on the arrangement now arrived at between the two partners it is not clear, but it was provisionally agreed between them that they should occupy the house in turn, four years at a time.

The first to move in was Mr. Unthank. He was vigorously sceptical regarding the alleged ghost or ghosts. However, shortly after his arrival in the house he heard a mangle going all night. On discovering the next day that there was no mangle on the premises he became judiciously silent as to his unbelief in the hauntings, and if he experienced further upsets during his stay he kept them well and truly to himself.

When Mr. Unthank had completed his four-year term, Mr. Joseph Procter brought his family from North Shields to live at the mill house. Procter was a much respected man, upright of manner and diligent in business, and both he and his wife were members of the Society of Friends, Mrs. Procter having belonged to a Quaker family in Carlisle. Her husband, a teetotaler, was further described as being " a man of the most lofty morality and intelligence " who was good and kind to his family and to his employees. The family brought with them from North Shields a servant girl named Mary Young, and it is some measure of the loyalty generated by the family that she elected to stay with them during the next eight years, though several times, in the general distress caused by the hauntings, she was sorely tempted to leave.

The drama of Willington mill house began in January 1835, the first strange noises being heard by a nursemaid. She heard them for about eight weeks, noticing them usually each evening, when she was in the nursery on the second floor, watching for one of the children to go to sleep. Above her was a room that was very little used, and to and fro in this room went tireless heavy footsteps, until the window in the nursery shook and rattled with their tread. At first the nursemaid took little notice of the noise, until she remembered with a shock that there could be nobody in the room, and, filled with alarm, told her mistress. Mrs. Procter found that the testimony of the nursemaid was supported by a servant girl in the kitchen who had also heard the mysterious footsteps. Soon, however, no such corroboration was needed, for all the members of the family were hearing the noises; and the weird sounds were heard, too, by a new nursemaid who had not been told about them. A man, wearing very heavy boots, seemed to be stamping to and fro in the disused room. Family and servants listened at the door, and then rushed in to surprise the intruder, only to find no one there. Some sat vigil in the room, others even slept in it, yet without seeing anything that would explain the tramplings which all had heard, and continued to hear.

The noises went on at frequent intervals. Joseph Procter did his best to find the cause of them, but in vain. The floorboards were taken up, but nothing was found; then the boards were covered with meal, in order to detect footmarks, but the ghost of the mill house trod with too light a step even to leave a trace on the flour strewn floor. And the noises went on.

There was another disturbing feature of the ghost. Most ghosts pass through doors, and even when they seem to open them, the doors are found locked as before. The Willington ghost, however, not merely passed through doors but left them open. On one occasion, when family prayers were being conducted by Mr. Procter, a noise began in the room above and heavy footsteps descended the stairs. They passed the room door, then proceeded to the front door; the bar was removed, the lock turned, two bolts drawn back, the latch lifted, the door flung open, and the footsteps passed into the front garden. Mr. Procter stopped reading, went out into the passage and found the door wide open. Mrs. Procter was almost fainting, and her husband, disturbed as he was, filled himself with gloomy reflections as to the opportunities which such a ghostly habit would afford to burglars.

The noises went on, and on. Sometimes the sounds were like a pavior at work with his rammer thumping on the floor, making all things rattle and shake that were not fixtures. Again they were like a donkey galloping round the room overhead; at another time it was as if a shovelful of scrap iron had been thrown upon the fireplace and fender. It became very difficult to get servants to remain in the house —few would stay longer than several weeks. Heavy footsteps were heard going up and down stairs, door handles turned, doors creaked as if they were opening, and occasionally the room would be filled with bluish smoke and sticks would crackle as if they were burning, but when the door was opened no fire was to be seen. At other times it was as if newspapers were being crumpled and trampled about football fashion. Once Mary Young counted 120 taps on the washtable, as if someone was striking it with a pencil. Another time the noisy ghost manifested itself so vigorously in Mr. Procter's bedroom that he adjured it in the following words : " If thou art a good spirit, why not stay in thy own place? If thou art a bad spirit, why torment me and my house?" With a great noise the restless spirit then seemed to take its departure for that night. Next night, however, it was back and as busy as ever.

On some days it seemed as though a man or woman were walking on the gravel path outside the house. Inside, there would be heard a sound like the winding of a clock upon the stairs. Beds shook, a man seemed to be dumping loads in sacks upon the floors, there was a hammering on the floorboards, the sound of bullets penetrating the floor, and footsteps approaching beds. There were sounds of doors being opened, and of people entering rooms; sounds of whistling and wheezing, laboured breathing, thumps and blows; the noise of moving chairs, of opening and shutting windows, of the banging down of box lids, and of thumping with fists. Sometimes it seemed as though a box were being trailed across the floor, or turned over; and a handbell was heard ringing. People lying in bed were certain that someone with bare feet was moving about at the foot of the bed, creeping on hands and knees; or there would be a rustling sound as if a woman dressed in silk was hurrying out of the room. In the dead of night there would be a sound as if some animal had jumped off a chair; or a child seemed to be walking about. And from various parts of the house came noises as though things were being thrown down, yet afterwards it was found they had not moved.

Occasionally doors would actually bang in the faces of people when no windows were open and there was no draught. From a closet there issued a clatter which caused the family to fear that all the china and the glass in the cupboard had been shattered to splinters; yet nothing was disturbed. On other occasions it seemed that peas or pebbles were being scattered on the floor, or on the lids of the tin boxes in the kitchen.

The noises were one thing, but then came the spectres.

One Whit Monday Mary Young was in the kitchen, washing the dishes after dinner, when she heard footsteps in the passage. On look-ing out she saw a woman in a lavender-coloured silk dress go upstairs and enter one of the upper rooms, above the sitting room. Mary went to Mrs. Procter and asked if she was expecting a visitor, telling her about the caller. Mrs. Procter was greatly alarmed. No, she said, she expected no visitors, but she had just heard a great noise in that room —" Nor will I stay any longer, but go with thee into the kitchen." That night the uproar in the mill house was the worst ever known, the noises being so violent that neither family nor servants got a wink of sleep.

Mary Young, having taken ill, went home for a few days, and her sister Isabella came to do her work. While Isabella was tidying one of the bedrooms she saw what she took to be a white towel lying on the floor. She walked towards it to pick it up, when it suddenly rose of its own accord, went behind a dressing table, over the top of it, back to the floor again, across the bedroom, under the door and downstairs. The noise it made in descending the stairs was distinctly heard by Mrs. Procter and other persons who were in different parts of the house.

Another afternoon Isabella was gazing out of the nursery window when she saw what appeared to be a white handkerchief, knotted at each corner, dancing wildly, leaping sometimes as high as the windows of the first floor. Occasionally it assumed different and peculiar shapes. One of the children, two-year-old Edmund, watched with Isabella. He was delighted, and shouted for joy: "Oh! Bonny pussy"; but his enjoyment was not shared by the bewildered Isabella.

Two sisters of Mrs. Procter who came on a short visit to the mill house had a terrifying experience. The first night, sleeping together in the same four-poster bed, they felt it lifted up beneath them. Fearful that a thief had hidden himself there for the purpose of robbery they gave the alarm, and a search was made but nothing found. On another night their bed was violently shaken and the curtains suddenly hoisted up all round to the tester, as if pulled by cords, and as rapidly let down again, several times. Again, a search produced no evidence of the cause. Next day the sisters had the curtains removed from the bed, resolving to sleep without them, as they felt that "evil eyes" lurked behind them. The following night, as both lay awake, they saw the misty, bluish-grey figure of a woman come out of the wall at the bed's head and through the headboard, in a horizontal position, and lean over them. Both saw the figure very distinctly, and as they lay frozen with terror it passed back again into the wall. From that night on neither sister would sleep in the room again, one of them even quitting the mill house entirely and taking lodgings in the house of the mill foreman.

As the hauntings continued, the Procters discouraged ordinary callers at the house, such as friends of the servants, in an effort to stop the rumours now being spread. Even Thomas Davidson, who was courting Mary Young, was asked not to enter the house, so it became his habit to stand waiting outside, after giving Mary, in the kitchen, the signal that he was there. On one such night, clear and cloudless, while waiting for Mary to appear, something attracted Thomas's attention. Looking towards the mill, which was separated from the mill house by an open space, he saw what seemed to be a whitish cat approach and come near to his feet. He gave it a kick, regarding it as "cheeky", but his foot touched nothing and the animal quietly strolled away, followed by him, until it suddenly disappeared from his gaze. Returning to his position near the kitchen window, and looking back in the same direction, Thomas again saw the cat appear. This time it came hopping towards him like a rabbit, coming quite as close to his feet as before. He kicked at it again, but as before, his foot went through it and he felt nothing. He went after it, but it disappeared at the same spot. He returned to the window, but the animal then made a third appearance, though with a certain difference. It was still of the shape of a cat or rabbit, but fully as large as a sheep, and quite luminous. On it came, as Thomas stood rooted to the spot, his hair on end, and went on to disappear as before.

Next day Thomas called at the mill and told Mr. Procter what he had seen. The harassed mill owner then revealed that he had seen the same strange animal himself on another occasion, in front of the house.

In the summer of 1840 an erstwhile ghost-hunter, Mr. Edward Drury of Sunderland, who had heard from friends in the locality of the alleged goings on at the mill house, wrote to Joseph Procter, giving his credentials and asking if he might be allowed to keep a night's vigil in the house. " On account of this report coming from one of your sect, which I admire for candour and simplicity," he wrote, " my curiosity is excited to a high pitch, which I would would fain satisfy. My desire is to remain alone in the house all night, with no companion but my own watch-dog. My hope is that if I have a fair trial I shall be able to unravel this mystery. . . ."

Drury was fortunate in that the Procter family were shortly going away for a time, so Procter acceded to his request. The family left home on June 23 1840, leaving the house in charge of an old servant, and in their absence Drury was given leave to conduct his night's vigil, with or without his dog. As it transpired, Drury seemingly had second thoughts about coming with only a dog for company, and instead of the animal brought a friend, Mr. Thomas Hudson. He also took the precaution of arming himself with a brace of pistols. And so, on the evening of July 3rd, Drury and Hudson arrived at the mill house, only to find Joseph Procter there; he had been recalled to the mill on business. However, the vigil went ahead as promised. After the house had been locked up for the night, Drury and Hudson made a detailed examination of every room to guard against trickery. They were well provided with lights, and after satisfying themselves that there was no one in the house besides Mr. Procter, his servant, and themselves, they got down to their vigil.

It was ten days before Edward Drury sufficiently recovered from the alarming experiences of that night to write a letter to Procter confirming what had happened.

After searching the house and finding it quite empty, Drury had felt there was no need for him to load his pistols. At 11 p.m. he stationed Hudson on the third-storey landing. Less than an hour later, at ten minutes to midnight, they both heard a noise as if a number of people were pattering with their bare feet on the floor, and a few minutes later, another noise as if someone was knocking with his knuckles among their feet. This was followed by a hollow cough from the room where the female apparition had been seen, and then the noise of someone unseen rustling against the wall in coming upstairs.

"At a quarter to one," Drury testified in his letter written afterwards, "I told my friend that, feeling a little cold, I would like to go to bed, as we might hear the noise equally well there. He replied that he would not go to bed till daylight. I took up a note which I had accidentally dropped, and began to read it, after which I took out my watch to ascertain the time, and found that it wanted ten minutes to one. In taking my eyes off the watch they became riveted upon a closet door, which I distinctly saw open, and saw also the figure of a female, attired in greyish garments, with the head inclining downwards and one hand pressed upon the chest as if in pain, and the other, the right hand, extended towards the floor with the index finger pointing downwards. It advanced with an apparently cautious step across the floor towards me. Immediately as it approached my friend, who was slumbering, its right hand was extended towards him. I then rushed at it, giving as Mr. Procter states, a most awful yell, but instead of grasping it I fell upon my friend, and I recollect nothing distinctly for nearly three hours afterwards. I have since learnt that I was carried downstairs in an agony of fear and terror."

It was Joseph Procter who carried him down, after hearing him shriek. Drury was beside himself with fright, crying out in agony: "There she is. Keep her off. For God's sake keep her off!" For nearly three hours he kept saying this, after which he came to himself, and said that not for ten thousand pounds would he put foot across the doorstep of the house again. As for his friend Mr. Hudson, who had dozed off and was awakened by the shriek, he had seen nothing.

In Drury's letter to the mill owner about what he called "that horrid and most awful affair," he said that no one could have gone into the house more sceptical of anything happening, but no one could be more satisfied than himself that the place was damnably haunted. "I am persuaded," he told Procter, "of the horrid apparition, that I would affirm that what I saw with my own eyes was a punishment to me for my scoffing and unbelief. Happy are those that believe and have not seen."

Joseph Procter replied to him: "Respected Friend, Edward Drury —I am glad to hear that thou art getting well over thy unlooked for visitation. I hold in respect thy bold and manly assertion of the truth in the face of that ridicule and ignorant conceit with which that which is called the supernatural in the present day is usually assailed. I shall be glad to receive thy detail in which it will be needful to be very particular in showing that thou couldst not be asleep, or attacked by nightmare, or mistake a reflection of the candle as some sagaciously suppose—I remain, thine respectfully, Joseph Procter. P.S. I have about thirty witnesses to various things which cannot be satisfactorily accounted for on any other principle than that of a spiritual agency."

John Richardson, an old and trusted servant of the Procters, sat up one night with an old Quaker gentleman who came to try to alleviate the situation with prayer. The old Quaker asked Richardson to get a Bible, and he would read a chapter. No sooner had he begun to read, however, than the candle began to jump in the candlestick and rock from side to side so strongly that the Quaker could not see to read. Yet the moment he stopped, the candle became quiet.

The Quaker looked at John Richardson and said : " Strange !" He began to read again, and again the candle began to sway from side to side. "Art thou afraid, John?" asked the Quaker. "No," replied John, "but I feel a peculiar sensation which I cannot describe." "Let us pray, John," said the Quaker. But immediately they got to their knees a terrific noise arose in the room, all the furniture seemed to be driven from its place, the candlesticks rattled on the table, newspapers seemed to be scattered to and fro in great profusion and the whole building seemed shaken. So much noise was there that Richardson could not hear a single word of the Quaker's prayer. Yet the moment the Quaker arose from his knees everything became quiet.

Another Quaker, who faced the invisible ghost with a bold : " Who art thou? In the name of the Lord, I bid thee depart," was answered by a mocking sound described by those present as being "like a spasmodic suction of the air through the teeth."

Inside and outside the mill house the ghost (or ghosts) continued to appear at intervals. Thomas Mann, the old mill foreman, together with his wife and daughter, and the frightened sister of Mrs. Procter who had chosen to lodge with them, were passing the mill house late one dark, moonless night when all four saw the apparition of a bald-headed man in a flowing robe like a surplice gliding backwards and forwards about three feet from the floor of the second storey, level with the bottom of the window. The figure seemed to enter the wall of the house on each side, thus presenting the watchers with a side view in passing.

" It then stood still in the window, and a part of the figure came through both the blind, which was closed down, and the window, as its luminous body intercepted the view of the framework of the window. It was semi-transparent, and as bright as a star, diffusing a radiance all around. As it grew more dim it assumed a blue tinge, and gradually faded away from the head downwards." Mann went to inform the family, but found the house locked up for the night.

In November 1841 Mrs. Procter's brother, Mr. J. Detchon Carr, paid a reluctant visit to the mill house, where he had already had some unhappy experiences. He had agreed to come only if Mr. Procter slept in the same room with him. In the evening of his day of arrival he went to have a talk with Thomas Mann and his wife about the ghost they had seen at the window. Afterwards he was preparing to return to the mill house when to their astonishment all three, in the darkness, saw another ghostly figure at the window of the "blue room" (so called because of the colour of its upholstery and decorations.) This apparition took the form of an animal about two feet high.

Telling the Manns to keep careful watch, Mr. Carr rushed off to the house and he and Joseph Procter scoured the blue room, but could find nothing. Leaving Procter in the room with a candle, Carr then hurried back to ask the Manns if the vision had remained in the window all during his absence, for it was still plainly visible. They replied that it had been there all the time, and all three now watched the spectre for a further half an hour, after which it began to shrink in size and gradually disappeared.

This was only the prelude to further manifestations inside the house that night. Bessy Mann and Isabella Young (taking her sister's place again) were sitting in the nursery with the children when Isabella felt a sharp blow on the back of her chair; then the night-table was physically moved from one side of the room to the other by an unseen body. Noises then began all over the house, and when bedtime came, one of the millers was sent for to sleep in the same room as Mr. Carr and keep him company; but the uproar was so terrible that all idea of sleep was abandoned by Carr and the Procters, who sat out the night with tired eyes.

Mr. Carr left next day by an early train, vowing he would never return to the place. That same night as he left, Isabella Young and Bessy Mann heard ghostly groans coming from a closet, and less than an hour later saw a whitish figure glide downstairs, cross the nursery floor and enter the closet. They fled.

A brother of Mr. Procter, described as "a gentleman in middle life and of a sensible, sedate and candid disposition," on a visit to the mill house found himself disturbed by the strangest noises. He had vowed before going that if he did hear noises he would speak out and demand to know the instigator of them, and his purpose. But when the occasion came, the brother was quite unable to make the challenge. As he lay in bed one night, he heard heavy steps ascend the stairs towards his room, together with the sound of someone striking the banisters with a thick stick as he went along. The footsteps came to the brother's door and he tried to call out, but his voice died in his throat. He then sprang from his bed and flung open the door, but found no one there. Yet even as he stood, puzzled, he heard the same heavy feet deliberately descending the stairs invisibly under his nose—and the same loud blows on the banisters as they went. Joseph Procter was roused by the noises and he and his brother quickly searched the house, but found nothing.

From the very onset of the disturbance the worried Procters had tried to keep them from their young children, and expressly ordered the servants not to mention the noises in front of the family. But the children very soon had their own experiences of the noises, and worse still, the apparitions. In fact the life of one of the boys was made so miserable by the hauntings that he had to be packed off to his mother's home in Carslisle.

One day one of his young sisters came to Mary Young and told her : " There's a lady sitting on the bed in Mama's bedroom. She has eyeholes but no eyes, and she looked so hard at me." When the family investigated, the room was empty. On a different occasion, another of the girls said that the previous night a lady had come out of the wall and looked into the mirror; she had something tied over her head, and had eyeholes but no eyes. One child lying in bed saw the figure of a man enter the room, walk to the window, push up the sash, put it down again, and then walk out of the room. His hair was light or grey, and he wore no hat. At another time a phantom boy was seen; and on several occasions the children had bizarre fun chasing up or down stairs the ghostly figure of an animal—" a funny cat or a bonny monkey."

All this and much more went into the day-to-day diary of the hauntings which Joseph Procter kept, and which ultimately found its way into the hands of psychical researchers. It furnished a very nearly complete record of the weird happenings at Willington mill house right up to the day the distressed family left it, for in 1847 Joseph Procter decided his family could take no more. They moved to North Shields, and afterwards to Tynemouth, and were never again troubled by ghosts.

They left behind them, at Willington, two main apparitions, one in the likeness of a man, which was luminous and passed through walls, and the other the figure of an eyeless female in grey, said to be seen sometimes sitting wrapped in a sort of mantle, with her head depressed and her hands crossed on her lap.

Six years after the family left the mill house the clairvoyant wife of a pitman was involved in an attempt to solve the mystery of the disturbances. This woman, though completely without knowledge of the Procter family or what had happened in the house, described many of the events there most accurately, and pronounced the two principal spectres to be a priest and a "grey lady". The priest, she said, had refused to allow the woman to confess a deadly crime committed at the spot many years before, and this was the troubling cause of the poor woman's apparition.

When, in the 1890s, W. T. Stead first put together the story of the Willington ghosts, from his own knowledge and the accounts of others, and letters, there were still living more than forty different people who had actually witnessed the ghosts at the mill house. As for the house itself, some time after the Procters left it was divided into two, and the foreman and chief clerk of the mill lived in it, remaining there for nearly twenty years, reputedly hearing noises and seeing visions, but choosing to put up with them. A converted rabbi then lived in the house for a time, and during his stay the manifestations partially returned. Then the house was divided up into tenements, and in the course of time became a slum. Still, at intervals, strange noises were heard in the building, but eventually it was demolished, and presumably the ghosts with it, for they were heard and seen no more in the locality.

MORE SPECTRES FROM MY NOTEBOOK

My notebooks are full of by-ways of ghostland down which I have travelled, sometimes to success, sometimes to failure. The pages roam over the years, recording names and events by the hundred. I find that many people are, at times, more fascinated by these pencilled records than by anything else, possibly for the infinite variety of ghostly happenings that they cover, and the always varying backgrounds to them.

Here then, taken at random, are some further excerpts from my notebooks.

When I was visiting St. Paul's Cathedral one summer's day, two Americans, I think man and wife, came to me in great excitement and said they had just had a very curious experience. "We were walking down that aisle," the lady said, pointing to the centre aisle, "when we both saw a great black cloud suddenly come out of the ground in front of us and ascend into the air. When about twenty feet up, it suddenly vanished."

I asked her if it was like smoke, and she said, "Oh, no, it was like nothing I've ever seen. It gave me the impression it was alive, and I was terribly frightened."

She certainly looked scared, for she was very white and trembling. The man with her, who appeared equally alarmed, corroborated her story. They left St. Paul's with me, and said they would go back again in a few days' time, when they had recovered from the shock, to see if the same thing happened. Whether they did go back I cannot say, for I never saw them again.

Another lady told me that when resting in St. Paul's one day, she saw a woman kneeling in one of the aisles, apparently searching for something. Thinking to help her, she got up and was walking towards the woman, when she felt someone touch her on the shoulder. She swung round at once, but there was no one in sight, and when she turned to look again at the woman, she, too, had disappeared, and not a trace of her was to be seen.

Several days later, when she was in the Cathedral at about the same time of day, the same thing happened. She saw the same woman kneeling in the same aisle, and as she was walking towards her, she again felt a tap on her shoulder. She glanced round immediately, but no one was there, and when she turned again the kneeling woman also had vanished. An eerie feeling then came over her and she got out of the Cathedral as quickly as possible.

Many strange stories have been told about the old Richmond Palace, where many English monarchs lived and several died. One of the several who died there was Queen Elizabeth I, concerning whose death Miss Strickland, in her interesting history, notes the following ghostly incident :

" As her mortal illness drew towards a close, the superstitious fears of her simple ladies were excited almost to a mania, even to conjuring up a spectral apparition of the Queen while she was yet alive. Lady Guildford, who was then in waiting on the Queen, leaving her in an almost breathless sleep in her privy chamber, went out to take a little air, and met Her Majesty, as she thought, three or four chambers off. Alarmed at the thought of being discovered in the act of leaving the royal patient alone, she hurried forward in some trepidation in order to excuse herself, when the apparition vanished away. She returned terrified to the chamber, but there lay the Queen in the same lethargic slumber in which she had left her."

Stories and traditions abound about the Palace, the old gatehouse and the mound, called Oliver's Mound, where in 1834 some workmen, when digging, found the skeletons of three people buried about three feet beneath the surface. Soon afterwards a tradesman passing by the gatehouse one night is said to have seen two men in armour fighting furiously. Amazed at the spectacle, he was standing watching them when a man, richly clad in clothes of a bygone age, came striding up to them, dagger in hand, and stabbed one of the combatants to the heart. As the wretched man fell without a sound to the ground, all the figures disappeared and the tradesman found himself merely staring into space.

Mr. Charles Green, an artist, told me another story of the Richmond Palace ghosts.

One evening a man and his son, who were engaged on repair work at the Palace, were leaving for home when a tall, gaunt woman in black emerged from behind a tree and walked ahead of them. She was carrying a sack over her shoulders with something so heavy in it that she staggered under the weight. The workman and the boy were studying her out of curiosity, for there seemed something unusual in her appearance, when to their horror a hand suddenly emerged from a hole in the side of the sack nearest to them. It was a large, coarse hand, and the thumb was missing. The mutilated state of the flesh suggested that it had been hacked or torn off.

The man and boy tried to run after the woman to stop her, but their limbs refused to move any faster, and when they tried to call out, they found that they could not. In this confused state they were compelled to follow the old woman, who never varied her pace and always kept the same distance ahead of them. On and on they went, right through the Palace grounds till they came to Oliver's Mound, when both man and boy felt a slight, though sharp, blow dealt them on the shoulder. Both turned round quickly to see who or what had struck them, and to their amazement saw no one and nothing. Turning back again they looked for the woman, but she had vanished. A few minutes later, while they were still looking around, wondering where she could possibly have gone, they heard a series of wild shrieks, followed by a succession of groans and gasps, which seemed to indicate only too plainly that someone was being done to death. The man and boy did not stop to investigate, they left the mound and ran hard for home.

The unearthing of the skeletons in the vicinity of the mound had some connection, so Mr. Green and others thought, both with the phantom fighters seen by the tradesman at the old gatehouse, and the spectral woman seen by the workman and his son.

When I was giving a talk at St. Ives, a woman member of the audience told of a strange incident in a shop in the West End of London.

A middle-aged couple were visiting the shop one day when they saw to their astonishment one of the women superintendents walking about with a speckled bird, belonging to a species they did not recognize, on her shoulder. Going up to her the wife said, " Whatever kind of bird is that on your shoulder, my dear?" Whereupon the woman turned ghastly white and fainted.

It subsequently transpired that whenever a member of the woman's family was about to die, a strange-looking bird would be seen hovering near the doomed individual. This instance proved no exception to the rule, for the superintendent, although in apparently perfect health at the time, developed ptomaine poisoning the next day, and died within a week.

For many years an inn at Sedgley, near Wolverhampton, had frequently changed hands owing to the occupants being badly scared by unearthly sounds at night—groans, sighs and spine-chilling cries—and the appearance on the stairs and in the rooms of the phantoms of an old man and other people, all of them resembling the long dead.

The inn was finally demolished, and under a hearthstone were found a number of human bones. Elderly people in the village remembered hearing of several mysterious disappearances, including that of an old man known as "Old Short, the moneyman". He had often stayed at the inn, which in his time bore a very bad reputation. That some of the bones were his was beyond doubt.

I have noted many other inn hauntings in my time, some rather similar in that they involve violence and murder, for after all, it is common knowledge that many inns of not so long ago had unsavoury reputations. But for a haunting of a most unusual nature, here is the story connected with a public-house at Bethnal Green, in London.

Near the site of the old schoolhouse in Bethnal Green there used to be a public-house known as the "Gibraltar". For many years it was kept by John Harris, a native of Birmingham and silver plater by trade. At first he conducted the "Gibraltar" in a most exemplary fashion, but having made a lot of money he gradually got lax, and in the end he had to close down, the local authorities refusing to renew his licence.

The old adage that misfortunes never come singly proved very true in Harris's case, for soon after his enforced retirement from business, his wife quarrelled with him over money and left him. One night, soon after her departure, he was sitting by his lonely fireside brooding over his misfortunes, which seemed almost too much to bear, when he suddenly heard the bell ring in the now deserted bar. Though rather startled, as he was alone in the house, having dismissed all his employees because he could no longer afford to keep them, he did not stir from his seat till the bell rang a second time. He then got up and went to the back door, thinking someone had entered that way and was indulging in a joke at his expense. But there was no one there.

Much puzzled, Harris was returning to the warmth and comfort of the parlour, for it was a cold winter's night, when the bell started ringing again, not so quickly as before, but more regularly, as if the hand that pulled it held it for a while. Greatly uneasy now, he armed himself with a poker, the first weapon that came to hand, and passed through the bar into the room beyond, where he saw a woman dressed in a brown costume, resembling that formerly worn by

Quakeresses, seated in a chair between the two back windows. At first he was too overcome by terror to speak, for although there was nothing actually frightening about the woman's appearance, there was something distinctly eerie about her. As he described it later, something told him at once she did not belong to this world, and he instinctively associated her with death.

Had he never done an evil thing he might have felt braver, but, guilty in the knowledge that he had been living a thoroughly bad life, he was sick and afraid. With a great effort he summoned up courage to speak.

"Who are you?" he demanded, clutching hold of the wall for support, for all the strength seemed to go out of his limbs.

"Who or what I am is not my business to relate," the strange woman replied, "but what you may hereafter become if you do not amend your life, is my business to warn you. You have but a few years to live, make the most of them and train up your daughter, Phoebe, in a good way. Be very particular whom she associates with, or she will come to a violent end. Remember her life is just now in your keeping, a short space of time will place it out of your power to avert the evil that awaits her. Your responsibility is very great. Recollect this, John Harris, and live accordingly." She had hardly ceased speaking before she tapped the ground with a long stick on which she had been leaning, and immediately disappeared, leaving Harris paralysed with awe and amazement.

No better proof of the truth of this story, which John Harris subsequently confided to a friend, could be afforded than the sudden change that now came over him. From being a scoffer at religion, a heavy drinker and hard swearer, he took to going first to church and then to chapel, and finally became a Methodist. He never touched a drop of alcohol again, and gave up using bad language. In short, he changed from a rogue into a really decent living person, and remained such till his death.

But it was too late for him to convert Phoebe. She had got involved with a gang of criminals and ended up on the scaffold.

In the course of time the old " Gibraltar " was pulled down, but right up to the year of its demolition it was regarded as haunted, in consequence of what Harris was always convinced he saw there.

The case of a ghostly dream which led to a conviction for murder, is associated with another London district, Cripplegate. In the neighbourhood of Cripplegate in the autumn of 1698, a man named Stockden was murdered. The motive of the crime was robbery, and the assassins escaped without leaving any clue to their identity. But Mrs. Elizabeth Greenwood, a neighbour of Stockden, dreamed that the murdered man came to her, and bidding her follow him led her to a house in Thames Street.

" In that house," she understood him to say, " Maynard, one of the men who robbed and murdered me, lives." She then awoke.

With the dream fresh in her memory, Mrs. Greenwood went the following morning to Thames Street, and recognizing a house there as the one she had seen in her dream, she asked whether a man named Maynard lived in it. She was told yes, and then left.

In another dream Mrs. Greenwood again saw Stockden, who gave her a minute description of Maynard and a certain wine-drawer. Both men were found from these descriptions and arrested.

In a third dream Stockden again appeared to Mrs. Greenwood and took her to a house in Old Street, where he said Marsh, another of his murderers lived. In the morning she went to the street and found her dream was true. Marsh did live in that particular house. Mrs. Greenwood had yet a fourth dream in which she thought the murdered man took her over a bridge in the Borough into a yard where she saw a man and his wife. Stockden told her they were the Bevils, and that the man was also one of the gang that had murdered him. In the morning she searched for the yard, accompanied by Stockden's housekeeper. The yard proved to be the Marshalsea prison yard, and walking about in it were the man and woman Mrs. Greenwood had seen in her dream.

The man was at once charged with the murder. He, Marsh and Maynard were tried, found guilty and executed. The wine-drawer, who was a friend of Maynard, was not convicted.

The night after the executions Stockden made his final appearance in a dream to Mrs. Greenwood, and said : " Elizabeth, I thank thee, the God of Heaven reward thee for what thou hast done."

All the details of this extraordinary case are recorded in law court history.

I turn now to the uncanny experiences of three young ladies. First that of Miss Frances Sinclair, while travelling by train between Chester and London.

On the train entering a tunnel, at about six in the evening, Miss Sinclair was quite positive there was no one in the compartment save herself and her small dog. Judge then her horror when she suddenly saw, seated opposite her, the huddled-up figure of what she took to be a man with his throat cut. He had two protruding, fishy eyes, which met hers in a glassy stare. He was dressed in mustard-coloured clothes, and had a black bag at his side. Miss Sinclair was at once seized with a violent impulse to destroy herself, and while her dog was burying its nose in the folds of her dress and showing every indication of terror, she was doing all she could to prevent herself jumping out of the carriage. Just when she thought she must succumb and was on the verge of opening the door, the tunnel ended, the apparition vanished, and her longing for self-destruction abruptly subsided.

Miss Sinclair had never before, she assured me, experienced any such sensations. She was far too upset to make inquiries about the incident, so whether any other people had also experienced the haunted railway compartment it is impossible to say.

Now to Miss Ann Featherstone. "About seven years ago," she told me, "my sisters and I were staying at a farmhouse at Chagford, on Dartmoor, near Gidleigh. We started one day to walk to Gidleigh, and went through the village and up a lane beyond, on to the open moor. There we found ourselves on a level piece of ground, with Kes Tor close by to our left, while on our right were three new-looking houses, with little gardens and wicket gates leading to them. I went into one to inquire if there were any rooms to let for the following year, and was shown over it, while my sisters waited on the moor for me. Strange to say, I forgot to ask the name and address of the place, but it seemed on a perfectly straight road from Gidleigh.

"When we got back to Chagford, we asked our landlady where we had been, and she said the name of the place was Berry Down, so the next year we wrote there for rooms, but on arriving we were astonished to find quite a different place—not on the open moor at all. We then set about looking for the three houses we had seen. We walked round Gidleigh in every direction, inquiring of the postman, clergymen, farmers and villagers, but none knew of any such houses, nor could we find the remotest traces of them.

"The day on which we saw them was bright and sunny, so we could not possibly have been mistaken, and moreover, we rested on the moor opposite them for some time, so that had they been mere optical illusions, we should have eventually become aware of the fact. Several old Gidleigh cottagers to whom we narrated the incident were of the opinion we had been 'Pixie led'. Is such a thing possible?"

Indeed it is, as amply proved by the number of similar cases on record.

And now to Miss Wheatman, who at the time of her story was living near Morland, in Westmorland. Miss Wheatman was returning home one night with two of her sisters after spending the day with some friends in a neighbouring town, when on reaching Skellaw Wark, in the Parish of Morland, they were all startled at suddenly seeing the shadowy figure of a tall, frightening looking man emerge from behind some trees and cross the path in front of them. He was quite nude and surrounded by an eerie yellowish-green light which seemed to emanate from within him. On reaching a big stone on the wayside the figure stopped and, raising one hand, shook it menacingly at them. Then, suddenly, he seemed to sink right into the ground and disappear. Hardly had this happened before another man, also of the most forbidding aspect, appeared on the scene and went through precisely the same performance, disappearing in the same mysterious and inexplicable manner.

Another figure followed it, and then another, until the appalled young girls had finally counted eleven. Then all was still. Miss Wheatman and her sisters, confused and highly upset almost flew the rest of the way home. Their mother, to whom they babbled out their incredible story, was even more upset than they were. She told them that the ghostly figures they had seen were undoubtedly the spirits of some skeletons which had been dug up some years previously at Skellaw Wark, and as the spirits were said to be evil, and that some misfortune always befell those who saw them, she could not help feeling extremely uneasy.

The mother's fears seemed only too well founded, for very soon after the incident Miss Wheatman lost her fiance, while her two sisters were both taken so badly ill that recovery seemed impossible, and it was many months before they were well again.

I investigated the history of Skellaw Wark, which was entirely unknown to the Wheatman sisters, and found that in or about the year 1827 eleven human skeletons, with gold bangles round their wrists, were unearthed there. The skeletons were believed to date back to considerably more than a thousand years ago, and the locality in which they were discovered had always been known to be haunted. It seems pretty certain, however, that the hauntings were far more frequent and insistent after the discovery of the bones than they were before it, and that the three young girls were by no means the only observers of the remarkable spectacle.

My authority for a most unusual haunting, that of a phantom herd of pigs, is a farmer who, as a boy, saw the whole strange sight in company with his parents, brothers and sisters.

Mr. Bonsell lived as a boy in a small house called the Moat Grange, in a very lonely spot near four crossroads connecting four towns. The house, which derived its name from the fact that a moat, now dry, surrounded it, stood near the meeting point of the four roads, which in earlier years had been the site of a gibbet; and the bodies of criminals hanged there had been buried in the moat.

The Bonsells had not been living long on the farm before they were awakened one night by the most dreadful noises, partly human and partly animal, which seemed to come from a neighbouring spinney. On going to a long front window overlooking the crossroads, the family saw a number of spotted creatures like pigs, screaming, fighting and tearing up the soil on the site of the criminals' cemetery. The sight was so unexpected and alarming that the Bonsells were appalled, and Mr. Bonsell senior was just about to light a lamp when a diabolical white face was pressed against the outside of the window-pane and stared in at them.

The children shrieked with terror, and their mother, falling to her knees, began to pray, at which the face at the window vanished and the herd of pigs, ceasing their disturbance, tore frantically down one of the high roads and disappeared from view.

Similar phenomena were seen and heard so frequently afterwards that the Bonsells eventually had to leave the farm. From inquiries made later they learned that the place had long borne the reputation of being haunted, something which the previous tenant farmer had prudently omitted to tell them. The pig-like ghosts were supposed to be the earth-bound spirits of the executed criminals, but whether this was so or not must, of course, be a matter of conjecture.

One aspect of haunted houses that is often overlooked is the pos-sibility of the disturbance being the work of elemental spirits—or more popularly, "nature spirits"—as against apparitions of once-living people. Elementals are nature ghosts that have never known human form, but which often strive to imitate it. They seemingly never suc-ceed, always some part of the human anatomy being beyond their capabilities of simulation.

These conclusions are reached both from long personal experience and the many scores of other cases reported to me. One or two brief examples from my notebook will serve to illustrate the point.

From a doctor in Northamptonshire : " I well remember as a boy, running upstairs into the top room of a certain house in Guilsborough and seeing a tall, thin figure of a man with an animal's head crouch-ing on the bed. I was so frightened when I saw it that I ran out of the room as fast as I could."

From a lady in Sussex : " Waking up one night, when a young girl, I saw a tall figure standing by my bedside. It appeared to have a light inside it, and gave the same impression that a hand does when held in front of a candle. I could see the red of the flesh and dark-blue lines of the ribs—the whole was luminous. What the face was like I do not know, as I never got so far, being much too frightened to look. It bent over me, and I hid my head in the bedclothes with fright. When I told my parents about it at breakfast, to my surprise no one laughed at me. Why, I do not know, unless the house was haunted and they knew it. My brother said he had seen a tall figure disappear into the wall of his room in the night."

From a well-known author : " A few weeks ago my brother and I, on going upstairs one evening, saw the figure of a man with a cone-shaped head suddenly stalk past us and, bounding up the stairs, vanish in the gloom. Though naturally very surprised, neither I nor my brother were in the least degree frightened—the phantom answered so well to our ideas of a bogey ! Nevertheless, we are not keen to see it again."

In this case, as in many, the presence of the elemental could have been due to either some prehistoric relic that lay buried near at hand, or to the loneliness and isolation of the place.

Finally, a rather more disturbing example which came to me from a reader in Wiltshire, immediately following the publication of one of my books. The correspondent writes of an incident which had occurred only ten days before.

" I was on a visit to my two sons in Markham Square, Chelsea. On the first night of my visit I slept in a room on the third floor facing the square. The room was not absolutely dark, as some light penetrated from the street lamps in the square, but as I lay with my face to the wall, all in front of me was dark.

" I fell asleep, and remained so for an hour or more, when I suddenly awoke with a great jerk, and found confronting me the most dreadful apparition you can imagine. It was a dwarfed, tubby figure with a face like a pig, perfectly naked, in a strong bright light. The whole figure resembled in appearance the scalded body of a pig of average size, but the legs and arms were those of a human being, male or female I could not be sure. It had bright yellow hair worn in ringlets extending barely as far as the shoulders.

" In ten or fifteen seconds it vanished, leaving me bathed in perspiration and trembling. But I slept off the rest of the night.

" When the landlady came to call me (she slept on the third floor back) she pointed out that a picture on the connecting door had fallen down between my bed and the next room. Doubtless it was the fall of the picture that waked me up with a start, but what of the apparition?"

What, indeed.

One of the oddest hauntings I have ever been called upon to investigate was that of a phantom aeroplane, which was said to hover at midnight over the spot where a plane had, some time before, crashed. This was at Shepperton-on-Thames, in the winter of 1932.

In 1929 a Vickers Vanguard had broken up 4,000 feet in the air and crashed in a field near Ferry Lane. The pilot, Captain E. R. Scholefield, and his mechanic, Mr. F. W. Cherrett, were killed instantly. Three years later in 1932, strange noises were heard at night which suggested that the whole tragic incident was being enacted again in chilling ghostly fashion. On hearing the phantom crash people dashed out of their homes to look for a wrecked plane, only to find nothing.

Among the principal witnesses to this strange occurrence were Captain W. J. Gibson and his wife, whose bungalow was situated only a few hundred yards from the scene of the real crash. They heard the phantom aeroplane not once, but four or five times, on successive nights, always shortly before midnight. As Captain Gibson had served with the Royal Air Force in the 1914-18 War and seen many crashes, there could hardly have been a more authoritative witness.

Mrs. Gibson described how, on the first occasion, she was sitting at home with her husband when he remarked that there was an aeroplane close by that was obviously in difficulties. "He had hardly spoken before there was the sound of a crash, and the crumpling up of a machine. It sounded so real that we both went to look for the wreck, but found nothing. Next morning we made inquiries and found that other people had heard the sound of the approaching aeroplane, followed by the crash. But even if the noises had not been confirmed by others we should not have doubted our own ears, especially as my husband had a good deal of experience of aeroplanes during the war."

Mrs. Harding, who lived at the bungalow next door, was equally emphatic about the ghost machine. She stated : "I was in a boat on the Thames when Captain Scholefield's plane crashed. One wing came off and crashed in the Thames near me. I therefore have a vivid recollection of the noises, and the sounds we have heard at night are exactly similar. I got out of bed the same night the Gibsons first heard the phantom, and looked out of the window to see what had happened. Now when I hear the noises I just say to myself 'Oh, there's that ghost aeroplane again.' I was quite sceptical about ghosts, but this thing has occurred so many times that I am bound to believe my own ears."

Not only was the phantom plane heard, but some residents told me they actually saw it, and that it was "surrounded with a leadenish blue light." Just before it dived and crashed, dogs in the houses round about started howling dismally. Mrs. Turpin, of the Anchor Hotel, on looking out one night just before the ghostly crash saw a "white and misty" aeroplane, and heard the droning of its engine.

It was strongly suggested by the worried residents that in order to lay the ghost, which was getting on everyone's nerves, a service should be held at the scene of the crash. However, after making half a dozen regular appearances the phantom plane suddenly stopped its visits, and was not seen again.

Sadler's Wells Theatre was always said to be haunted by the ghost of Joe Grimaldi, and after the old theatre had fallen into disuse, it was still to be seen there in one of the boxes. A box at Drury Lane Theatre was also long rumoured to be haunted by Grimaldi's ghost. Its white, painted face, it was reported, had been seen behind people sitting in the box, and would peer at the stage over their shoulders, fixing its eyes always on one or other of the performers.

Joe Grimaldi, probably the most renowned of all the clowns that have ever performed on an English stage, was the son of a Genoese clown and dancer. The father, known on account of his extraordinary strength as "Iron Legs", performed at Drury Lane when David Garrick was its manager. Grimaldi senior was a firm believer in the supernatural and used to visit alleged haunted houses and places, hoping he might see the ghost. It was his love of the weird that led him to invent the Skeleton Scene and the Cave of Petrifaction in pantomime, both of which deservedly gained great popularity. He had a perpetual dread of being buried alive, and ordained in his will that after the doctor had pronounced him dead his daughter should cut off his head "to make sure I am not alive." I am glad to say the daughter did not carry out her father's wishes to the letter, and instead of performing the desired operation herself, deputed someone else to do it in her presence.

Joe Grimaldi also appears to have been interested in things weird and ghostly, but not to quite the same extent as his eccentric father. He made his first appearance at Sadler's Wells before he was three years old, so it is not surprising that his ghost should haunt the theatre with which he was subsequently associated for so many years, and for which he must have conceived a very strong affection; most hauntings are rooted in and traceable to a very strong emotion of one sort or another. But it is more difficult to find a reason for Grimaldi's appearances in ghostly form at Drury Lane. I have always inclined to the belief that the ghost which occasionally manifested itself there was either that of Grimaldi senior or some clown of lesser note.

Much has been written about hauntings at other London theatres, but one in the provinces which I think is particularly worth recording is that at Leeds. As recently as the 1950s the Leeds City Varieties was said to be haunted by the ghost of a woman which some people believed was the wraith of that well loved artist, Florrie Ford. The theatre, which is more than 150 years old, saw the great days of the music hall; at one time its artists performed on a sawdust floor, and the biggest attraction was the free flowing beer.

There could be other ghosts attached to the place. Once, in the early hours, a strange tinkling of the grand piano on stage brought the night watchman into the auditorium. Shining his torch on the stage, he saw standing near the piano the shadowy figure of a man, which gradually disappeared. This happened again on another night, with the difference that when the watchman shone his torch on stage and disclosed the figure, the spectre moved across the stage and up the aisle towards him. The startled watchman reached for the house lights switch, and when the lights came on the ghost vanished.

But it is the female ghost that has caused the widest interest. Always dressed in white, she has been seen several times, and the same night-watchman said he not only saw it but also heard it speak, saying something like, " Don't be afraid, I've just come back to the old place. . . ." The watchman saw the apparition, which he described as " beautiful, with red hair," appear from the direction of the dressing rooms, carrying an apparently lighted candelabra. Though he gathered courage enough to ask who she was, the phantom made no reply and simply vanished into thin air.

I conclude with a simple haunting on a country road, at an early hour on a fine summer's night. I choose it because it is typical of so many sightings of ghosts in the open-air; which, because of their once-only nature are seldom given the attention they deserve. This incident happened in Dunbartonshire, and was witnessed by three people simultaneously. It is described by the principal witness.

" I was walking, about nine years ago, one night in August about ten o'clock, and about half a mile from the house where we are now sitting. I was going along the public road between the hamlets of Haldane's Mill and Balloch. I had with me two young women, and we were leisurely walking along, when suddenly we were startled by seeing a woman, a child about seven years old, and a Newfoundland dog jump over the stone wall on one side of the road and walk on rapidly in front of us. I was not in the least frightened, but my two companions were much startled. What bothered me was that the woman, the child and the dog, instead of coming over the wall naturally one after the other, as would have been necessary for them to do, had come over with a bound, simultaneously leaping the wall.

" Leaving my two companions, who were too frightened to move, I walked rapidly after the trio. They walked so quickly that it was with difficulty that I got up to them. I spoke to the woman but she never answered. I walked beside her for some little distance, and then suddenly the woman, the child and the Newfoundland dog, disappeared. I did not see them go anywhere, they simply were no longer there. I examined the road minutely at the spot where they had disappeared, to see if it was possible for them to have gone through a hole in the wall on either side, but it was quite impossible for a woman and a child to get over a high dyke on either side. They had disappeared, and I only regret that I did not try to pass my stick right through their bodies, to see whether or not they had any resistance.

" Finding they were gone, I returned to my lady friends, who were quite unnerved and who, with difficulty, were induced to go on to the end of their journey."

When our informant and his companions got to Balloch they asked the bridge-keeper whether a woman, a child and a dog had passed that way, but he had seen nothing; nor, despite numerous inquiries, had anyone in the district ever seen the trio, either real or ghostly.

The apparitions had vanished as suddenly as they appeared.

MR. WYETH AND MR. NEAL

IN THE 1920s the activities of Mr. Arthur Wyeth and Mr. Walter
Neal, quite apart from their little publicized exorcism of the "demon
mummy" of Amen-Ra, drew special attention by reason of the unique
partnership formed between two very ordinary men. Certainly there
was no glamour or mysticism about them, you would not have noticed
them in the street; both had reached their forties and lived quiet,
normal lives in North London. Even their partnership had come
about by the merest chance.

Mr. Wyeth, as I recall, was a short, dark, rather plump man, while
Mr. Neal was tall and sturdy, with something of a military bearing.
In fact he had once been a tramcar driver.

Their first meeting was at St. Albans in 1908, where Mr. Wyeth
had gone on business. As he later described it, " I was standing in the
street when a stranger approached whom I felt was a friend. It was
Mr. Neal. We greeted each other in a natural fashion, as if we had
known each other for years, and went to look at the Cathedral together. We remained ordinary friends for years, never dreaming that
either of us had any unusual interest in common, until one day in
1914, when Mr. Neal came to me and said, 'What is a mirage? I
have just seen a most extraordinary thing at Worthing.'

" He explained that while sitting on the sea front, and looking
towards the Isle of Wight, he had seen in the air a castle, with men
on the battlements fighting with others, horses and soldiers and spears,
turrets and drawbridges—all as real as if actually built on the waters
of the Channel. I asked him to describe the castle. It seemed to me
to be like Carisbrooke, on the Isle of Wight, and when I showed him

86

some photographs I had of the place he recognized them immediately."

Mr. Wyeth, unlike his friend, had in the past read some books to do with the ghostly world and psychic matters generally. Now, as he related, "I was amazed at this apparition that such a common-sensible man as Neal had experienced. I wondered if he could see more than most people. I said, ' Close your eyes and look at me. What do you see in your mental vision?' He replied, ' Why, you're all in a sort of colour.' I told him, ' That means you're a seer,' to which he replied, ' What the devil's that?' ' A clairvoyant,' I said. ' A person who can see our spirit bodies as well as our earthly ones.'

" We afterwards talked and talked over this strange business until we found we met each other in our dreams. Neal would ask me questions during the night as to what I was thinking, and would write everything down. I would do the same for him."

After months of discussion between themselves the two men decided to put their psychic partnership to the test, in the case of a haunted house. Their experiment was successful in detecting and even clearing the ghost from the premises, as were several more; and so their reputation grew and they were invited to investigate cases in various parts of the country. They discovered to their own surprise that Neal's newly found powers as a seer were quite constant, and that although Wyeth could not see ghosts (and in fact I believe he never did see one), his power lay in an ability to effect their release.

The two men were very reluctant to make any claims for them-selves, and of course they did have some failures, but by reason of their successes they were for a time in great demand, no less on the lecture platform, and it is interesting to look at a few of their more notable cases.

They were called to a haunted flat in Hampstead, where the occupants had been worried by knockings and weird noises. The family had all had vivid dreams of a strange intruder dressed as a clergyman, though no one had actually seen this person during their waking moments. Nerves were strained by constant tapping noises and the sound of furniture being thrown about at night.

Mr. Neal, keeping vigil, saw the ghost of an old clergyman walking about the flat, dazedly looking at unfamiliar furniture and unfamiliar people. " He was trying, I could see, to make his presence known to those friends whom he thought must still be there. We made inquiries and found that this old man used to live in the neighbourhood about sixty years ago, a very lonely life he led, and that, in this house, his dearest friends had lived. In their house he was always welcome."

They effected the release of the ghost from the flat, but then the people in the lower flat became troubled. It seemed that, being un-able now to enter the top flat, where he had wandered for years, the ghost knocked on the staircases and doors lower down. This time his release was effected entirely. As Mr. Neal added, " There was nothing repulsive or horrifying about this poor ghost, he was just a blind, lost, lonely old thing, holding out his hands for friendship and clutching the empty air."

In Lincoln's Inn, the partners investigated a house in which disturbances had been felt, and noises heard, over a period of nearly 250 years. " When we went to this house," said Mr. Wyeth, " there was a strange atmosphere of pain and tragedy and almost unbearable tension. We waited for what was to come, and presently Mr. Neal saw a man dressed as a cavalier of the reign of King Charles. He was agonized, wringing his hands, frenzied. ' I want my wife,' he kept saying. ' I am innocent. I want my wife !' We were able to secure his release, and then, delving into records, found out his history. He was a soldier who lived on the Isle of Dogs, and his wife was accustomed to visit some friends in Lincoln's Inn. Sometimes he accompanied her, sometimes not. Sometimes he would go to fetch her at the end of the day.

" One day he went to the house and could obtain no answer. He forced his way in, to find his lady lying on the floor with a dagger in her heart. Falling on his knees beside her, he snatched the dagger away and fell in a dead faint, holding the dagger in his hand. He was found so, thrown into Greenwich Jail, and accused of the murder. And, in spite of his protestations, he was found guilty and executed. It seemed clear to us, from the evidence we sifted, that the wife had actually been killed by someone who had been disappointed in his love for her and taken his revenge."

The two men encountered a much uglier case in a big house in a South London suburb. This had been opened as a boarding school by three elderly women. Children came, and a staff was installed. Not long afterwards some of the children started to do automatic writing, much to the distress of their mistresses. They stopped these activities by the children, but then they themselves were beset by feelings of uncleanness. They were three nice, fine women who had never in all their lives read any ugly books or talked of any ugly subject, and one can imagine their horror when they were afflicted by terrible dreams. Waves of terror went through the place and the children became unmanageable, until at last the school had to be closed down.

Mr. Wyeth and Mr. Neal were called in after other investigators had failed to find the cause of the haunting. They made systematic investigations. Mr. Neal looked clairvoyantly into every room, and all over the garden, and stated there were many earthbound spirits there. Mr. Wyeth gave these spirits release. Then the partners, searching old records again, found that on the site of the school there used to be a ring where a secret society of black magicians celebrated their rites. One day at dusk in the year 1511, a little boy gathering fruit in the woods which then covered the district came upon the ring. He fled, near crazed with terror, and his father told the watch. A deputation of citizens armed themselves and surrounded the spot, led by the boy, and fell on the ring. Many of the magicians escaped into the thick woods but a number were killed immediately, and it seemed that in sudden death they had gone on pursuing their evil practices. Later on the woods were cleared and the little hillock levelled for houses to be built, and the three poor women and their pupils had come in for the evil that still hung about the place. After the partners' visit the school was re-opened, and there was no recurrence of the trouble.

A similar instance of evil seeping down through the centuries attended what I think is one of the more extraordinary cases dealt with by the partners.

The owner of a house in Cheshire was afflicted by a terrible nervousness that resulted in neuritis. She was a lady who had been very fond of playing the violin, but for four years she had been unable to touch the instrument. Horrible noises were heard in the house, sounds of terror and pain, and the rushing of water, while an impalpable fear, a sort of creeping apprehension, lay over all. It was as though the occupants of the house were wrapped in a cloud of dread through which it was almost impossible for them to breathe.

For seven years this had gone on, gradually getting worse and worse. When the two ghost-hunters visited the house they found an astonishing state of affairs, Mr. Neal detecting no fewer than twenty-five earthbound spirits there.

" In the middle of the house I saw the apparition of a waterfall. It spread over to the garden. There was a flat piece of rock underneath the waterfall, and on the rock stood the figure of an old, old man, with several indistinct spirits at his feet. He was the founder of a secret society that existed in the Middle Ages to celebrate all sorts of horrible rites, including human sacrifice. They called themselves the Druid Kings. To prove his power, this old man would stand on a flat rock underneath a great waterfall (the rocks over which this waterfall came were levelled many centuries ago, and the water diverted to another channel). This Druid King anticipated modern science in one thing. He believed that if the glands of young people were taken and made into a potion, the drinker of the potion would live for ever. This is not far beyond the rejuvenating monkey gland we hear so much about, and not very different from the sheep's thyroid gland extract which doctors now use.

" When children could not be found, this man killed adults. The people in the neighbourhood lost children and friends, but no one dared to do anything. Every morning he would stand on his rock, defying the elemental power of Water, and anyone who tried to emulate him was washed off and drowned. One day a friar came by, a man of great repute for holiness, and the terrified people of the neighbourhood begged him to ask the saints for help against the horror in their midst. The monk prayed all night, and, the next morning, when the Druid took up his position as usual, there was standing beside him whom he could not see, one whose power for good was stronger than evil. The Druid was dashed into the water and drowned, and then the villagers, encouraged, fell on his followers and avenged the ghastly murders of their children and friends. These evil slain haunted the place because they were destroyed suddenly in the midst of their rites, and the rites were so important to them that they simply 'had no time' for death. They just went on doing what they were doing when they died."

After the partners gave release to the spirits, the cloud vanished from the house. The owner regained her good health, and the violin that had been silent for four years was soon being played again.

Throughout their investigations, Mr. Wyeth and Mr. Neal kept a level-headedness which was commendable and they made no extravagant claims. According to Mr. Neal, investigating the ghosts of clergymen or cavaliers was a more or less simple matter, " as people troubled by such a haunting do not mind talking about it. But when sensitive, pure-minded people get horrible dreams and visions they find it almost impossible to talk about them. Yet the victims of these things are quite innocent. There is nothing to be ashamed of, any more than there is any disgrace in getting smallpox from an affected house."

These are my own sentiments precisely.

A BARGAIN WITH A GHOST

GHOST HUNTING, it is fair to say, is made up of fifty per cent failure. Failure, that is, at special vigils held in the hope of witnessing apparitions seen by others. For most ghosts just will not appear to order, much as some self-styled " investigators " try to engineer it otherwise. Conditions must also be right, and as we have, as yet, little knowledge of these required conditions, failure must often follow.

However, in some fortunate cases, including a number in my own personal experience, it is not the ghost hunter who has gone seeking the ghost, but rather the reverse.

This happened with Cheiro (Count Louis Hamon), in a case which I consider in its completeness to be almost the perfect story of a domestic haunting. Cheiro on this occasion did not go looking for the ghost; it came to him. He had been abroad for some time, and on returning to London, started looking round for a suitable house he could rent. He was tired of flat life and determined to have a spacious house in which he could move around at ease. He was unashamedly fussy in his requirements, insisting on trees and a garden, but also wishing to be in the centre of active life in the city. Such a combination was not easy to find, but after a long search, find it he did.

The story is given, with Cheiro's permission, in his own words.

" One afternoon at the end of an unusually warm summer by a mere chance I came across exactly the type of place I required. It was an old-fashioned house, standing back from the main thoroughfare with quite a large garden, and several high trees that sheltered and concealed it from the passing traffic. No agent had given me the address. There were no bills up, ' To be Let ', or ' To be Sold ', yet I intuitively felt that I should make some attempt to get possession of this house which so attracted me. As I have all my life tried to follow my intuitions I at once determined to make an effort to get particulars about the property. There would be no harm in making inquiries, I thought.

" I pushed open the high, old fashioned heavy oak door in a high wall which cut the place off from the street, and as it closed behind me I found myself in an instant in quite another world. Outside, the roar of buses and traffic; inside the high walls, peace, quiet and a strange feeling of old world isolation. In the centre of the badly kept garden a quaint fountain splashed and dripped as if Time for it had ceased to exist. By its side grew some bedraggled flowers and wandering nasturtiums, and further back was an old wooden seat in the last stages of decay.

" The house itself, with its low, diamond-shaped windows, looked rather gloomy, yet there was something about it that appealed to me so strongly that without hesitation, I went up to the porch and pulled the chain of a heavy iron bell. Instead of a servant answering as I expected, an elderly gentleman opened the door. For a moment I was completely nonplussed and hardly knew what to say. Then I rattled off some excuse about having heard that the house might be to let. The old man, although rather deaf, was very courteous but firmly replied that I had made a mistake. I was turning to leave when a woman came out of the hall.

" ' My dear,' he turned to her, ' just imagine, this gentleman has called to ask if the house is to let.' I again attempted to apologize for my intrusion, but was cut short by the woman saying : ' How you could have heard such a thing, sir, I do not know, but although I have not mentioned it to my husband, I've been thinking of putting the house in some agent's hands. Will you come in?'

" I gladly assented. We entered an oblong, quaint-looking lounge hall. I glanced at the wooden beams across the ceiling, the dark oak panelling nearly black with age, the wide open hearth and Tudor-shaped fireplace, then rather hesitantly the woman pulled aside some curtains and disclosed at the farther end, a small chancel or chapel with a stained glass window.

" ' How delightful !' I said in surprise.

" ' I'm glad you think so,' she said. ' We don't like the idea of the chapel so we keep it curtained off, but come and see the rest of the rooms.' Before we had gone far I had inwardly decided that I would take the house if the terms were at all suitable. ' Why do you want to leave the place?' I asked impetuously. There was an embarrassed look in her eyes as she replied.

" ' The trouble is,' she said, ' no servant will stop, no matter what

I pay them. I will not try to deceive you. The servants' rooms are in the back, the old part. They claim to hear noises, queer knocks, and sometimes they think they see things. Lately the knocks have begun in other rooms. My husband is so deaf he doesn't hear them, but it has been rather too much for me, and I will be glad to go if I can get anyone to take over the lease.' Then she added : 'We have not been here long. My husband came in for this house on the death of his uncle twelve months ago. He was a very eccentric man and lived alone for some years with his old butler in the front part. The back rooms he would never allow anyone to use.' "

The talk of " knockings " did not deter Cheiro, if anything they added lustre to the house. Within half an hour he had come to terms with the couple, with the stipulation that the house would be handed over to him promptly and empty, at the end of a fortnight.

" When the day came for me to take possession, I was as happy as a child with a new toy. There was something about the place that appealed to me in an extraordinary way. I walked through the dusty rooms and told them out loud how I would have them done up, how the old oak would be taken care of and polished, and the diamond-paned windows cleaned as they had not been cleaned for years. I am not the only one who has ever felt that way over a house, I'm sure. There was one room, however, I would not touch. It was in the old part of the building, off the stairs below the level of the hall. What there was about this room I could not explain, no suggestion I made seemed to fit in with it, and the decorator I had employed was equally at a loss what should be done, so in the end I turned the key in the door and left it as it was.

" At last the day came when I could begin to send in some furniture, and as quickly as I could I fitted up two rooms, one for my secretary, a man some twenty years older than myself, and the other for my own use. By living in the house I argued I would be able to get rid of the decorators more quickly than coming to see them every day.

" At this stage I had no need to worry about employing servants, as we could get our meals outside and simply sleep in the place. Did I say sleep? From the very first evening such a thing was impossible. The first night my secretary and I got home about ten o'clock. We went through the basement, saw all doors and windows properly fastened, groped our way through the decorator's ladders in the hall and little chapel downstairs, and turning off the electric lights, got up into our respective bedrooms. The place was as quiet and still as if we were in the middle of the country. The hum of traffic in the distance had a soothing effect on one's nerves, like the sound of waves rising and falling on a sanded shore. I had an electric light over my bed so I read for a while, then switched it off and turned over to sleep.

"I felt very happy about the house, the decorators were doing their work quickly, and I could see in my mind's eye how everything would look when they had finished. Suddenly I gave a jump. Away down in the bottom of the house there was a noise—it sounded like the opening and shutting of a door in the basement. Rapidly my mind went over all the doors and windows we had fastened. It must have been the wind, I thought, then I remembered how still the night was, and how, when we had passed through the garden, I had noticed there was not a leaf stirring on the trees.

"Again I heard a noise. This time I sat up in bed and listened intently. There could be no mistaking now what I heard; it was a heavy footstep on the basement stairs leading up to the hall. Sitting bolt upright in the dark I listened. The steps entered the hall. I imagined I could see someone walking in and out of the decorator's ladders, then they sounded nearer, and the footsteps came to the uncarpeted staircase leading to our bedrooms. I felt I dared not switch on my electric light—that if I did, the gleam under my door might lead the mysterious 'steps' direct to my room.

"The staircase creaked. I remembered as I came up to bed noticing a loose board on one of the treads—it was on the landing turning towards my door. It seemed ages before the footsteps came nearer; whoever it was did not seem in any particular hurry. The loose board was reached—it made exactly the same noise as it had done when I walked on it on my way up to bed—then a few more steps and the shuffling feet were at my door.

"How strangely one's mind works in a moment of tension. I knew I had fastened the brass bolt (a habit gained from living abroad). I knew it would resist a good pressure when the pressure came, as I felt it must. I wondered if the man outside were broad-shouldered, what he looked like, if he would wear a mask, and a hundred other things of a like nature passed rapidly through my brain, but never for one moment did the idea come to me that the person outside my door was not human.

"I hardly dared to breathe. I slipped from bed, gripped a heavy poker from the fireplace, and with the other hand on the electric light switch, waited for the bursting open of the door. Instead, something came which to my excited senses seemed a thousand times worse. Suddenly, as if from bony knuckles, there was a sharp rat-tat-tat, tat-tat, on the central panel of the door. I could feel my hair stand on end. The fear of a burglar had passed, and in its place had come a dread of the unknown. Again came the chilling knock. I switched on the light, and I don't know what possessed me—rushed to the door, pulled the bolt, threw the door wide open and stood facing . . . the darkness of an empty landing, and nothing more. But just as I sighed with relief, for answer came something that made my blood freeze. Right by my side, in the bright light of the electric lamp, on the open door about level with my head, the rat-tat-tat was repeated even clearer and sharper than before.

" Jumping back, I slammed the door with a bang that echoed down the empty stairs. I shot in the bolt, shivering with fright, and sat down on my bed and waited—for what I did not know.

" Morning came at last, and with it courage. As the first streaks of dawn stole through the windows I pulled up the blinds and welcomed the sight and sound of waking traffic. I put on my clothes, opened the door of my room and stepped on to the landing. How natural everything seemed, the early morning sun now streaming in through the windows, the uncarpeted stairs seemed to welcome me. The loose board made me jump for a moment as it recalled the foot-fall of the night before, but it was only for a moment, the next I was laughing at myself. I did exactly as so many others would have done under similar circumstances. I told myself, in very forceful language, that I was nothing more or less than a damned fool to have allowed myself to imagine I heard footsteps coming up those stairs; and as for believing I had heard knocking on my door, I told myself that any man who could work himself into such a state was only fit for the nearest lunatic asylum.

" At that moment my secretary, Parkins, opened his door. ' Well,' I said, ' did you have a good night?' ' Did you?' he grunted. I laugh-ingly told him what I had heard, putting it all down to a bad case of nerves. But he was a blunt man and would have none of it. He also had heard noises. 'I'm damned if I'll stop in this house another night,' he said. ' There's no money in the world would make up for it, that's all I've got to say.'

" ' Well,' I said, ' what are we going to do about it?'

" ' There's nothing to do, sir, except give the house up, give the keys back to the people who had it, and ask them to return the money you've spent on it. If they don't agree quietly, bring them to court, and I'll guarantee there's no sane jury that wouldn't give a verdict in your favour.'

" I told him that was all very fine, but the wife had admitted to me she could not keep a servant in the place, that they had heard knocks and noises. She had virtually confessed the place was haunted, so I had taken it at my own risk.

" ' Well, sir, what _are_ you going to do?' Parkins asked.

" I'm going to keep the house whatever happens," was my reply. " And furthermore, I'm going to keep you, too. Yes I am, my friend.

You've too much good old North of England blood in you to be frightened out by a ghost.'

"He took rather more talking round than that, but eventually he agreed to stay. That night we returned to the house about ten o'clock. We lit a fire in my room, put two easy chairs before it, fortified ourselves with sandwiches and good strong coffee, and determined to see things out till dawn. The first few hours passed quietly enough, but about one o'clock we were dozing off to sleep in our chairs when suddenly we started up. There was no mistaking what we heard, a shuffling footstep on the landing. It came nearer, stopped at the door, a pause, then clear and sharp came a determined knocking on the middle of the door. We jumped from our chairs and stood staring at one another like two helpless children.

"Then came a sharp click from the empty landing—the electric light had been switched on. 'Great God! That can't be a ghost,' Parkins exclaimed. We each took up a poker from the grate and I pulled back the bolt and threw the door open as I had done the night before. This time the landing was flooded with light. Gripping our iron pokers we stepped out on the stairs. I peered over the banisters. 'Parkins,' I whispered, 'the lights are on in the hall. We can't leave them like that, we must go down and turn them off.'

"Side by side, step by step, we went down together, very slowly. What we expected to find I don't know. 'It can't be a ghost with such light about,' Parkins kept repeating as if to keep up his courage. We reached the last step of the stairs and saw before us the hall flooded with light, with every lamp on. On our left, the dining-room door was wide open, and the room in darkness. We looked at the shining brass electric switches in a row just inside the door—something seemed to call our attention to them—then click, click, click, one after another they were switched on before our eyes, and the empty room became a blaze of light.

"We felt rooted to the spot, but only for a moment. Out there somewhere in the middle of the empty room we heard a hollow, croaking kind of laugh, a sneering laugh. It came closer to us, we almost felt it. We did not wait for more, but with one bound had reached the landing and were soon behind the closed door of my room.

"When the decorators came to their work next morning they found all the lights on, even in the basement. We let them think what they liked about our carelessness, we were glad to go back to our beds and sleep. We slept all the more soundly, I think, by reason of the welcome sound of the painters' ladders.

"When night came again Parkins and I, after a good dinner, both felt quite courageous as we set off for home. He chiefly because he had acquired the loan of a mongrel dog for company in his room. For in spite of all that had occurred, he was still as strongly of the opinion that our nightly intruder was human, and someone who for some reason wished to frighten us out of the house. Parkins had left the dog shut up in his room during our absence.

" I must admit I was not quite so confident as we closed the garden door behind us and looked up at the dark windows of the empty house. I had had experience with dogs before, when ghost-hunting, and had seen them show more terror than humans on coming into contact with anything uncanny. Still, as I put the latch-key in the front door there was something very comforting in hearing a vigorous barking from the room Parkins slept in, which continued while we switched on and off the lights and came up the stairs. The poor animal went mad with delight to see us. He had been lonely, shut up for several hours.

" We first watched him devour the supper we had brought him, and then with that 'brave Horatius feeling' that men get when they have a dog for a companion, we all three went down to the basement to ensure that the doors and windows were closed and fastened. The dog seemed afraid of nothing. He sniffed and barked in every room. There was one place, however, where his Irish-Scotch blood got a setback that puzzled him. We had been out in the yard seeing that the heavy iron bar was across the door leading into the back alley. We had returned into the passage and shot the bolt home into the inside door, remarking as we did so, that bolts in the days that the house was built were certainly not made for ornament. We had examined the windows in every part, and had reached the threshold of the small room on the half-landing which up to then the painters had not touched.

" Calling the dog to follow, Parkins struck a match. It was the only room in the house that had no electric light. Parkins called again, and the dog answered with a whine. The animal was crouching down on the doorstep, every hair standing up like a bristle, and trembling in every limb. The match went out. We went up to my room, the dog following close to our heels. He was still trembling, and I threw a cushion for him close to the fire. I patted his head and he licked my hand. 'What do you think of your dog, Parkins?' I could not help but ask.

" He did not answer. He poured me out a cup of coffee. I took the hint and did not pursue the subject. We had been sitting quietly for some time, the distant hum of the streets had died down, a neighbouring clock had struck one, the house seemed very still, even the dog at our feet had gone to sleep. I was about to suggest that we should follow his example, when Parkins started up.

" ' What was that?' he whispered.

" I had heard nothing. I looked at the dog. He was now sitting bolt upright, but with ears lying down at the back of his head. He evidently remembered the fright he had had a few hours ago. I was beginning to think I was the bravest of the three, when away downstairs came the ominous sound of feet. We could hear them entering the dining-room, then the hall. They stopped at the foot of the stairs, then came on with a tread far more heavy and distinct than on the former occasion. Parkins and I instinctively grabbed the two iron pokers, the dog stood between us, with his head back sniffing the air.

" Suddenly there was a bang on the door, this time, thank heavens, accompanied by a human voice.

" ' What the hell's going on in this house?'

" The dog was already at the door, barking like fury. Parkins got him by the collar. A heavy push made the door tremble, the brass bolt surprisingly flew off, the door shot open, and there stood before us the finest sample of a London policeman my eyes had ever seen. He certainly looked particularly good to us at such a moment, but he was decidedly out of temper.

" ' What the hell's going on in this house? I'd like to know,' he repeated. We hardly knew what to say. He went on : ' Five minutes ago your back door was closed and barred, I had just tried it on my first round when I heard the bolt being drawn and the door opened before my eyes. I entered the yard, found the passage door open, every light in the place on, and you two gentlemen and a dog alone here in an empty house. What's your game? That's what I want to know.'

" It was no use trying to look dignified under such circumstances or to try to explain about ghosts. So I meekly said that my friend and I had not carelessly left the back doors open as he had imagined. We had very carefully bolted them before coming upstairs, and there was no explanation that we could offer for their being found open.

" ' Well, I've got to search the house from top to bottom,' he said. ' There must be someone concealed on the premises you don't know about, so come along with me and bring the dog.'

" We searched the house from the attic to the cellars, the policeman's bull's-eye lantern shooting its beams into every corner. The dog followed us all over the house except in the small room off the stairs where he had had his previous fright. Into that room he absolutely refused to go. Each time we tried to induce him to enter he lay down crouching on the doorstep, trembling in every limb. The constable jotted remarks in his notebook, as he would have to make a report about finding the doors open, he said. We finally saw him out into the back alley, put the big bolt back into its place and returned to my room. Nothing more happened that night. When daylight came, Parkins retired with the dog, and I went to bed.

" Whether it was the effect of the policeman's visit or the presence of the dog, I cannot say, but for a few weeks after that we had no disturbances of any kind. Then one afternoon Henry Hamilton, the dramatist, dropped in to see me. ' I quite envy you having this quaint old house in the heart of London,' he said. ' But tell me, have you had any queer experiences in it since moving in ?'

" ' What kind of experiences do you mean ?' I asked.

" ' Well,' he went on, ' when friends of mine lived here some years ago they heard noises and knocks all over the place, and on that account they gave the house up. I will write down and place in an envelope a message spelled out to me by knocks in this very room. Lock it up in your desk, and don't open it until at some time a message is again rapped out—then compare the two and let me know if they are alike.'

" I promised I would do this, but as some weeks went by without knocks or disturbances taking place, I had quite forgotten about the envelope, until one night my attention was drawn to it in a remark-able manner. I had asked a few friends to dinner, a kind of house warming party. After dinner we sat round the fire in the lounge, hav-ing coffee and cigarettes, when for no apparent reason a series of decided knocks began on a crystal bowl containing flowers that I always kept before an image of Buddha at the far end of the little chapel. Someone suggested very seriously, that we should sit round a table and ask the ' ghost ' to spell out its name.

" I took a writing pad and pencil, and turning to where the knocks had been heard, said aloud : ' I will call out the letters of the alphabet —please knock at the letter you want. At the end I will read out the word. If it is correct rap three times, if not correct, rap once.'

" The message that came out clearly and distinctively was : ' My name is Karl Clint. I lived here about a hundred and twenty years ago. If you go down to the empty room off the stairs you will hear more.'

" Taking our chairs, we moved to the empty room—the same room which, it will be remembered, the dog that Parkins brought refused to enter. As there was no electric light in this room we placed a candle on the mantelpiece and sat round a small table we had brought down with us. We had hardly taken our places before the knocks again commenced, this time much stronger than before, and on the centre of the wall immediately above where the candle stood. The message that came was : ' I am Karl Clint. I own this house. In this room I murdered Liddell. I buried him underneath.'

" ' Who was Liddell ?' I asked.

" ' He was Arthur Liddell.'

" ' Do you want us to do anything about it ?'

" ' No. You can do nothing.'

" ' Do you want any prayers said?' someone asked.

" ' No,' very emphatically.

" ' Can we help in any way?'

" ' No! I want to be left alone in my own house. Why can't people keep away?'

" This was followed by a loud bang on the door, and at the same moment the candle was extinguished. In the darkness we groped our way out and were only too glad to get upstairs. I opened the sealed envelope in my desk. It was almost word for word with what I had taken down.

" The next day I looked up the archives and records of the parish. I found that between 1740 and 1800 the old part of the house had been a kind of farm owned by an Austrian or German named Karl Clint. This man had been mixed up with the disappearance of Arthur Liddell, who was last seen in the company of the man Clint. Years later all trace of Karl Clint had been lost. The farm land had become covered with streets and the property changed hands many times. The records gave me no further information.

" Things went on quietly in the house for some weeks after this, until the time came when I made plans to make some use of the empty room in question. The first thing I did was to put in electric light. That night I was awakened several times by knocks on my bedroom door. Two of the servants also heard them, and immediately gave notice. I telephoned my friends and asked them to come over the next evening at nine o'clock. I had now determined to solve the mystery one way or the other, as to continue to live under such conditions appeared to me impossible.

" I had some experience of the results that could be at times obtained by the materialization seances given by a blind medium named Cecil Husk. I determined to have this man with us to see if we could get something more tangible than messages by knocks. I had some time previously attended seances where Husk was the medium, at which forms developed and spirit voices of persons I recognized had spoken to me. Perhaps, I thought, it will give the ghost who haunts this house an opportunity of showing more definitely what he wants me to do.

" I should explain that from the kind of life I had led for many years, and from the hundreds of confessions that men and women had poured on my ears, I had lost all sense of prejudice or the desire to judge or condemn any person, no matter what crime they might have committed. Saints and sinners had become alike to me; in both there was evil and in both good. The sinner might have become the saint if circumstances had been equal, and the saint might as easily have been the sinner if he had been exposed to the same temptation. So it was that I would as gladly have helped the spirit of this self-confessed murderer, Karl Clint, as I would some long dead bishop struggling to break the chains of Purgatory.

" Nine o'clock came. My friends were punctual to the minute. I went to meet the blind medium and helped him into the dining-room where the chairs had been placed round the central table. I put the medium in the centre of the group, and switched off the main lights, leaving a small lamp with a red shade burning at the far end of the room.

" I had scarcely reached my seat opposite the medium before manifestations commenced in the shape of very decided knocks on the ceiling, the chandelier and a mirror hanging on the wall. Distinct footsteps were heard apparently coming from the unused room; they stopped at the door. A grey kind of shadowy cloud formed inside. It grew thicker, and came directly over to where I sat. Then out of it a head and shoulders formed, and in another second I was looking into the face of Karl Clint.

" I knew it was Karl Clint. He had no need to repeat his name. That weary, haunted, broken look, told me in a flash his loneliness, his heartweariness, and murderer though he may have been, my soul went out to him in sympathy and pity. Everyone present could see the face I was looking at. It was decidedly a German or Austrian type of head; as the features developed more clearly one could almost distinguish the texture of the skin and see the reddish colour of the hair and close-cropped beard. In appearance the face was that of a man between forty-five and fifty years of age, an intelligent looking man but of the peasant or farmer class.

" Perhaps on account of the sympathetic look in my eyes the face in a few moments became still clearer. We could see that the lips were making a tremendous effort to speak. Several times they opened, but no sound came. At last, and how it was accomplished I can offer no explanation, a voice did come, at first only a kind of whisper—we strained every nerve to listen—a few guttural words, then more, until every person in the room could hear the following conversation.

" ' Why are these people in my house?'

" ' They are my friends,' I answered. ' Won't you tell me something about yourself?'

" ' I am Karl Clint,' the lips said. ' I lived here as far as I can make out one hundred and twenty years ago, but time makes no difference to me now. It is people who appear to change. Why have you come here?'

" ' Because I liked your house. Perhaps I can help you by living here?' I answered quickly.

" ' No one can help me,' the voice said, in a curiously sad way. ' I only want to be left in peace.'

" ' But you are not at peace. If you were, you would not come and frighten people as you do.'

" ' I can't get away, since the night I died I am here all the time.'

" ' You told us you murdered Liddell—why did you commit such a crime?'

" ' Liddell would not leave the woman I lived with alone. I loved Charlotte more than man ever loved a woman. He was always coming here, tempting her with his money. One night he went too far. I killed him as I would a mad dog. People call such an act a murder, but I would do the same over again if he and I were living. I dug a hole in the earth under the room downstairs. I filled it with quicklime. I put his body in it and what is left of it is there still as far as I can tell.'

" ' What became of Charlotte?' I asked.

" ' She died a few years later. She helped me to get rid of the body, but she never got over the worry and the dread of my being found out. I buried her in the graveyard not far from here."

" ' And what became of you?'

" ' After she died I went back to Germany. I never knew a moment's happiness after Charlotte went—life for me was torture—in the end I committed suicide.'

" ' And then?'

" ' I can't tell you how it came about, but one day I seemed to wake up in the room downstairs, and I've been here ever since.'

" ' But would you not like to leave the place and get away?'

" ' Why should I? This is the only place I called home. I was happy here with the one woman I ever loved. It was the only happiness I ever knew, why should I leave—there is no place else for me to go.'

" ' But Charlotte?' I said.

" ' Charlotte is here with me. We live the old happy days over and over—till Liddell comes, and then I kill him again.'

" ' But surely there is something I can do to help you?'

" ' There is one thing you can do,' the voice replied. ' Leave the room downstairs untouched. Put two chairs and a table there, and allow no one to enter it after dark. If you will do this, you can have the rest of the place to yourself, and I won't give you any trouble.'

" I pledged my word I would carry out my side of the bargain. That night two chairs and a table were placed in what I now called ' his room '. I locked the door and put the key in my safe, and from that night on I had no more annoyances or noises of any kind.

" The day came for me to give the house up and live in a different part of London. A few evenings before I left I thought I ought to have another seance—out of sentiment, perhaps, to say goodbye to my ghost friend, who had so faithfully kept to his side of the bargain.

" Without much waiting, Karl Clint appeared.

" ' Karl,' I said, ' I am moving to another house. I thought I would like to say goodbye and thank you for having kept to your side of the arrangement. For the last time I am going to ask is there anything I can do to help you before other people take over this house?'

" To my great surprise, the answer came clear and distinct.

" ' I want to go with you, you are the only one I ever met who has shown sympathy with me. Behind the panelling in my room you will find a painting I had made of Charlotte. I put it there when she died and it has been hidden there ever since. Take it with you, hang it somewhere in your home, and perhaps when the time comes for you to pass into the shadow land, you will have at least two humble but loyal friends to greet you.'

" I found Charlotte's picture behind the panelling—it is on the wall over my desk as I write."

So ends Cheiro's story, quite the most remarkable, I think, in his eventful career. After giving up the house in question he was warned that if he mentioned its address in connection with the strange occurrences that had taken place, he would be sued for heavy damages. He therefore lodged the address in the keeping of lawyers, together with a deposition, as conclusive evidence of the truth of his story. It would serve no purpose to mention the address here, and thus break an undertaking which he steadfastly kept.

Cheiro's own death in Los Angeles in 1936, at the age seventy, was not without its strangeness.

Four days before his death a brisk, efficient English nurse, Mrs. Edith Phelan, was called in to attend him. She was present when he died, and what happened then is best described in her own words.

" I was sitting at the head of the stairs except at the last moment. They were deserted, and yet they creaked as though an army of people were coming and going. When the doctors called me about midnight, I noticed he was sinking. I told his wife he couldn't last long. They were just asking me how long, when the clock struck one—yet my wristwatch showed 12.15. Twice again, at about ten-minute intervals, the clock struck one. At the last moment the whole house was filled with an overpowering fragrance of flowers. There was none in the room, yet we all smelled the fragrance.

" I cannot deny the evidence of my senses, yet I cannot believe them. I am a registered nurse. I have seen hundreds of people die and I do not believe in ghosts. I came to this house four days before my patient died, and I did not even know his name."

On a final bizarre note, Cheiro's widow (Countess Mena Hamon) kept his ashes in a metal box, and for nine years carried them about with her wherever she went, three times crossing the Atlantic with them. Finally, in fulfilment of a promise made to her husband on his deathbed, the Countess had the ashes interred at Meltham, Yorkshire, in the grave of her son by her first marriage.

OLD JEFFREY

IT MAY seem strange to include John Wesley, the vigorously unorthodox founder of Methodism, among the ghost hunters, but it is thanks to him that we have a complete record of one of the most interesting hauntings of earlier times.

Wesley did not exactly have to go hunting the ghost, for it appeared in his father's parsonage when John was a boy. What he did do, in the later years of his life, was to publish in his own publication, the *Arminian Magazine,* a full account of the ghostly happenings based on his father's diary, together with his own experiences and those of the rest of the family. The carefully written statements of each member of the household, their letters written at the time, and the results of Wesley's own further inquiries all combined to make the story of Epworth parsonage one of the best authenticated hauntings on record.

Over the years Wesley's absorbing story has receded into history, to become one of those happenings alluded to only briefly by later authors, and annoyingly never explained. I feel it is time to take a proper look at it again.

When it all took place, in the year 1716, John Wesley was just thirteen years old. His father, the Reverend Samuel Wesley, was rector of Epworth, a small market town in Lincolnshire, and the family lived in the old parsonage there. After the second day of December 1716 things were never quite the same again, for it was on that night that the long period of disturbances began. As John Wesley himself describes :

" While Robert Brown, my father's servant, was sitting with one of

105

the maids, a little before ten at night, in the dining-room which opened into the garden, they both heard someone knocking at the door. Robert rose and opened it, but could see nobody. Quickly it knocked again and groaned.

" ' It is Mr. Turpine,' said Robert, ' he used to groan so.'

" He opened the door again twice or thrice, the knocking being twice or thrice repeated, but still seeing nothing, and being a little startled, they rose up and went to bed. When Robert came to the top of the garret stairs he saw a handmill, which was at a little distance, whirled about very swiftly. When he related this he said, ' Nought vexed me but that it was empty. I thought if it had been but full of malt he might have ground his hand out for me.'

" When he was in bed, he heard as it were the gobbling of a turkey-cock close to the bedside, and soon after, the sound of one stumbling over his shoes and boots; but there was none there, he had left them below. The next day he and the maid related these things to the other maid, who laughed heartily and said, ' What a couple of fools you are. I defy anything to fright me !' After churning in the evening she put the butter in the tray and had no sooner carried it into the dairy than she heard a knocking on the shelf where several puncheons of milk stood, first above the shelf, then below. She took the candle and searched both above and below, but, being able to find nothing, threw down butter, tray and all, and ran away for life."

More shocks came the next evening between five and six o'clock.

" My sister Molly, then about twenty years of age, sitting in the dining-room reading, heard as if it were the door that led into the hall open, and a person walking in that seemed to have on a silk night-gown, rustling and trailing along. It seemed to walk round her, and then to the door, then round again; but she could see nothing. She thought, ' It signifies nothing to run away, for whatever it is, it can run faster than me.' So she rose, put her book under her arm and slowly walked away. After supper she was sitting with my sister Sukey (about a year older) in one of the chambers and telling her what had happened. She made quite light of it, telling her, ' I wonder you are so easily frightened. I would fain see what would frighten me.' Presently a knocking began under the table. She took the candle and looked, but could find nothing. Then the iron casement began to clatter. Next the catch of the door moved up and down without ceasing. She started up, leaped into bed without undressing, pulled the bedclothes over her head and never ventured to look up until next morning.

" A night or two after, my sister Hetty (a year younger than Molly) was waiting as usual between nine and ten to take away my father's candle, when she heard someone coming down the garret stairs, walking slowly by her, then going slowly down the best stairs, then up the back stairs and up the garret stairs, and at every step it seemed the house shook from top to bottom. Just then my father knocked, she went in, took his candle, and got to bed as fast as possible. In the morning she told it to my eldest sister, who told her, 'You know I believe none of these things, pray let me take away the candle tonight, and I will find out the trick.'

" She accordingly took my sister Hetty's place, and had no sooner taken away the candle, than she heard a noise below. She hastened downstairs to the hall where the noise was, but it was then in the kitchen. She ran into the kitchen, when it was drumming on the inside of the screen. When she went round it was drumming on the outside, and so always on the side opposite to her. Then she heard a knocking on the back kitchen door. She ran to it, unlocked it softly, and, when the knocking was repeated, suddenly opened it, but nothing was to be seen. As soon as she had shut it, the knocking began again. She opened it again, but could see nothing. When she went to shut the door, it was violently knocked against her; but she set her knee and her shoulder to the door, forced it to, and turned the key. Then the knocking began again; but she let it go on and went up to bed. However, from that time she was thoroughly convinced that there was no imposture in the affair.

" The next morning, my sister telling my mother what had happened, she said, ' If I heard anything myself, I shall know how to judge.' Soon after she begged her mother to come into the nursery. She did, and heard, in the corner of the room, as it were the violent rocking of a cradle; but no cradle had been there for some years. My mother was convinced it was preternatural, and earnestly prayed it might not disturb her in her own chamber at the hour of retirement; and it never did. My sister now thought it was proper to tell my father. But he was extremely angry and said, ' Sukey, I am ashamed of you. These boys and girls frighten one another, but you are a woman of sense, and should know better. Let me hear of it no more.'

" At six in the evening he had family prayers, as usual. When he began the prayer for the King, a knocking began all round the room, and a thundering knock attended the *Amen*. The same was heard from this time every morning and evening while the prayer for the King was repeated.

" As both my father and mother are now at rest, and incapable of being pained thereby, I think it my duty to furnish the serious reader with a key to this circumstance. The year before King William died, my father observed that my mother did not say *Amen* to the prayer for the King. She said she would not, for she did not believe the Prince of Orange was King. He vowed he would never cohabit with her until she did. He then took his horse and rode away, nor did she hear anything of him for a twelvemonth. He then came back and lived with her as before. But I fear his vow was not forgotten before God."

Sukey (Susannah) Wesley also described the violent knockings which ensued when the words "Our most Gracious Sovereign Lord" were applied by her father to the newly enthroned German king of England, George I. It all seemed to point to the unquiet spirit of the parsonage having a Jacobite's hatred of the newest Protestant interloper to follow the deposed Catholic James II. Sukey further tells us that when her father first discovered that the ghost seemed to object to State prayer, he decided for the future to have three collects instead of two, which showed that he had not only courage, but also the courage of his political convictions. One Friday night when they had attended service in church the family devotions were shortened by the omission of the "Prayer for the Royal Family", and no knocking occurred, which Samuel Wesley considered good evidence. "Always at the name of the King it began to knock, and did the same when I prayed for the Prince. This was heard by ten persons."

John Wesley, continuing his story, introduces the testimony of the Reverend Mr. Hoole, of the adjoining parish of Haxey, whom he questioned about the haunting. This was Mr. Hoole's statement:

"Robert Brown came over to me and told me your father desired my company. When I came, your father gave me an account of all that had happened, particularly the knocking during family prayer. That evening, to my great satisfaction, we heard no knocking at all. But between nine and ten a servant came in and said, 'Old Jeffrey is coming' (that was the name of one that had died in the house) 'for I hear the signal.' This, they informed me, was heard every night about a quarter before ten. It was towards the top of the house, on the outside, at the north-east corner, resembling the loud creaking of a saw, or rather that of a windmill, when the body of it is turned about in order to shift the sails to the wind.

"We then heard a knocking over our heads, and Mr. Wesley, catching up a candle, said 'Come, Sir, now you shall hear for yourself.' We went upstairs, he with much hope, and I, to say the truth, with much fear. When we came to the nursery, it was knocking in the next room; when we went there, it was knocking in the nursery; and there it continued to knock, though we came in, and particularly at the bed (which was of wood) in which Miss Hetty and two of her younger sisters lay.

"Mr. Wesley, observing that they were much affected—though asleep, sweating, and trembling exceedingly—was very angry, and, pulling out a pistol, was going to fire at the place whence the sound came. But I snatched him by the arm and said, 'Sir, you are con-

vinced that this is something preternatural. If so, you cannot hurt it,
but you give it power to hurt you.' He then went close to the place
and said sternly, ' Thou deaf and dumb devil! Why dost thou fright
these children who cannot answer for themselves! Come to me, in
my study, that am a man!' Instantly it knocked his knock (the particular knock which your father always used at the gate) as if it
would shiver the board to pieces, and we heard nothing more that
night."

Commenting on this statement by Mr. Hoole, John Wesley says:
" Till this time my father had never heard the least disturbance in his
study. But the next evening, as he attempted to go into his study, of
which none had the key but himself, when he opened the door it was
thrust back with such violence as had like to have thrown him down.
However, he thrust the door open and went in. Presently there
was a knocking first on one side, then on the other, and, after a
time, in the next room, wherein my sister Nancy was. He went into
that room and, the noise continuing, adjured it to speak, but in vain.

" He then said, ' These spirits love darkness, put out the candle, and
perhaps it will speak.' My sister did so, and he repeated the adjuration;
but still there was only knocking and no articulate sound. Upon this
he said, ' Nancy, two Christians are an overmatch for the devil. Go
all of you downstairs, it may be when I am alone he will have the
courage to speak.' When she was gone, a thought came into his head,
and he said, ' If thou art the spirit of my son Samuel, I pray knock
three knocks and no more.' Immediately all was silence, and there was
no more knocking at all that night.

" I asked Nancy (then fifteen years old) whether she was not afraid
when my father used that adjuration. She answered she was sadly
afraid it would speak when she put out the candle, but she was not at
all afraid in the daytime, when it walked after her, only she thought
when she was about her work, he might have done it for her and saved
her the trouble."

Sukey Wesley records how from the first to the last day of a whole
month the noises continued—groans, squeals, tinglings, knockings,
" and my father's particular knock, very fierce." The noise occurred
everywhere, and was followed into almost every room of the house,
both day and night. Some members of the family sat alone, and when
they heard the noise spoke to it, asking it to tell them who it was, but
the only result was more noise, and never a voice.

John Wesley describes how his sisters eventually became so
accustomed to the noises that they were no longer much frightened
by them. " A gentle tapping at their bed-head usually began between
nine and ten at night. They then commonly said to each other,
' Jeffrey is coming, it is time to go to sleep.' And if they heard a noise

in the day, and said to my youngest sister, 'Hark, Kezzy, Jeffrey is knocking above,' she would run upstairs and pursue it from room to room, saying she desired no better diversion."

Wesley goes on to describe other incidents of the mysterious haunting.

" My father and mother had just gone to bed, and the candle was not taken away, when they heard three blows, and a second and a third three, as if it were with a large oaken staff, struck upon a chest which stood by the bedside. My father immediately arose, put on his nightgown, and, hearing great noises below, took the candle and went down; my mother walked by his side.

" As they went down the broad stairs, they heard as if a vessel full of silver was poured upon my mother's breast and ran jingling down to her feet. Quickly after there was a sound as if a large iron bell were thrown among many bottles under the stairs, but nothing was hurt. Soon after, our large mastiff dog came, and ran to shelter himself between them.

" A little before my father and mother came into the hall it seemed as if a very large coal was violently thrown upon the floor and dashed all in pieces, but nothing was seen. My father then cried out, ' Sukey, do you not hear? All the pewter is thrown about the kitchen.' But when they looked, all the pewter stood in its place.

" Then there was a loud knocking at the back door. My father opened it, but saw nothing. It was then at the front door. He opened that, but it was still lost labour. After opening first one, and then the other, several times, he turned and went up to bed. But the noises were so violent all over the house that he could not sleep till four in the morning.

" Several gentlemen and clergymen now earnestly advised my father to quit the house. But he constantly answered, ' No. Let the devil flee from me, I will never flee from the devil.' But he wrote to my eldest brother, at London, to come down. My brother was preparing to do so, when another letter came informing him the disturbances were over, after they had continued (the latter part of the time day and night) from the 2nd December to the end of January."

But it was not the end, for the disturbances still went on intermittently. Wesley's father, in his diary, records some curious incidents not given by the son. For instance, he says, " I have been thrice pushed by an invisible power, once against the corner of my desk in the study, a second time against the door of the matted chamber, a third time against the right side of the frame of my study door, as I was going in."

On December 25 he records, " Our mastiff came whining to us, as he did always after the first night of its coming, for then he barked violently at it, but was silent afterwards, and seemed more afraid than any of the children."

John Wesley tells us more about the behaviour of this dog. "At first, while the disturbances continued he used to bark and leap and snap on one side and the other, and that frequently before any person in the room heard any noise at all. But after two or three days he used to tremble, and creep away before the noise began. And by this the family knew it was at hand, nor did the observation ever fail."

Before the noise came into any room, says Wesley, " the latches were frequently lifted up, the windows clattered, and whatever iron or brass was about the chamber rang and jarred exceedingly.

" When it was in any room, let them make what noise they would, as sometimes they did, its dead, hollow note would be clearly heard above them all. The sound very often seemed in the air in the middle of a room, nor could they ever make any such themselves, by any contrivance.

" It never came by day till my mother ordered the horn to be blown. After that time scarce anyone could go from one room into another but the latch of the room they went to was lifted up before they touched it."

The horn-blowing idea was Mrs. Wesley's, after the suggestion had been made that the disturbances may be due to scurrying animals— cats, dogs, rats, or even weasels. She had a horn blown all over the house to scare away the rats or weasels, but to no avail. The noises simply got worse.

However, Mrs. Wesley did seem to find some agreement with the spirit. " From the time of my mother desiring it not to disturb her from five to six, it was never heard in her chamber from five till she came downstairs, nor at any other times when she was employed in devotion."

John's sister Emily, asked for her report on the affair, wrote to her brother : " A whole month was sufficient to convince anybody of the reality of the thing. I shall only tell you what I myself heard, and leave the rest to others.

" My sisters in the paper-chamber had heard noises, and told me of them, but I did not much believe till one night, about a week after the first groans were heard, which was the beginning. Just after the clock struck ten I went downstairs to lock the doors, which I always did. Scarce had I got up the west stairs, when I heard a noise like a person throwing down a vast coal in the middle of the fore kitchen. I was not much frighted, but went to my sister Sukey and we together went all over the lower rooms, but there was nothing out of order. Our dog was fast asleep, and our only cat in the other end of the house. No sooner was I got upstairs and undressing for bed, but I heard a noise. . . . This made me hasten to bed. But my sister Hetty, who sat always to wait on my father going to bed, was still sitting on the lowest step of the garret stairs, the door being shut at her back, when, soon after, there came down the stairs behind her something like a man in a loose night-gown trailing after him, which made her fly rather than run to me in the nursery."

This sudden visual appearance of the ghost was seen by others. Mrs. Wesley saw it, but " like a badger." The manservant also saw the same spectral animal " sat by the dining-room fire," although when he chased it into the kitchen it seemed to him more like a blurry white rabbit.

Samuel Wesley commented drily on the upsets : " It would make a glorious penny book." Once or twice it was thought " Old Jeffrey " had gone, but then the noises reappeared, driving Mrs. Wesley to exclaim piteously : " I am quite tired of hearing or speaking of it." In all, the haunting went on for five months, then the parsonage was quiet again.

The curious sequel, however, is that Emily Wesley believed herself followed by the noisy spirit throughout her life. When writing to her brother John, thirty-four years after the disturbances at Epworth, she referred to " that wonderful thing called by us Jeffrey " as still visiting her before any special illness.

It was Emily who, during the parsonage haunting, had given the ghost its nickname.

PHANTOM DOGS AND CATS

SOME, NOT all, dogs seem to be able to scent the advent of death, and generally indicate their fear of it by the most dismal howling. In my experience there is little doubt that dogs sometimes see a ghostly presence hovering close when death is about to take place. I have had this presence described to me by several people who also claim to have seen it, as a very tall, hooded figure, clad in a dark, loose, flowing costume, its face never discernible.

It would, of course, be foolish to say that a dog howling in a house is invariably a sign of death, but when the howling is accompanied by unmistakable signs of terror, as in the cases to which I refer, then it can be that someone in the house, or a person connected with someone in the house, will shortly die.

When investigating a haunted house I have generally taken a dog with me, for early experience taught me that a dog seldom fails to give notice, in some way or another, either by whining or growling, or crouching shivering at one's feet, or springing on one's lap and trying to bury its head in one's coat, of the proximity of a ghost.

For example, I had a dog with me when keeping vigil in a well-known haunted house in Gloucestershire. The dog, my only companion, and I sat on the staircase leading from the hall to the first floor. Just about two o'clock the dog gave a loud growl. I put my hand out and found that the animal was shivering from head to foot. Almost directly afterwards I heard the loud clatter of fire irons from somewhere away in the basement, a door banged, and then something, or someone, began to ascend the stairs.

Up, up, up came the footsteps, until I could see first of all a bluish light, then the top of a head, then a face, white and luminous, staring up at me. A few more steps and the whole thing was disclosed to view. It was the figure of a girl of about sixteen with a shock of red hair, on which was stuck, all awry, a dirty little, old-fashioned servant's cap. She was clad in a cotton dress, soiled and bedraggled, and had on her feet a pair of elastic-sided boots, which looked as if they would fall to pieces at each step she took. But it was her face that riveted my attention most. It was startlingly white and full of an expression of the most hopeless misery. The eyes, wide open and glossy, were turned direct on mine. I was too appalled either to stir or to utter a sound. The figure came right up to where I stood, paused for a second, and then slowly went on; up, up, up until a sudden bend in the staircase hid it from view. For some seconds there was a continuation of the footsteps, then there came a loud splash from somewhere outside and below, and then silence.

I did not wait to see if anything further would happen. I made hasty retreat, and the dog, who was apparently even more frightened than I, fled with me. We both arrived home considerably shaken.

Over and over again, on similar occasions, I have taken a dog along with me, and the same thing has occurred : the dog has made some noise indicative of great fear, remaining in a state of stupor during the actual presence of the apparition.

As to phantoms of dogs themselves—usually dead pets re-appearing —I have had literally hundreds of cases brought to my notice. Most are fragmentary, as with the following two occurrences. The first comes from a man in America.

" Five years ago we had a little puppy about six months old. I used to train him to always go round the back way to come into the house. One day he got hurt and run over, being instantly killed by a street car. A day or two after the accident I was going in my front door and I saw the dog go up the steps in front of me, as plain as I ever saw him in my life. It seemed he knew that I had taught him he must not go in the front way, because he would go a few steps and then turn round and look at me, as though he wanted to see how I was taking it, and I positively saw him go to the full length of the hall into the house, a distance of about twenty feet, before he disappeared. I saw him do this at least three times in the two months that we stayed in that flat. I told at least half a dozen people of the incident at the time it happened, and I can vouch for its authenticity."

And this from Portsmouth : " Two or three years ago I visited a medium. I had been seated only a few minutes when a little pug-dog of hers looked up in the direction of my knees and down towards my feet, growling and howling in a most strange manner.

" ' What on earth is he looking at?' I asked.

" 'Oh,' said the medium, ' there's a little fox-terrier lying across your feet, one half of his face is quite dark and the other half white, but he has such a peculiar black patch over the eye that one would think it was a black bruise.'

" Now, sir, I had such a little dog in India, but this lady did not know of him, and would never have known had he not, as I after-wards found out, died out there. This is not only a case of an appear-ance of an animal after death, but also a case in which it was seen by another animal, as also by the medium. I am also told that the pug-dog who had this vision of my dog was once seen to pounce upon what seemed to the medium to be several cats, near the copper in the scullery of the same house. The medium asked a neighbour if the previous occupants had had any cats. ' Oh, yes,' replied the neighbour, ' and badly the poor things were served, for they were cruelly thrown into the copper, which was full of boiling water.' "

Here is another poignant little haunting. " I had a collie who lived to a good old age. She was deaf and infirm, and one hind leg was paralysed, so that it dragged as she walked. I was taken ill, not seriously, but the poor old dog would insist on coming and lying in my room. The doctor insisted on her being destroyed. I felt that her life was no pleasure to her, and so she was painlessly put down.

" On three successive days afterwards in the afternoon, I heard her come upstairs, dragging her hind leg. I heard her steps come along the long passage which had my room at the end, and lost them about half-way up. On the third day I called out and spoke to her, putting out my hand as if she would come and put her head under it, and told her all was right. I never heard her any more."

One of the most extraordinary hauntings involving the phantom of a dog—indeed, a case unique in all its strange aspects—was first brought to light by that dedicated ghost hunter, W. T. Stead. It came to him through an old friend, the Reverend Harry Kendall, a Congregational minister of Darlington, but there was nothing hearsay about it. The story comprised a quite dramatically straightforward deposition made by one James Durham, who stated :

" I was night watchman at the old Darlington and Stockton Station at the town of Darlington, a few yards from the first station that ever existed. I was there fifteen years. I used to go on duty about 8 p.m. and come off at 6 a.m.

" I had been there a little while—perhaps two or three years—and at about 12 o'clock or 12.30 I was feeling rather cold with standing here and there, so I said to myself ' I will away down and get some-thing to eat.' There was a porter's cellar where a fire was kept on and a coalhouse was connected with it. So I went down the steps, took off my overcoat, and had just sat down on the bench opposite the fire and turned up the gas when a strange man came out of the coalhouse followed by a big black retriever. As soon as he entered, my eye was upon him, and his eye upon me, and we were intently watching each other as he moved on to the front of the fire.

" There he stood, looking at me, and a curious smile came over his countenance. He had a stand-up collar and a cut-away coat with gilt buttons and a Scotch cap. All at once he struck at me, and I had the impression that he hit me. I up with my fist and struck back at him. My fist seemed to go through him and struck against the stone above the fireplace and knocked the skin off my knuckles. The man seemed to be struck back into the fire, and uttered a strange, unearthly squeak. Immediately the dog gripped me by the calf of my leg, and seemed to cause me pain. The man recovered his position, called off the dog with a sort of click of the tongue, and then went back into the coalhouse followed by the dog. I lighted my dark lantern and looked into the coalhouse, but there was neither dog nor man, and no outlet for them except the one by which they had entered.

" I was satisfied that what I had seen was ghostly, and it accounted for the fact that when the man had first come into the place where he sat I had not challenged him with any enquiry. Next day and for several weeks, my account caused quite a commotion, and a host of people spoke to me about it, among the rest old Edward Pease, father of railways, and his three sons, John, Joseph and Henry. Old Edward sent for me to his house and asked me all particulars. He and others put this question to me : ' Are you sure you were not asleep and had the nightmare?' My answer was quite sure, for I had not been a minute in the cellar and was just going to get something to eat. I was certainly not under the influence of strong drink, for I was then, as I have been for forty-nine years, a teetotaler. My mind at the time was perfectly free from trouble.

" What increased the excitement was the fact that a man a number of years before, who was employed in the office of the station, had committed suicide and been carried into this very cellar. I knew nothing of this circumstance, nor of the body of the man, but Mr. Pease and others who had known him, told me my description exactly corresponded to his appearance and the way he dressed, and also he had a black retriever just like the one which gripped me. I should add that no mark or effect remained on the spot where I seemed to be seized. (Signed) *James Durham*. Dec. 9th, 1890."

The Reverend Mr. Kendall went very closely into James Durham's story and gave the reasons why he accepted it fully. The arguments he used strike me as being so concise and sensible that I think it is not out of place to quote them here.

" First," said Mr. Kendall, " he (Durham) was accustomed as a watchman to be up all night, and therefore not likely from that cause to feel sleepy. Secondly, he had scarcely been a minute in the cellar, and feeling hungry was just about to get something to eat. Thirdly, if he was asleep, at the beginning of the vision, he must have been awake enough during the latter part of it when he knocked the skin off his own knuckles. Fourthly, there was his own confident testimony. I strongly incline to the opinion that there was an objective cause for the vision, and that it was genuinely apparitional."

So interested was Mr. Kendall in the case that he visited the station and was taken into the cellar where the manifestations took place. His guide, an old official of the North Road Station, told him he well remembered the clerk, a man of the name of Winter, who committed suicide there, and showed Mr. Kendall the exact spot where Winter had shot himself with a pistol. In dress and appearance Winter corresponded minutely with the phenomenon described by James Durham, and he had certainly owned a black retriever.

Although, as I have said, ordinary hauntings featuring dog phantoms are quite numerous, the most common forms of animal phenomena seen in haunted houses are undoubtedly those of cats. The number of places reported to me over the years as being haunted by cats is almost incredible, and I remember at one time being notified of four different houses in a single street in Whitechapel, all suffering the hauntings of a spirit cat, or cats. This state of affairs may be accounted for by the fact that until recent years cats, more than any other pet animals, tended to meet with sudden and unnatural ends, especially in the poorer districts.

However, as with dogs, a good number of cat hauntings are of the simple type, the return of a much loved pet, as instanced by the following episode taken from my investigations in early years.

" One evening my son and I were quietly reading in full gaslight, our small grey cat lying on the sofa a short distance from where I sat. Suddenly I saw on my knee a large red and white cat which had belonged to us in India, which was a very dear family friend and as fond of us as a child. On leaving India we were obliged to give him to a friend and in the end he shared the usual fate of pets in that country, making a meal for some wild animal.

" 'Rufie-Oofie ', in his spirit shape, purred vigorously, rubbing his head against me and giving every sign of delight at seeing us again. I did not speak, but in a few minutes my son looked up and said ' Mother, Rufie-Oofie is on your knee,' at which the spirit cat jumped down and went to him to be petted. Then the cat returned to me, and walked along the sofa to where our present cat, ' Kim ' was asleep. The spirit cat, with a look of almost human fun, patted Kim's head, at which he awoke with a start. Rufie-Oofie continued to make playful dabs at Kim's ears, Kim following each movement with glaring eyes, distinctively seeing and realising that another cat was invading his sofa, but not in the least angry with him and quite ready to play.

"After a few minutes the spirit cat came back to my knee, whereupon the earth cat displayed jealousy which Rufie-Oofie resented, but before they came to actual 'words' the spirit cat vanished."

And here is another typical example. "My son had the following experience at the age of four years in our Worcestershire home. He was an only child and spent much of his time in the company of a cat which shared his tastes and pursuits even to the extent of fishing in the River Weir with him, the cat being far more proficient at the sport than the boy. When the cat died we none of us dared to break the news to the child, and were much surprised when he asked us to say why his cat only came to play with him at nights nowadays. When we questioned him about it, he stoutly maintained that the cat was there in bodily form every night after he went to bed, looking much the same but a little thinner."

For a cat haunting with a difference, we are indebted to a husband who wrote down the following account from his wife, who was brought up in Germany. I will quote it as he gave it, in her own words.

"When I was a little girl living with my family near Michelstadt, in the Odenwald, I remember an old woman like an old witch, whose name was Louise, and who was called 'Pfeiffe Louise' because she exhibited pipes for sale in her cottage window, along with the cheap dress-stuffs, needles and threads, and simple toys for children which were her stock-in-trade. She had a favourite cat which was devoted to her, but its attachment doesn't seem to have been enough to make her happy, for she married a young sergeant named Lautenschlager, who might have been her son, or indeed her grandson, and who, as everyone said, courted her for her money.

"During her last illness, the devoted cat was always with her. It kept watch beside the body when she was dead and refused to be driven away. In a fit of exasperation Lautenschlager seized it, carried it off, and drowned it in the little River Mumling, at a place where the road from Michalstadt to the neighbouring village of Steinbach runs near the water's edge. It was bordered with poplars then, but chestnut trees shade it now.

"Soon after Louise was buried Lautenschlager married again, and opened an eating-house in Steinbach, where he established his second wife. He had a sister whom he placed in the cottage of poor 'Pfeiffe Louise'. She carried on the business, and every day Lautenschlager used to walk over from Steinbach to see how the sister was getting on, returning in the evening to his wife, who used to relate to my mother that he frequently came home terrified and bathed in perspiration, for as he passed the place where he had drowned the cat, its ghost used to come out of the river and run beside him along the dark road, sometimes terrifying him still more by jumping in front of him.

" After a few years the second wife died, and Lautenschlager married a third. The little cottage business had prospered, and in its place he now had a considerable draper's shop in Michelstadt. He continued to walk over from Steinbach, where the third wife now lived in the eating-house, and the ghost of the cat continued to frighten him by appearing at nightfall as he walked beside the river.

" I can remember hearing his third wife describe his dread of it, and my mother has told me how both the sister and the second wife used to say the same thing, though I was too young then for them to tell me about it. Lautenschlager also complained to the country people who came to dine at his eating-house. He considered himself an ill-used man, and felt that the supernatural powers were treating him very hardly, and subjecting him to a real persecution. I have only the conversation of his wife and the gossip of the village to vouch for his sincerity, and the genuineness of the apparition is supported only by Lautenschlager's word, but his evident anger and agitation were accepted as genuine, and no one dreamed of doubting his word. He was not at all a dreamy or imaginative man, and did not drink. His passion was merely momentary. He was not only a draper and caterer, but a usurer, and realized something of a fortune by lending money on good security to peasants and farmers who, it was said, did not consider how they bound themselves when they signed the papers he put before them.

" Lautenschlager continued to be haunted by the cat-ghost at irregular intervals for more than twenty years, and it made a marked change on his character. He became serious, and during the years before his death would only talk about religion and read sacred literature."

THE RESIDENTS OF RAMHURST

It surely goes without saying that it requires much patience to be a
ghost hunter. For instance, you cannot hope to witness in a single
night's vigil ghostly events which have occurred at intervals sometimes
over a space of years. Nor is it possible always to find a tidy ending
to a haunting, to explain the probable cause of it down to the last
small mysteries. However, if you dig hard enough it is surprising what
you can find at times, and certainly a ghost hunter named Robert
Dale Owen had this persistence and reaped its reward, in the case of
Ramhurst Manor.

In the middle years of the last century this beautiful old country
house near Leigh, Kent, was the scene of a rather poignant haunting.
As the house dated from the year 1270 it perhaps offered just the
right setting for it. The 1850s being a time when more often initials,
rather than names, were given in true ghost stories, we have to be
content with initials in the case of Ramhurst, but this does not in any
way detract from the authenticity of the story.

In October 1857 Mrs. R., the wife of an English officer of high rank,
took up residence at Ramhurst. From the time she moved in, Mrs.
R. and the servants were disturbed by strange knockings, unaccountable voices, and the sound of mysterious footsteps. The ghostly voices
were generally, but not invariably, heard coming from an unoccupied
room. Sometimes it was as if someone was talking in a loud tone, and
other times as if someone was reading aloud. Occasionally it was a
sound like someone screaming.

The servants were very frightened and although they did not
actually see anything, the cook one day told Mrs. R. that in broad

daylight she had heard the rustle of a silken dress close behind her. The dress seemed to touch her, but when she turned suddenly round, thinking it to be her mistress, to her great surprise and horror she could see no one.

Mrs. R.'s brother, a young officer, who enjoyed staying at Ramhurst for the country shooting, was highly sceptical of the ghostly noises, which he claimed must be the voices of his sister and a woman friend of hers sitting up chatting at night. But twice, when a voice which he thought resembled his sister's rose to a scream, he rushed into her bedroom between two and three o'clock in the morning with a gun in his hand, only to find her sleeping quietly.

On the second Saturday in October Mrs. R. went by horse carriage to the railway station at Tonbridge, to meet her young friend Miss S., whom she had invited to spend some weeks with her. Miss S. seems to have been blessed with some psychic powers or " second sight ", for she had seen ghosts at times from early childhood.

On their return to Ramhurst at about four o'clock in the afternoon they drove up to the entrance of the manorhouse, whereupon Miss S. immediately saw on the threshold the appearance of two figures, apparently an elderly couple, dressed in clothes of a bygone age. They appeared to be standing on the ground. Miss S. did not " hear any voice ", and not wishing to make her friend uneasy, deliberately refrained from mentioning what she had seen.

Miss S. saw the same figures, in the same clothes, several times during the next ten days, sometimes in one of the rooms of the house, sometimes in one of the passages; and always by daylight. The couple appeared to her " surrounded by an atmosphere nearly of the colour usually called ' neutral tint '." On the third occasion they spoke to her psychically. They said they were husband and wife, and that in former days they had possessed and occupied the manorhouse, and their name was Children. They appeared sad and downcast, and when Miss S. asked the cause of their melancholy, they replied that they had idolized this property of theirs, that their pride and pleasure had centred on its possession, that its improvement had engrossed their thoughts, and it troubled them to know that it had passed away from their family, and to see it now in the hands of careless strangers.

To Miss S., the ghost-seer, the voices of the apparitions were not only perfectly audible, but also intelligible, though no one else heard them. Meanwhile, Mrs. R., detecting that something unusual had occurred to her friend in connection with the haunting, questioned her, and was then told by Miss S. what she had seen and heard from the apparitions.

Always afterwards, when the noises occurred, Mrs. R. looked for the ghosts, but to no avail. She had given up hope of seeing them when a month later she had a surprise. She was hurriedly dressing for dinner, her brother, who had just returned from a day's shooting, having called to her impatiently that the meal was served and he was famished. At the moment of completing her toilet, and as she hastily turned to leave her bedroom, there in the doorway stood the same female figure which Miss S. had described, identical in appearance even to the old point-lace on her brocaded silk dress, while beside her on the left, but less distinctly visible, was the figure of her husband. They made no sound, but above the figure of the woman, as if written in phosphoric light in the dusky atmosphere that surrounded her, were the words " Dame Children ", together with some other words, conveying the message that, having never aspired beyond the joys and sorrows of this world, she had remained " earth-bound ".

These last words Mrs. R. scarcely paused to decipher, for another call from her impatient brother urged her forward. The woman's figure, filling up the doorway, remained quite still. There was no time for hesitation, Mrs. R. closed her eyes, rushed through the apparition and into the dining-room, throwing up her hands and exclaiming to Miss S. : " Oh, my dear, I've walked through Mrs. Children ! "

This was the only time Mrs. R. saw anything of the apparitions during her stay at Ramhurst, and it was quite enough for her. She afterwards kept her bedroom well lit by a blazing fire, and also by candles, while a lighted lamp was kept burning all night in the corridor.

Miss S. however, had several more encounters with the ghostly couple, and from her conversations with them learned that the husband's name was Richard, and that he had died in 1753. From the clothes they wore Miss S. deduced that they were of the period of Queen Anne or one of the early Georges, she could not be sure which as the fashions were so very similar.

Deeply impressed with the mystery, Mrs. R.'s husband on his return tried to solve it by making inquiries among the servants and in the neighbourhood, but without success. No one knew of the house ever being owned or inhabited by people named Children, though a nurse in the family, Miss Sophy, had spent all her life in the vicinity.

Four months later, when Mrs. R. and her husband had given up all hope of unravelling the mystery, Sophy went home for a holiday to her father's home at Riverhead, near Sevenoaks. During her visit she called on a sister-in-law, aged seventy, who fifty years ago had been a housemaid at Ramhurst Manor. Sophy asked her old sister-in-law if she had ever heard of a family named Children at the Manor, and was told there was no such family there in her time, but she did remember having been told by an old man, that in his boyhood he had helped to keep the hounds of the Childrens, who were then living at Ramhurst.

On her return from holiday Sophy told Mrs. R. of her discovery. So now it was established that a family named Children had once really occupied the manorhouse, but beyond that Mrs. R. was unable to learn anything about them.

That is where our ghost hunter, Robert Dale Owen, came in. In December 1858, fourteen months after the hauntings began, he heard about it from Mrs. R. and Miss S. Then, having accepted an invitation to spend Christmas week with some friends living near Sevenoaks, Owen determined to make further inquiries about the haunted manorhouse, and its former occupants. He sought out the nurse, Miss Sophy, and questioned her closely, but was unable to get from her any more about the hauntings than he already knew. Nor did his inspection of the churches and graveyards of Leigh and Tonbridge bring to light any fresh information about the Children family, except that a certain George Children had left, in the year 1718, a weekly gift of bread to the poor, and that another George Children, his descendant, who had died about forty years previously and who had not lived at Ramhurst, had a marble tablet in Tonbridge Church erected to his memory.

Then Owen was referred to a neighbouring clergyman, who lent him a document that contained the following extract from the Hasted Papers, which are preserved in the British Museum :

" George Children . . . who was High Sheriff of Kent in 1698, died without issue in 1718 and by will devised the bulk of his estate to Richard Children, eldest son of his late uncle, William Children of Hedcorn, and his heirs. This Richard Children, who settled himself at Ramhurst, in the Parish of Leigh, married Anne, daughter of John Saxby, in the parish of Leeds, by whom he had issue four sons and two daughters. . . ."

Now Mr. Owen knew that the first of the Children to live at Ramhurst was named Richard, and that he had settled there in the early part of George I's reign; but he was still ignorant of the date of Richard's death, which, it will be recalled, was given by the apparition as 1753. Then, being referred by an antiquarian friend to Hasted's History of Kent, published in 1778, Owen found the following paragraph :

" In the eastern part of the parish of Lyghe (now Leigh), near the river Medway, stands an ancient mansion called Ramhurst, once reputed a manor, and held of the honour of Gloucester. . . . It continued in the Culpepper family for several generations. . . . It passed by sale into that of Saxby, and Mr. William Saxby conveyed it by sale to Children. Richard Children resided here, and died possessed of it in 1753, aged eighty-three years. He was succeeded to it by his eldest son, John Children of Tonbridge. . . ."

And so Owen verified the last remaining particular, the date of

Richard Children's death. The history also made it clear that Richard Children was the only representative of the family who lived and died at Ramhurst, his son John having decided to live instead at Ferox Hall, near Tonbridge, which then became the family seat. In 1816 the family, through no fault of their own, lost all their property and were compelled to sell Ramhurst, which was then turned more into a farmhouse than a family residence.

Here, obviously, began the sadness of the ghostly Mr. and Mrs. Richard Children, who, my own researches show, had made considerable alterations at Ramhurst during the first years of their occupation, to turn it into a home that was their pride and joy.

Thus, forty years after the sale of Ramhurst—and a hundred years after their own deaths—the couple returned to impress their melancholy upon Mrs. R. After her departure they were never seen again.

THE MURDERER'S RETURN

WHEN I was on a visit to the village of Guilsborough, in Northampton, some years ago, my host quietly produced an old pamphlet which he thought might interest me. In this casual way did I come upon the strange case of the murderer's ghost.

The pamphlet's intriguing title was : " The Guilsborough Ghost, or a Minute Account of the Appearance of the Ghost of John Croxford, Executed at Northampton, August 4, 1764, For the Murder of a Stranger in the Parish of Guilsborough." The pamphlet was first printed in 1764. It was then reprinted in 1819 (by F. Cordeaux, Northampton), and again in 1848 (by G. Henson, Letterpress and Copperplate Printer, Bridge Road, Northampton). Its author was an unnamed parson who was chaplain to Northampton Gaol at the time of the execution.

Briefly, the John Croxford of the title, and three other men named Seamark, Gee and Butlin, were tried at the Northampton Assizes and all convicted of the brutal murder of a Scottish pedlar, identity unknown. The pedlar, who was passing through Guilsborough with his goods, called by chance at the home of Seamark—in fact, a shepherd's hut. It was at this hut that the four men, all with unsavoury reputations, used to meet, and the luckless pedlar walked right into their lair. They robbed and afterwards cruelly murdered him, and in order to prevent discovery, bundled his body into a coal oven and disposed of him in the fire. This was proved at the trial on the evidence of Mrs. Ann Seamark and her ten-year-old son, who was an eye-witness to the affair—the child saw the whole horrible act while peeping through the crevices of a room above.

125

The four men were executed on August 4, 1764, and John Croxford's body hung in chains on Hollowell Heath, in the parish of
Guilsborough, near the spot where the murder was committed.

The pamphlet was published within weeks of the execution, and
its author, the prison chaplain, was at pains to go into detail regarding
the crime and the trial, before getting down to the main purpose of
his "troubling the world with his narrative", which he emphasized
was a "plain and conscientious account" of how the ghost of the
murderer John Croxford had returned to him eight days after the
execution. The chaplain, who of course attended the four men on the
scaffold, recalled first the way they had acted after conviction.

"Clear and conclusive as the evidence was against them, no
arguments even after condemnation, though delivered and enforced
with the utmost energy, precision and perspicuity by a learned and
worthy divine, were able to reach their hardened hearts and prevail
for an open and unreserved confession of their guilt. Even at the
gallows, in their last addresses to the people, they insisted on their
innocence in the strongest terms imaginable, wishing the heaviest
penalties an offended God could inflict might be their portion in the
next world, if they were guilty of the murder that was laid at their
charge, and for which they were about to suffer.

"Thus did they divide the sentiments of the crowd that many more
were brought over to a full persuasion of their innocence, while others
were left halting between two opinions, and severely agitated with
conflicting doubts.

"But mark the event. After having instructed my people, as a
teacher in the knowledge of the Scriptures, I used to spend the super-
fluous hours of the Lord's Day in perusing some part or other of the
Old and New Testament. Accordingly on August 12, 1764, being the
Sabbath, I returned as usual to my study, the door of which is secured
by a lock with a spring bolt, and sat down to my accustomed evening
devotion; the business of this day by rotation lying where St. Paul
in his Epistle to the Corinthians, proposes, maintains and proves the
resurrection of the body. Struck with the sublimity of his thoughts,
boldness of his figures and energy of his diction, and convinced by the
number and weight of his arguments, and looking with a pleasing
foretaste of happiness into futurity, I was on a sudden surprised with
the perfect form and appearance of a man, who stood erect at a small
distance from my right side. Conscious that the door was locked, and
that there was no other means by which my visitor could have entered,
I was considerably surprised, surprise turning into abject terror, when,
glancing with irresistible fascination at the man, I perceived something indefinably but most unmistakably unnatural.

"Feeling sure that I was in the actual presence of an apparition,

I contrived by an almost superhuman effort I admit, to sum up sufficient courage to speak, my voice seeming dry and unrecognizable. I addressed the figure in the power and spirit of the Gospel, inquiring on what errand it was sent, what was intended by such an application, and what services could be expected from a person of so little note and mean abilities as myself. Every second tended to strengthen my composure, and when it spoke in a voice rather more hollow and intense, perhaps, than that of an ordinary human being, my fears were instantly dissipated.

" I was now able to take a close stock of it, and observe that in features, general appearance and clothes, it closely resembled any ordinary labouring man; it was in its expression and colouring only that it differed—its eyes were lurid, its cheeks livid. Raising one extremely white and emaciated hand it desired me to compose myself, saying that as it was now strictly limited by a Superior Power, and could do no one act but by the permission of God, I had no reason to be afraid, abrupt as was its appearance, and that if I would endeavour to overcome the visible perturbation I was in, it would proceed in the business of its errand.

" At this announcement my heart fluttered with an excitement I found difficult to control. Was that wonderful mystery that had hitherto enshrouded the existence and composition of the Unknown about to be revealed to me? Was I going to be initiated into those secrets hitherto denied to human beings? Eagerly promising to control myself, and lost to all else, save the fascinating presence of my guest, I settled down to listen to anything the apparition might have to say. Commencing in a clear and solemn tone, it stated its name was John Croxford, and that it was one of those unhappy prisoners executed at Northampton on the 4th day of August, 1764.

" A cold chill ran down my spine at this announcement, and as I stared at the figure, absolutely transfixed with awe and astonishment, I suddenly and for the first time, recognized it. It was indeed the exact counterpart of John Croxford, one of the murderers whose execution I had so recently attended and about whose guilt I had been, and still was, in no little perplexity.

" It had been, so it continued, the ringleader and principal of the gang of miscreants, most of whom it had corrupted, debauched and seduced to that deplorable method of life, and it was particularly appointed by Providence to undeceive the world and remove those doubts which the solemn protestations of their innocence to the very hour of death had raised in the minds of all who heard them. It explained that the reason all the murderers had so persistently insisted on their innocence lay in the fact that, while the blood of their victim was still warm, they entered into a sacramental obligation, which they sealed by dipping their fingers in the blood of the deceased and licking the same, by which they bound themselves not to confess, if condemned to die for it on the evidence of others.

"They were further encouraged to such measures (said the apparition) since as Seamark himself was a confederate in the murder, they concluded the evidence of his wife would not be admitted; that as the child was so young, they presumed no judge or jury would pay the least regard to his deposition; that as Butlin had but lately entered into a confederacy with them, and no robberies could be readily proved against him, they thought it would be impossible for one of his age to begin a career of wickedness with murder; that if they could invalidate the evidence on behalf of Butlin, it must be of equal advantage to them all; and that, though disappointed of this view in court, and condemned to die on the above evidence, they were still infatuated with the same notion even at the gallows, and expected a reprieve for Butlin when the halter was about his neck, and consequently, if such a reprieve had been granted, as the evidence was as full and decisive against Butlin as against them, the sentence for the murder must have been withdrawn from all, their execution deferred, and perhaps transportation only their final punishment.

"When the figure had said so much, it paused, and taking advantage of its sudden lapse into silence, I asked it if the evidence of the woman and child was clear, punctual and particular, to which it replied, ' It was as circumstantial, distinct and methodical as possible, varying not in the least from truth in any one particular of consequence, unless in the omission of their horrid sacrament, which she might possibly neither observe nor know.' I then asked why they had behaved with such impropriety, impudence and clamour upon their trial, to which it replied that they had been somewhat elevated with liquor, probably conveyed to them, and that by effrontery and a seemingly undaunted behaviour they hoped to intimidate the woman, throw her into confusion and perplex her deposition, thereby rendering the evidence precarious and inconclusive, or at least give the Court some favourable presumptions of their innocence.

"I next inquired whether they knew the name of the person murdered, whence he came, and what reasons they had for committing so horrid a barbarity. The figure again replied. It said that the man was a perfect stranger to them all, and that the murder was committed more out of wantonness and the force of long-contracted habits of wickedness than necessity, as they were at that time in no want of money. They first found occasion to quarrel with the pedlar through a strange propensity to mischief, for which it could not account, but from God's withdrawing His grace and leaving them to all the extravagance and irregularities of a corrupted heart, long-hardened in the ways of sin. The man, being stout and undaunted, resented their ill usage, and in his own defence proceeded to blows. Two only, Gee and Croxford, were at first concerned, but finding him resolute, they called up Seamark and Butlin who were at a distance behind a hedge. They then all seized the pedlar, notwithstanding which he struggled with great violence to the very last against their united efforts, nor did they think it safe to trifle any longer with a man who gave such proofs of uncommon strength; with much difficulty they dragged him down to Seamark's yard, and there committed the murder as represented in Court.

" I now inquired if there was any licence in his bag or pockets, that they might discover his name or place of abode. The figure shook its head and went on to explain that the paper left behind in its, Croxford's, writing was of a piece with the rest of their conduct in this affair—it was a hardened untruth, abounding with reflections so false, as scandalous and wicked as was the Father of Lies himself, who had gradually brought them from one step of iniquity to another, to the place of Purgatory in which they now were. It declared further that though their bodies were unaffected with pain, their souls were in darkness under all the dreadful apprehension of remaining there for eternity, far beyond what the liveliest imagination, while influenced by the weight and grossness of matter, could conceive. Their doom had been not a little aggravated by their final impenitence, impiety and profaneness in adjuring God by the most horrid implications, to attest the truth of a palpable and notorious falsehood, and by wishing that their own portion in eternity might be determined in consequence thereof. Language, it added, was too weak to describe, and mortality incapable of conceiving a ten-thousandth part of their anguish and despair even at present, and happy would it be for succeeding ages if posterity could be induced to profit by their misfortunes, and be influenced by this account to avoid the punishment of earthbound spirits.

" The figure delivered this harangue with such perspicuity and with such an emphasis and tone of voice, as plainly evinced the truth of what it spoke, and claimed my closest attention and regard. As it seemed to hint that I was singled out to acquaint the world with these particulars, I told it that the present age was one of incredulity and agnosticism, that few gave credit to fables of this kind, that the world would conclude me either a madman or an impostor, or brand me with the odious imputations of superstition and enthusiasm. Therefore, true credentials were necessary, not only to preserve my own character, but also to procure respect and credit to my relations.

" To this the figure instantly responded that what I observed was perfectly right, and that unless some proper attestations were given to accounts of this nature, they would be considered by the rational part of mankind as mere tales, invented only to amuse the credulous or frighten children on a winter's evening into obedience; in short, that they would have no weight, and disappoint the ends of Providence, who intends them for the good and benefit of the world. Therefore, in order to encourage my perseverance in supporting the truth of this appearance and embolden me to publish a minute detail of it, it would direct me to such a criterion as would put the reality of it beyond all dispute. It accordingly told me that in such a spot, describing it as minutely as possible, in the parish of Guilsborough, was deposited a gold ring, which belonged to the pedlar whom they murdered, and moreover on the inside of it was engraved this motto : ' Hanged he'll be who steals me, 1745 '.

"Continuing, the figure said that the above wording on the ring had struck it (Croxford) as so ominous when he read it, that it at once buried the object, hoping thus to elude the sentence denounced at random against the unlawful possessor of it, and even escape the vindictive justice of Heaven itself by such a precaution. If I found not every particular in regard to this ring exactly as it related to me, then I might conclude there was not a single syllable of truth in the whole, and subsequently no obligation lay upon me to take any further concern in the affair.

" The figure now ceased speaking, and I suddenly became aware of two things—the lateness of the hour and the strange silence. I glanced at the window to see if there still remained any lights in the houses of my neighbours, and on my turning round again, I found the figure had gone. Furthermore, the lamp, which had burned low all the time it was present, was now once again giving its accustomed light. Bitterly disappointed at so abrupt a disappearance, just when I had overcome my fear and was preparing to put to the phantom certain questions with regard to the other world, I sat down and canvassed over the whole matter to myself, reflecting seriously upon every particular. I laid particular stress in my cogitations upon the circumstance of the ring, the singularity of its motto and the minute description of the spot where it was alleged to be secreted, and was induced to conclude from the coherence and punctuality of the whole story that it must be true.

" Accordingly I set out in the morning to Guilsborough, and in the spot that the phantom had described to me found the ring with the words : ' Hanged he'll be who steals me, 1745 ' engraven on it. Assured now that my visitor of the night before was indeed the spirit of the unfortunate Croxford. I hastened back to Northampton, resolved to make the whole matter public and so dissipate the doubts certain folk still entertained regarding the guilt of the executed man."

The chaplain's statement concluded with a fervid exhortation to piety, coupled with an equally strong warning against indulgence in any kind of vice or crime.

In spite of the many intervening years, I found that the story of the murder and the ghost was still discussed by the people of Guilsborough, some of whom pointed out to me not only the spot where the crime was committed and the ring subsequently found, but the exact spot where the gibbet, on which the body of John Croxford was hung in chains, stood.

Evil as Croxford had been during his lifetime, I think one may gather from the chaplain's story that the murderer tried to make amends for his misdeeds after death.

THE WAILING BANSHEES

ONE OF the questions put to me most frequently over the years has been : " What really is a Banshee?"

It is a question easily answered. The Banshee is a family ghost. Moreover, it is a ghost which can be positively and unerringly identified, for it manifests itself only to members of really old Irish families. As there are few such families left in Ireland, so the Banshee hauntings have become fewer and fewer. However, the Banshee does sometimes travel; when, and only when, it accompanies abroad a descendant of one of these ancient families.

As to its origin, in spite of arbitrary assertions made from time to time, no one truly knows. In fact the Banshee would seem to have a number of origins, for there is not one kind of Banshee only, but many. Each Irish clan possesses a Banshee of its own, as does the O'Donnell clan, which dates back in unbroken line to Niall of the Nine Hostages. The O'Donnell Banshee, as I can testify from personal experience, is very different in appearance, and in its manner of making itself known, from the Banshee of the O'Reardons, the O'Flahertys or the O'Neills.

Some Banshees have been known to manifest themselves as very beautiful women with lovely long hair; raven black, burnished copper or brilliant gold. These are the creatures which, understandably enough, have been most popularized in fiction. Their star-like eyes, full of tender pity, are either dark or tearful, or of the most exquisite blue or grey. Some, again, appear as haggish, wild-looking creatures seized by the utmost despair; while a few—fortunately, only a few— incline to take the form of something that is wholly devilish and frightful.

As a general rule, however, the Banshee is not seen, it is only heard, and it announces its presence in a variety of ways, sometimes by groaning, sometimes by wailing, and sometimes by the most blood-curdling screams, which I can only liken to the screams a woman might make if she were being violently done to death. Occasionally I have heard of Banshees clapping their hands, and tapping and scratching at walls and window-panes, and, not infrequently, signalling their arrival by terrific crashes and thumps. Also, I have met with the Banshee that simply chuckles—a low, short, but terribly expressive chuckle, which makes ten times more impression on the mind of the hearer than any other ghostly sound he has heard, and which no lapse of time is able to efface from his memory.

I myself have heard this sound, and as I write this I fancy I can hear it again—a Satanic chuckle full of mockery, as if made by someone in the full knowledge of coming unpleasant events. In my case the unpleasant surprise certainly came, though had I never before believed in the ghost world, after hearing that chuckle my cynical arguments would have dissipated and died.

There is one remarkable instance of a number of Banshees manifesting themselves simultaneously. It occurred before the death of a member of the Galway O'Flahertys. The doomed one was a woman of unusual piety who, though ill at the time, was not thought to be in a serious condition. Indeed she got so much better that several of her acquaintances came to her room to enliven her convalescence, and it was while they were all there, talking together happily, that singing was suddenly heard, apparently outside the bedroom. They listened, and could distinctly hear a choir of sweet voices singing some extraordinary plaintive air, which made them turn pale and look at one another apprehensively, for all felt intuitively it was a chorus of Banshees. Nor were their fears mistaken, for the patient unexpectedly developed pleurisy and died within a few days. And again, at the actual moment of death, the same chorus of spirit voices was heard sweetly singing.

In all my researches I have never come upon a parallel case, though in several instances two Banshees have been heard at once.

Among the more well-known cases of Banshee hauntings is that related by Ann, Lady Fanshawe, in her memoirs. It seems that Lady Fanshawe experienced this haunting when on a visit to Lady Honora O'Brien, daughter of Henry, fifth Earl of Thomond, who was then in all probability living in the ancient castle of Lemaneagh, some thirty miles from Limerick. After going to bed rather early on the first night of her stay there, and being joined later by her husband, Lady Fanshawe was awakened at one o'clock by the sound of a voice, and drawing aside the hangings of the four-poster bed, she saw looking in through the window at her, the face of a woman. The moonlight was very strong and Lady Fanshawe could see every feature with startling distinctness, but at the same time her attention was apparently riveted on the extraordinary pallor of the cheeks and the intense redness of the hair. Then, to quote her own words, the apparition " spake aloud, and in a voice I never heard, thrice ' Ahone ', and then with a sigh, more like wind than breath, she vanished and to me her body looked more like a thick cloud than substance.

" I was so much affrighted that my hair stood on end, and my nightclothes fell off. I pulled and pinched your father, who never awakened during this disorder I was in, but at last was much surprised to find me in this fright, and more when I related the story and showed him the window opened; but he entertained me with telling how much more these apparitions were usual in that country than in England."

The following morning Lady Honora, who did not appear to have been to bed, told Lady Fanshawe that a cousin of hers had died in the house at about two o'clock in the morning, and expressed a hope that Lady Fanshawe had not been subjected to any disturbances.

" When any die of this family," she explained, " there is the shape of a woman appears in this window every night until they be dead." She said the apparition was believed to be that of a woman who, centuries before, had been seduced by the owner of the castle and murdered, her body being buried under the window of the room in which Lady Fanshawe had slept. " But truly," she added by way of apology, " I thought not of it when I lodged you here."

Another well-known case of the Banshee is a further incident involving the Galway O'Flahertys. In the days of much inter-clan fighting in Ireland, when the O'Neills frequently embarked on crusades against their alternate friends and enemies the O'Donnells, and the O'Rourks embarked on similar crusades against the O'Donovans, it happened that one night the chief of the O'Flahertys, arrayed in all the brilliance of a new suit of armour, and feeling more than usually cheerful and fit, marched out of his castle at the head of his retainers, who were all, like their chief, in good spirits and talking and singing gaily. They had not gone far, however, when a sudden silence ensued, to be abruptly broken by a series of agonizing screams coming from just over their heads. Instantly everybody was sobered and naturally looked up, expecting to see something that would explain the extraordinary disturbance. Nothing, however, was to be seen, except a vast expanse of cloudless sky in which shone a brilliant moon. Yet despite the fact that nothing was visible, everyone felt a presence that was at once sorrowful and weird, and which they instinctively knew was the Banshee, come to warn them of some approaching catastrophe.

The next night, when the chieftain and his followers were again marching forth, the same thing happened; but after that, nothing of a similar nature happened for about a month. Then the wife of the O'Flaherty, during the absence of her husband on one of these foraging expeditions, had an alarming experience. She had gone to bed one night and was restlessly tossing about, unable to sleep, when she was terrified by a succession of shrieks coming apparently from just beneath her window, and which sounded like the cries of a woman in great trouble or pain. She looked out, but could see no one. She then knew that she had heard the Banshee, and the next day her forebodings were only too fully realized. With a fearful knowledge of its meaning, she saw a cavalcade, bearing in its midst a bier, slowly and sorrowfully winding its way towards the castle. She did not need to be told that the foraging party had returned, and that the surviving warriors had brought back with them the lifeless and mutilated body of her husband.

A more recent haunting of an especially poignant nature is that of the Kenealy Banshee. Dr. Kenealy, the Irish poet and author, lived in his early years in a wildly romantic and picturesque part of Ireland. Among his brothers was one, a mere child, whose gentle nature made him beloved of all, and the entire household and neighbourhood were grief-stricken when the boy fell into a decline and his life was despaired of by the doctors. As time went on he grew weaker and weaker, until the moment arrived when it was obvious that he could not possibly survive another twenty-four hours. At about noon, the room in which the young boy lay was flooded with a stream of sunlight, which came pouring in through the windows from the summer sky; in such brilliant weather it seemed almost incredible that death could be hovering quite so near the house. One by one, members of the family visited the bedroom to take what each felt might be their last look at the sick boy while he was still alive. Presently the doctor arrived, and as they were all discussing in hushed tones the condition of the poor child they heard someone singing, apparently in the grounds, immediately beneath the window. The voice seemed to be that of a woman, but divinely soft and sweet, and charged with a pity and sorrow that no earthly being could ever have portrayed. Now loud, now hushed, it continued for some minutes, and then seemed to die away gradually.

"What a glorious voice!" one of the listeners exclaimed. "I've never heard anything to equal it."

"Very likely not," someone else whispered—"it's the Banshee. . . ."

So enthralled were they by the singing that it was only when the final note had faded that they became aware that their beloved patient had died. It seemed as if the boy's soul, with the last whispering notes of the dirge, had joined the beautiful, pitying Banshee, to be escorted by it into the realms of the unknown. Dr. Kenealy commemorated the strange event in one of his poems.

The story of another haunting by a sympathetic Banshee is told in Kerry, in connection with a family which used to live there. According to my informant the family consisted of a gentleman farmer, his wife, their son, Terence, and a daughter, Norah.

Norah, an Irish beauty of the dark type, with black hair and blue eyes, possessed numerous admirers, but none she favoured so much as a certain Michael O'Lernahan. This young man was not particularly liked by either of her parents, but her brother took to him, and also Michael was reputed to be rich for that part of Ireland. Accordingly, he was invited pretty freely to the farm, and no obstacles were placed in his way. At last he proposed, and Norah accepted, but no sooner was their announcement made than they both heard, just above their heads, a low, despairing wail, as of a woman in great distress.

Though they were much alarmed, being convinced that the sounds came from no human being, neither seems to have regarded the phenomenon as a warning, and they continued their courtship as if the incident had never occurred. A few weeks later, however, Norah noticed a sudden change in her lover; he was colder and more distant, and invariably preoccupied. At last the blow fell. One evening he failed to call, though expected as usual, and as no explanation was forthcoming the following morning, nor on any of the succeeding days, the parents made inquiries and found he had become engaged to another girl living only a few minutes' walk from the farm.

This was too much for Norah, who, although neither unusually sensitive nor particularly highly strung, fell ill, and shortly afterwards died of a broken heart. It was not until the night before she died, however, that the Banshee paid her a second visit. Norah was lying on a couch in the parlour of the farmhouse, her mother sitting beside her, when a noise was heard that sounded like leaves gently beating against the window-panes, and almost directly afterwards came the sound of singing, loud and full of intense sorrow and compassion, obviously that of a woman.

" 'Tis the Banshee," the mother whispered, immediately crossing herself and at the same time bursting into tears.

" The Banshee," Norah repeated. " Sure I hear nothing but that tapping at the window and the wind, which seems all of a sudden to have risen."

The mother made no response. She simply sat with her face buried in her hands, sobbing bitterly and muttering to herself : " Banshee ! Banshee !"

Presently, the singing having ceased, the mother got up and dried her tears. Her anxiety, however, remained. All through the night she could still be heard every now and then, crying quietly and whispering to herself, " 'Twas the Banshee, the Banshee. . . ." And in the morning, Norah, suddenly growing alarmingly ill, died before the doctor could be summoned.

A case of Banshee haunting which is somewhat unusually pathetic was told to me in connection with a Dublin branch of the once powerful clan of McGrath.

The family, consisting of a widow and two young children, Isa and David, at that time occupied an old, rambling house not five minutes' walk from Stephen's Green. Isa seems to have been the mother's favourite, she was undoubtedly a very pretty and attractive child, while David, possibly on account of his pronounced likeness to his late father, with whom it was an open secret that Mrs. McGrath had never got on at all well, received rather more than his fair share of scolding. He was left very much to himself, and all alone, in a big empty room at the top of the house, and forced to amuse himself as best he could. Occasionally one of the servants, inspired by a fellow feeling, used to look in to see how the boy was getting on and bring him a toy bought out of her own meagre savings; and now and again Isa, clad in some costly new dress, would put her head in at the door, either to bring him some message from her mother, or merely to call out " Hello." Otherwise David saw no one, at least no one belonging to this earth. He only saw at times, he affirmed, strange-looking people who simply stood and stared at him without speaking, people who the servants, girls from Limerick and the west country, solemnly assured him were either fairies or ghosts.

One day Isa, who had been sent upstairs to tell her brother to go to his bedroom to tidy himself, as he was wanted immediately in the drawing-room, found him in a great state of excitement.

" I've seen such a beautiful lady," he said, " and she wasn't a bit cross. She came and stood by the window and looked as if she wanted to play with me, only I daren't ask her. Do you think she will come again?"

Isa laughed. " How can I tell? she said. " I expect you've been dreaming as usual. What was she like?"

" Oh, tall, much taller than mother," David replied, "with very blue eyes and kind of reddish-gold hair that wasn't all screwed up on her head, but was hanging in curls on her shoulders. She had very white hands which were clasped in front of her, and a bright green dress. I didn't see her come or go, but she was here for a long time, quite ten minutes."

Isa laughed again. " It's another of your fancies, David," she said. " But come along, hurry, or mother will be angry."

A few minutes later David, looking very shy and awkward, was in the drawing-room being introduced to a gentleman who, he was told, was to be his stepfather.

David seems to have taken a strong dislike to the man from the start, and to have foreseen in his mother's coming marriage nothing but trouble and misery for himself. In this he was absolutely right, for he became subjected to the strictest discipline. Morning and afternoon he was kept hard at his books, and any slowness or inability to master a lesson was treated as idleness, and punished accordingly. The moments he had to himself in his beloved nursery now became few and far between, for directly he had finished his evening preparation, he was given his supper and packed off to bed.

The one or two servants who had befriended David, unable to tolerate the new regime, gave notice and left, and there was soon no one in the house who showed any consideration whatever for the poor, lonely boy.

Things went on in this fashion for some weeks, and then a day came when the lad felt it impossible to go on living any longer. His health had deteriorated, and this, together with the fact that he was utterly broken in spirit, made it impossible for him to concentrate on his studies. But his entreaties were only taken for excuses, and when, in an unguarded moment, he let slip some sort of reference to unkind treatment, he was at once accused of rudeness by his mother, and, at her request, summarily punished.

It was more than he could stand. That night he was sent to bed as usual immediately after supper, and Isa, who happened to pass by his room an hour or so afterwards, was surprised to hear him apparently engaged in conversation. Peeping in at the door she saw him sitting up in bed, evidently addressing space, or the moonbeams, which pouring in at the window fell directly on him.

" What are you doing?" she asked. " And why aren't you asleep?"

The moment she spoke he looked round, and greatly disappointed said : " Oh, she's gone—you've frightened her away."

" Frightened her away? Why, what rubbish !" Isa said. " Lie down at once, or I'll go and fetch mother."

" It was my green lady," David went on breathlessly, far too excited to pay any heed to Isa's threat. " She told me I should be no more lonely, that she was coming to fetch me some time tonight."

Isa laughed, and telling him not to be so silly, but to go to sleep at once, she went downstairs to join her parents in the drawing-room.

That night, at about midnight, Isa was awakened by loud and plaintive singing, in a woman's voice, apparently coming from the hall. Very alarmed she got up, and on opening her bedroom door saw her parents and the servants, all in their nightclothes, huddled together on the landing, listening.

" Sure, 'tis the Banshee," the cook at length whispered. " I heard my father speak about it when I was a child. She sings, he said, more beautifully than any grand lady, but sorrowful like, and only before a death."

" Before a death?" said Isa's mother. " But who is going to die here, woman? Such nonsense—we are all of us perfectly sound and well." As she spoke the singing stopped, and in the silence that followed everyone went back to their beds.

Nothing more was heard during the night, but in the morning, when breakfast time came there was no David, nor was he in his bedroom. A thorough search was made, and he was eventually discovered, drowned in a cistern in the roof.

The malevolent Banshee is invariably depicted as a horrible hag with ugly, distorted features, her outstretched arms calling down curses on the unfortunate person she knows is about to die. In fact most " experts " on the subject seem to encourage the idea that all malignant Banshees are cast in one mould, and all beautiful Banshees in another, whereas from my own personal experience I would say that Banshees, whether good or bad, are just as individual as any member of the family they haunt.

It is told of a certain ancient Mayo family that a chief of the clan once made love to a very beautiful girl whom he betrayed and sub-sequently murdered. With her dying breath the girl cursed her murderer and swore she would haunt him and his for ever. Years rolled by, the chief married, and with the passing away of all who knew him in his youth, he came to be regarded as a model of absolute propriety. In these circumstances he was sitting one night before a big, blazing fire in the hall of his castle, outwardly happy enough and surrounded by his sons and daughters, when loud shrieks of exultation were heard coming, it seemed, from someone standing on the path close to the castle walls. All rushed out to see who it was, but no one was there, and the grounds as far as the eye could reach were absolutely deserted.

Later, after the household had gone to bed, the same demoniacal disturbances took place; peal after peal of wild, malicious laughter rang out, followed by a discordant moaning and screaming. This time the aged chieftain did not accompany the rest of the household in their search for the originator of the disturbances. Possibly in that moaning and screaming he fancied he could detect the voice of the girl he had murdered; and possibly he accepted the manifestations as a death-warning. The following day he was waylaid out of doors and brutally done to death.

The haunting of this particular Banshee still continues, the same phenomena occurring at least once to every generation of the family, before the death of one of its members. Happily, however, the haunting does not now precede a violent death, though in this respect only does it differ from the original.

I learned of another haunting by this same species of Banshee when I was in Ireland visiting a relative living in Black Rock. My relative, Jane, told me that when she was in her teens, some friends of hers, the O'Dees, lived in a big old-fashioned country house somewhere between Ballynanty and Hospital, in the County of Limerick. The family consisted of Mr. O'Dee, who had been something in India in his youth, and was now very much of a recluse, though much esteemed locally on account of his extreme piety and goodheartedness; his wife, who despite her grey hair still retained traces of more than ordinary good looks; their son Wilfred, a handsome but decidedly headstrong young man in his twenties; and their daughter Ellen, a blue-eyed, golden-haired girl.

Jane was on especially close terms with the daughter and son, and it became generally accepted that she and Wilfred would "make a match of it." The first of the ghostly happenings that she experienced in connection with the O'Dees occurred on the actual day Wilfred took the long-anticipated step and proposed to her.

Jane was out walking one afternoon with both brother and sister when Wilfred, taking advantage of Ellen's sudden fancy for going on ahead to look for dog-roses, passionately declared his love, and apparently did not declare it in vain. The trio then, in more or less exalted spirits—for Ellen had of course been let into the secret—walked home together. As they were passing through a big wooden gateway into the garden at the rear of the O'Dees' house, they saw a tall, spare woman, with her back to them, digging away furiously.

" Hello," said Wilfred—" who's that?"

" I don't know," said Ellen, puzzled. " It's certainly not Mary." (Mary was the old cook, who, like many servants of that period, did not confine her labours to the kitchen but performed all kinds of odd jobs as well.) " Nor is it anyone from the farm," Ellen continued. " But what on earth does she think she is doing? Hey, there !"

The woman instantly turned round, and the trio received a violent shock. The light was fading, for it was late afternoon, but what light there was seemed to be entirely concentrated on the face before them, making it appear luminous. It was a broad face with pronounced cheekbones, a large mouth, the thin lips of which were fixed in a dreadful leer, and very pale, obliquely set eyes that glowed balefully as they met the startled gaze of the young people.

For some seconds the evil-looking creature stood in dead silence, apparently gloating over the consternation her appearance had caused.

Then, suddenly shouldering her spade, she walked slowly away, turning round every now and then to cast the same malevolent look at them, until she came to the hedge that separated the garden from a long disused stone quarry, when she seemed suddenly to fade away in the uncertain twilight.

For some time no one spoke or stirred, but continued gazing after her in a kind of paralysed astonishment. Wilfred was the first to break the silence.

" Where has she gone?" he said.

" Ask another," said Ellen shivering. " There's nowhere she could have gone except into the quarry. Come on, let's be away, I'm chilly."

They started off, but had only gone a few yards when from the direction of the quarry there came a peal of mocking laughter, so evil that all three quickened their steps and hurried on to the house in silence. They went straight to Mr. O'Dee and told him what they had seen.

He looked unusually pale. " Very possibly," he said, " she was a tramp or gipsy. There may be others, we must take care to keep all the doors locked. Whatever you do, don't mention a word about it to your mother or the cook, as they are both nervous and easily frightened."

All three gave their promise, and no more was said. But Jane, who was then escorted home before it got thoroughly dark, subsequently learned that during the night, when all the O'Dee household had gone to bed, peal after peal of the same mocking laughter was heard just under the windows, first of all in the front of the house, and then in the rear. Next day came the news that the business concern in which most of Mr. O'Dee's money was invested had gone smash, and the family were practically penniless.

It began to look as if they would have to sell up their house, and many people believed that it was only to avoid this, and to enable her parents to keep a roof over their heads, that Ellen accepted the attentions of a wealthy Englishman in Limerick, and soon married him. But it was a desperately unhappy union. Barely able, even from the first, to tolerate her bullying husband, Ellen grew to loathe him, and at last, unable to endure the life any longer, she eloped with an officer stationed in the neighbourhood. The night before she did this, Jane and Wilfred again heard the malevolent laughter, which pursued them for some distance along the moonlit lane and across the common leading to the spot where Jane lived. After this the laughter was not heard again for two years, when Jane again experienced the phenomena.

She was spending the evening with Mr. and Mrs. O'Dee, discussing the homecoming of Wilfred, who was expected back from the West

Indies almost any day. After their long betrothal it had been arranged
that she and Wilfred should marry as soon as possible after his arrival.
They were all three engaged in animated conversation (the old people
had unexpectedly come into a little money, and that, too, had considerably contributed to their cheerfulness) when Mrs. O'Dee, fancying
she heard someone calling to her from the garden, got up and went
to the window. She then, still looking out and apparently unable to
remove her gaze, beckoned to them, saying, "Quick, both of you.
There's a most awful old woman in the garden staring hard at me—
she frightens me so."

Jane and Mr. O'Dee at once jumped up and ran to her side. There
they saw, gazing up at them, a face which Jane immediately recognized
as that of the woman she had seen two years previously, digging in
the garden. The old hag seemed to remember her too, for as their
glances met, a gleam of recognition crept into her light eyes, and a
moment later gave way to an expression of such hate that Jane caught
hold of Mr. O'Dee for protection. Evidently noting this action the
old woman leered horribly, and then, drawing a kind of shawl or hood
tightly over her head, moved away with a gliding motion, vanishing
round an angle of the wall.

Mr. O'Dee rushed into the garden, but although he searched everywhere could find no trace of the sinister-looking visitor. He had hardly
finished explaining this to the others when close to the house came
several peals of laughter that terminated in one loud, prolonged wail.

Mrs. O'Dee was on the verge of fainting. "What can be the meaning of it?" she said. "That surely was no living woman."

"No," her husband admitted, very reluctantly. "It was the Banshee
—the O'Dee Banshee, which for some reason possesses a great hatred
of my family. We must prepare again for some evil tidings. But," he
went on, steadying his voice with an effort, "with God's grace we
must face it, for whatever happens it is His Divine Will."

A day or two later, to her great and lasting distress, Jane learned
that Mr. O'Dee has been sent word that Wilfred was dead. The young
man had been stricken down with fever, believed to have been caught
from one of his fellow-passengers, and had died on the day that he
should have landed; on the very day, in fact, that his parents and
fiancée together had heard and seen the Banshee.

Soon after this tragedy Jane, who never married, left the neighbourhood and went to live with friends near Dublin. Although from time
to time she corresponded with the O'Dees, she never again heard anything of their Banshee.

Years later, however, Jane encountered a Banshee of another kind.
In Dublin she became acquainted with two old maiden ladies named
O'Rorke, who lived in a semi-detached house close to Lower Merrion

Street. The sisters were very reticent with regard to their family history, but Jane believed they originally came from the south-west. There seemed to be something peculiar about their house, as one room was invariably kept locked, and all reference to it carefully avoided. Jane often had it on the tip of her tongue to ask about the room, but could never quite sum up the courage to do so. One afternoon, however, when she was calling on the sisters, something happened which put an end to all speculation.

The elder of the two sisters, Miss Georgina, had just handed Jane a cup of tea and was about to pour out another for herself, when into the room with her cap all awry and her eyes bulging, rushed one of the servants.

" Good heavens," Miss Georgina exclaimed. " Whatever's the matter?"

The servant could hardly get her words out fast enough. " Miss, someone's got into that room you keep locked and is making the devil of a noise. Cook and I both heard it—a groaning and a chuckling, and a scratching, as if the creature was tearing up the boards and breaking all the furniture and all the while keening and laughing. For the love of heaven, ladies, come and hear it for yourselves. Such goings on. Ochone! Ochone!"

Both sisters turned pale, and Harriet, the younger one, was on the brink of tears.

" Where is cook?" asked Miss Georgina, who was by far the stronger minded of the two. " If she is upstairs, tell her to come down at once. Miss Harriet and I will go and see about the noise—there's really no need to make all this fuss, it's sure to be either mice or rats."

The servant scoffed. " Mice or rats? 'Tis some evil spirit, sure, and cook is of the same mind." And with that she flounced out, slamming the door behind her.

The sisters, asking Jane to excuse them, left the room, and returned shortly afterwards looking very white and distressed.

" I am sure you must think all this very odd," Miss Georgina said to Jane, " and I feel I owe you an explanation. But I must beg of you not to repeat a word of what we tell you to anyone."

Jane readily gave her promise, after which Miss O'Rorke began. " We have in our family," she said, " a Banshee. Being Irish you will not laugh, of course, as many English people do, at what I say. You will know that many of the really old families possess Banshees.

" Well, unlike most Banshees ours is appallingly ugly. So frightful indeed, that just to see it is sometimes fatal. One of our great uncles to whom it appeared died from shock, and a similar fate overtook another of our ancestors who also saw it. The Banshee seems to be strongly attracted to an old gold ring which has been in the possession of the family for hundreds of years. Both ancestors were wearing this ring at the time the Banshee appeared to them, and it is said to confine its manifestations to the immediate vicinity of the ring. That is why our parents always kept the ring strictly isolated in a locked room, the key of which was never for a moment allowed out of their possession. We have followed their example. This is the simple explanation of our locked room."

" And the noise," said Jane—" was that the Banshee?"

" I fear it was," Miss Georgina replied solemnly, " and that we shall shortly hear of a relative's death, or a grave catastrophe to some member of the family. A dear cousin of ours in County Galway has been seriously ill for some weeks, and it may be that her time has come."

She was partly right, but wrong on the most important point. For within a few days of the noisy Banshee's visit, a member of the family did suddenly die. It was not the sick cousin, it was Miss Georgina's own sister, Harriet.

I will conclude these notes of the Banshee in Ireland with two brief stories from widely different sources. The first is from a cousin of the head of one of the oldest Irish clans, whom I approached for a first-hand account of their family Banshee. From a long letter, I quote the following :

" Yes, I have heard the Banshee cry. It is simply like a woman wailing in the most unearthly fashion. The first time I heard her, a woman member of the O'Neill family was in this house, and she subsequently died on that night between midnight and three a.m., when we all of us heard the Banshee wailing at one end of the house.

" I heard the Banshee also at my mother's death, and at the death of my husband's eldest sister. The cry is not always the same. When my mother died, it was a very low wail which seemed to go round the house. When my sister-in-law died, I was awakened by a loud scream in my room in the middle of the night. She had died at that very instant.

" I also heard the Banshee one day, while riding in the country. The wailing came from a distance.

" I am told that the Banshee, who follows old families, is heard by the whole village. Some people say she is red-haired, and wears a long, flowing white dress; and she is supposed to wring her long, thick hair.

" Others say she appears as a small woman, dressed in black; and such an apparition did appear to me in the daytime before my mother-in-law died."

My second and final story comes from a rather colourful " character " encountered in my youth, one that could have leapt out from the pages of any storybook, but who was in fact a very real and live person.

Mrs. Broderick was a well-known vendor of oranges and chocolate in Bristol, where I attended day-school, and she used to visit our house every week with her wares. The old woman seemed to take a particular interest in me because I was Irish, one of " the real O'Donnells," as she said, and frequently used to halt her basket to tell me stories of her girlhood in Cork. And so it was that one day, with a deep earnestness that was most unlike her usual jocular self, she told me of her experience of the Banshee.

Mrs. Broderick said that in her girlhood she lived with her parents, who were small farmers, in a village just outside Cork. She was very fond of the sea, and often walked into Cork and went boating with young friends in Queenstown harbour. On one occasion she and another girl, Mary Rooney, and two young men, went for a sail with an old fisherman they knew, who took them some distance up the coast in the direction of Kinsale.

There had been a slight breeze when they started out, but it dropped suddenly as they were tacking to return home, and since the sail had to be taken down and oars used, both the young men volunteered to row. They pulled steadily till they saw an old ship, so battered and worn away as to be little more than a mere shell, lying half in and half out of the water in a tiny cove. As the weather was beautifully fine and no one was in a great hurry to get home, it was suggested that they pull up to the wreck and examine it. The old fisherman was reluctant, but he was soon won over, and the two men and Mary Rooney boarded the old hulk, leaving the less adventurous Mrs. Broderick and the old fisherman in the boat.

The evening shadows from the trees and rocks had now spread to the glistening shingles of the beach, but there was still a daytime freshness and clarity about the scene. Mrs. Broderick, leaning on the side of the boat and trailing one hand in the water, could hear her friends talking and laughing as they tried to steady themselves on the sloping boards of the old hulk, and presently one of them, named O'Connell, suggested they should go below deck and explore the cabins. As they descended, their voices gradually grew fainter until they faded completely.

Suddenly, from one side of the wreck that was partly under water, there rang out the screams of a woman who had been suddenly pounced upon and either stabbed or treated in some equally savage and violent manner.

Mrs. Broderick clutched the fisherman tightly by the arm and exclaimed : " Oh, no, the saints above, it's Mary—they're murdering her ! "

But the old man shook his head. " 'Tis no woman, that," he said hoarsely. " 'Tis the Banshee, and I would not have had this happen for the whole blessed world, I with my mother so ill in bed with the rheumatism. . . ."

" Are you sure?" Mrs. Broderick asked him nervously, clutching him even more tightly. " Are you sure it isn't Mary in trouble?"

" Sure," replied the fisherman. " That's the way the Banshee always screams. 'Tis her right enough, 'tis no human woman." And he crossed himself, dipped the oars into the water and began to pull slowly away.

The screaming stopped, and moments later the three young people came trooping on to the hulk, showing no signs whatever of alarm. They were quite surprised to be asked if they had heard anything, and laughingly replied that they had not. " Only," O'Connell added frivolously, " the kiss young Mike stole from Mary. That's all!"

But for O'Connell that was not all. When he arrived home he found that during his absence his mother had died suddenly, and at exactly the same hour that Mrs. Broderick and the fisherman had heard the Banshee's scream.

THE BANSHEES ABROAD

THE BANSHEE today is heard more often abroad than in Ireland. She has followed the true Irishman everywhere, even to the Poles. A notable case first recorded by Lady Wilde is the experience of a branch of the O'Grady clan who settled in Canada.

The spot chosen by this family for their house was wild and isolated, and one night at two o'clock, when all were in bed, they were aroused by a loud cry coming apparently from just outside the house. It was an unearthly sound suggestive of the greatest bitterness and sorrow, and it brought terror to all the listeners. Despite their feeling that it could have come from nothing human, an exhaustive search of the premises was made, but all to no avail.

Next day the head of the household and his eldest son went boating on a lake near the house, and failed to return to dinner. Various members of the family were sent out to look for them, but no trace of them could be found, nor was any solution to the mystery forthcoming till two o'clock that night, when, exactly twenty-four hours after the sorrowing cry had been heard, some of the searchers at last returned, bearing with them the wet and lifeless bodies of both father and son.

Then once again the weird wailing was heard, and the grief-stricken family remembered how their father had often spoken of the Banshee as having haunted their branch of the clan for countless generations.

Turning to my own files, here is a case of Banshee haunting relating to a branch of the southern O'Neills who settled in Italy. It was described to me in Paris by Mrs. K. Dempsey, who was an eye-witness of the phenomena.

Mrs. Dempsey, while staying at an hotel in the north of Italy, noticed among the guests an elderly man whose marked features, and intensely sad expression, quickly arrested her attention. She saw that he kept aloof from his fellow guests, and that every evening after dinner, he retired from the drawing-room as soon as coffee had been handed round, and went outside and stood on the veranda overlooking the shore of the Adriatic.

She made inquiries about the man and was told that he was the Count Fernando Asioli, a wealthy Florentine citizen, who, having recently lost his beloved wife, tended to avoid any close conversation. At this Mrs. Dempsey was even more interested, for it was not long since she had lost her husband, and so it was in sympathetic mood that, on seeing the Count go out as usual one evening on to the veranda, she resolved to follow him and try to exchange a few words.

She was about to cross the threshold of the veranda when to her astonishment she found that the Count was not alone. Standing by his side, with one hand laid caressingly on his shoulder, was a tall, slim girl, with masses of red-gold hair hanging loose to her waist. She wore an emerald green dress of some filmy substance, but her arms and feet were bare, and stood out so clearly in the moonlight that Mrs. Dempsey, who was something of an artist, noticed with a thrill that they equalled any she had seen in Greek or Florentine sculpture.

Puzzled as to who the unconventional girl could be, Mrs. Dempsey remained for a second or two watching, and then, afraid lest she should attract their attention and be thought to be spying, she withdrew. The moment she returned to the drawing-room she asked a woman who generally sat next to her at mealtimes who the girl was she had just seen with the Count. But her friend, shaking her head, could only suggest that the girl was some newcomer, a guest who had arrived at the hotel and gone on to the veranda while they were all at dinner. Her curiosity aroused, Mrs. Dempsey's friend then walked towards the veranda. She returned shortly, very puzzled.

"You must have been mistaken," she whispered. "There is no one with Count Asioli now, and if anyone had come away we should have seen them, for there is no other way than through this room."

"But I am quite sure I did see a girl there," Mrs. Dempsey replied, "and only a minute or two ago. She must have got out somehow."

At this moment the Count, entering the room, took a seat next to them, which ended their conversation. The next night, however, the events of the proceeding night were repeated. Mrs. Dempsey followed the Count on to the veranda, saw the girl in green standing with her hand on his shoulder, came back and told her neighbour, and the latter, on hastening to the veranda to look, once more returned declaring that the Count was alone. After this a slight argument took place between the two women, the one declaring her belief that it was all an optical illusion, and the other emphatically sticking to her story that she had actually seen the girl she had described.

They parted that night both a little ruffled, though neither would admit it, and the following night Mrs. Dempsey, as soon as she saw the Count go on to the veranda, fetched her friend.

" Now," she said, " come with me and see for yourself."

The pair of them went to the veranda, and, opening the door gently, peeped out.

" There she is," Mrs. Dempsey whispered, " standing in just the same position."

The sound of her voice, though so low as to be scarcely heard even by her companion, seemed to attract the attention of both the girl and the Count, for they turned round simultaneously. Mrs. Dempsey, whose gaze was solely concentrated on the girl, saw a beautiful face of neatly chiselled, but by no means coldly classical features, with wide eyes of a marvellous blue, and smooth, broad brow. It was the face of a young girl barely out of her teens, and it was filled with an expression of infinite sorrow and affection.

Mrs. Dempsey was so enraptured that, to quote her own words, she " stood gazing at it in speechless awe ", and was only torn away from it by the sudden voice of the Count.

" I hope, ladies," he was saying, " that you do not see anything disturbing in my appearance tonight. I seem to be the object of your concern. May I ask why?"

Though so polite, he was quite plainly annoyed. Mrs. Dempsey hastened to explain.

" It is not you," she faltered, " it is the lady—the lady you have with you. I fancied I knew her."

" The lady I have with me?" said the Count, much surprised. " What do you mean?"

" Why the lady . . ." Mrs. Dempsey began, and then she glanced round. The Count was standing in front of her, but quite alone. There was no girl in green, nor any other person on the veranda saving themselves, and immediately beneath the veranda, some thirty feet below, glimmered the white shingles of the deserted seashore.

" She's gone," Mrs. Dempsey said, " but I'm positive I saw her— a girl in green standing beside you." Then for the first time she felt afraid, and trembled. Mrs. Dempsey's friend, who was very embarrassed, and still, apparently, had not seen the girl, excused herself politely and left.

The Count, who had been studying Mrs. Dempsey intently, now came closer and in friendlier tones said : " Will you please describe the girl? Was she old or young, dark or fair?"

"Young and fair, very fair," Mrs. Dempsey said. "But please come inside, for I've received something of a shock, and can perhaps talk to you better in the light, with people around."

He did as she asked, and became more and more interested as she went on with her description, interrupting her every now and again with questions. Was she sure the girl had blue eyes? And how could she tell what colour the eyes were by the light of the moon only? Mrs. Dempsey replied that the girl's whole body seemed to be illuminated from within, in such a manner that every detail could be seen, almost as if she had been standing in the full glare of an electric light.

When she had finished, Mrs. Dempsey was further questioned by the Count. Had she, he asked, ever been told that he was partly Irish? When she shook her head, he went on : "Then I must tell you I am. My great-great-grandfather assumed the name of Asioli in order to come into some property when the family, which came from the south of Ireland, settled in Italy many years ago. But what will be of considerable interest to you is the fact that this branch of the O'Neills, the branch to which I belong, is haunted by a Banshee, and this Banshee has, I believe, now appeared to you. The description of it given me by various members of my family tallies with the description you have given of the girl you saw standing by me. But it is puzzling, because she is said to reveal herself only when an O'Neill is about to die. As I am the last of my line, I cannot see any reason for her having now appeared three nights in succession—unless, of course, it is to predict my own end !"

The Count now talked on in good humour, obviously taking this suggestion very lightly. Next day, however, summoned unexpectedly to Venice on urgent business, he was hurrying to the railway station when he suddenly fell dead. He was said to have died of a heart attack. As for Mrs. Dempsey, she was left in the unsettling position of possessing extraordinary information which she felt unable to confide to anyone; until, years later, she told it to me.

There are many instances on record of Banshee manifestations occurring on the battlefield, either immediately before or after battle, or even while the fighting was actually taking place. Before the Battle of the Boyne, several Banshees were heard singing in the air over the Irish camp, the truth of their prophecies being verified by the death roll of the next morning.

Some of my own immediate ancestors took part in this battle, and according to a family tradition one of them both saw and heard the Banshee. He was sitting in the camp with several other officers, including his brother Daniel, the night before the fighting, when, feeling an icy wind coming from behind and blowing down his back, he turned to look for his cloak, which he had discarded a short time before owing to the heat from the fire close beside them. The cloak was not there, and as he turned round still further to look for it, he saw the figure of a woman, swathed from head to foot in a mantle of some dark flowing material, standing a few feet behind him. Much surprised, but supposing her to be a relative or friend of one of the officers, for her mantle looked costly and her golden hair, though hanging loose on her shoulders, was evidently well cared for, he continued to gaze at her with curiosity. He saw she was shaking with what he at first imagined to be laughter, but from the constant clenching of her hands and heaving of her bosom, he finally realized that she was weeping, and when a sudden gust of wind blew back her mantle, he caught a full view of her face.

Her cheeks were as white as marble, and her eyes the most appealing he had ever seen. He was about to ask if he could help her, when, on someone calling out to him, she at once began to melt away, fading into the soft background of grey mist that was creeping towards them from the river.

Some hours later, when the troops were all lying down, trying to snatch a few hours sleep, he thought he saw her again in dim shadow outline, the fair face with big sorrowful eyes gazing pityingly first at one and then at another of his companions, but particularly at one, a young boy, who lay wrapped in his military cloak close beside the smouldering embers of the fire. She approached this youth, and bending over him stroked his short, curly hair with her fingers.

Believing he must be asleep and dreaming, my ancestor rubbed his eyes vigorously, but the outlines were still there, momentarily becoming stronger and more distinct, until he realized with a little jump of his heart that she actually was there, just as certainly as she had been when he had first seen her. He was so intent on watching her that he did not notice that one of his comrades had seen her too, until the latter, who had raised himself into a half-sitting posture, spoke. Then, just as before, the figure melted away and seemed to become absorbed in the dark, shadowy background. A moment later he heard, just over his head, a loud moaning and wailing that lasted for several seconds and then died away in one long, protracted sob.

The deaths of most of his companions of the night, including that of the curly-headed boy, occurred on the following day.

On foreign battlefields, too, the Banshee has made frequent appearances to soldiers of Irish birth. She often manifested herself to Irishmen engaged on active service abroad during the Napoleonic Wars, and also to those caught up in the American Civil War. The following incidents were all told to me for the first time by members of the families concerned.

Miss Julia O'Higgins, an aged lady living, prior to World War I, close to Fifth Avenue, New York, and visiting, when I met her, a friend in the Rue Campagne, Premiere, Paris, told me she well remembered her grandfather telling her when she was a child that he had heard the Banshee at Talavera, the day before the great battle there. He was serving with the Spanish Army, having married the daughter of a Spanish officer, and had no idea at the time that there were any men of Irish extraction in his corps. Camping with about a hundred other soldiers in a valley, and happening to wake in the night with a great thirst, Lieutenant O'Higgins made his way down to the banks of the river that flowed near by, drank his fill, and was returning to camp when he was startled to hear an agonizing scream, quickly followed by another, and then another, all coming apparently from the camp. Wondering what could have happened, and thinking it must in some way be connected with one of the thieving Spanish women who prowled about everywhere at night, robbing and murdering with equal impunity wherever they saw a chance, he hurried back, only to find on his arrival no sign whatever of any intruder, though the screaming was going on as vigorously as before. The sounds seemed to come first from one part of the camp and then from another, but to be always overhead, as if made by invisible beings hovering at a height of some six feet or more above the ground; and although Lieutenant O'Higgins had at first thought these sounds to come from one person only, on listening hard he could detect several different voices—and all female. As he stood there, not knowing what to do, the wailing and sobbing grew more and more harrowing, until it affected him so much that, hardened as he had become to all kinds of misery and violence, he, too, felt like weeping out of sheer sympathy. Then came the sound of a musket shot, as a sentry fired off in the dark (a false alarm, it transpired), and the wailing and sobbing abruptly stopped.

On mentioning the odd circumstance to one of his brother officers in the morning, the officer showed little surprise. "You must have heard the Banshee," he said. " Poor Doyle, who fell at Corunna, often used to tell me about it, and you can be sure there are some Irishmen in camp now, and it was their funeral dirge you were listening to."

What he said proved to be true, for on making inquiries Lieutenant O'Higgins discovered that three of the soldiers who had been sleeping near him that night had Irish names, and hours later all three perished on the bloody field of Talavera.

Miss O'Higgins also told me of the experience of an O'Farrell, who was with the Spanish in the same war. It was the day before the fall of Badajoz to the British, and O'Farrell, who was in Badajoz at the time, as a prisoner of the French, was invited

to supper with some Spanish-Irish friends of his named McMahon
The French were as a rule rather more lenient to their Irish prisoners
than to their English, and O'Farrell was allowed to walk about
Badajoz more or less at will, having given a pledge that he would not
go outside the boundaries of the town without special permission.

On this night O'Farrell left his quarters in good spirits. He liked
the McMahons, and in fact was in love with their youngest daughter,
Katherine. His case seemed to be hopeless, however, as Mr. McMahon,
who was a man of limited financial means, had sworn that none of his
daughters would marry unless it were to someone wealthy enough to
ensure them being well provided for should they be left a widow.
As O'Farrell had nothing but his soldier's pay, he saw no prospect of
his ever being able to propose to Katherine. Had he been strong
minded enough, he told himself, he would have said goodbye to the
girl and never allowed himself to see or even think of her again, but
this he could not do. So he had kept accepting invitations to her
father's house and meeting her whenever the slightest opportunity
presented itself.

On this night O'Farrell found himself once more speeding to meet
Katherine, vowing that it should be the last time. He arrived at the
house too early, and was shown into a room to wait. Large glass doors
opened out of the room on to a veranda, and walking out to this,
O'Farrell leaned over the iron railings and gazed down into the
courtyard and garden below, in the centre of which was a fountain
with a marble statue of a beautiful maiden not unlike his beloved
Katherine. He was looking dreamily at it when sounds of music, of
someone playing a sad and plaintive air on the harp, came to him
through the open doorway to which his back was turned. Surprised,
for none of the family as far as he knew were harpists, he turned
round, but to add to his surprise there was no one there. The room
was just as empty as when he had been ushered into it, and yet the
music unquestionably was coming from inside it. There was a peculiar
far-offness in the sounds which was like nothing he had ever heard
before. He remained on the veranda, prevented by a strange, uneasy
feeling from venturing into the room.

He was frozen in this attitude, half standing, half leaning against the
framework of the glass door, while the harping stopped and he heard
moaning and sobbing, as of a woman in violent grief. Fighting
his fears, he again looked into the room, but could see no spot
where anyone could possibly be in hiding, and nothing that would
in any way account for the sounds. Then the door opened, and
Mr. McMahon, followed by Katherine and his other daughters,
came into the apartment, at which moment the strange sounds
ceased.

"Why, what's the matter, Mr. O'Farrell," said one of the younger girls, laughing. "You're as white as a sheet. You haven't seen a ghost, have you?"

"I haven't seen anything," O'Farrell retorted, annoyed at her flippancy. "But I have heard some rather odd sounds."

"Odd sounds?" said Katherine. "What on earth do you mean?"

O'Farrell regarded the smiling faces edgily. "When I was on the veranda just now," he said, "I distinctly heard the sound of a harp in this room, and shortly afterwards I heard a woman weeping."

Mr. McMahon gave him a warning glance, and said hastily : "It must have been someone outside in the street, we do have street musicians visit us. O'Farrell, I've something to say to you about the English and their rumoured new attack on the town. . . ."

When he had drawn O'Farrell aside the father whispered to him : "Please, on no account refer to that music again. It was undoubtedly the Banshee, the ghost that my forefathers brought over from Ireland, and it is only heard before some death occurs in the family. Perhaps a relative of ours is ill."

Next day Badajoz was stormed and entered by the British, and in the wild scenes that ensued when the town was delivered up to pillage, the victorious soldiery got completely out of hand, and many Spanish men and women perished, as well as French. Among the casualties were the entire McMahon family.

This connection of phantom music with the Banshee is by no means an isolated case. I have been told of several others. During the American Civil War, for example, a ship transporting Confederate soldiers was making for the port of Charleston one evening, when a young Irish officer leaning over the bulwarks and gazing pensively into the sea, was astonished to hear the sweet sounds of music coming from, so it seemed to him, the depths of the blue waters. Thinking he must be dreaming, he called a brother officer to his side and asked him if he could hear anything.

"Yes," said the second officer. "Music, and what's more, singing. It's a woman, and she's singing some tender air. How the devil do you account for it?"

"I don't know," the first man replied. "Unless it's the Banshee. It sounds very like the ghost that my mother described to me. I only hope it doesn't predict the death of one of my near relatives."

It did not do that, but oddly enough, and unknown to the young man at the time, a namesake of his, whom he subsequently found was a second cousin, stood not ten yards from him at the very moment he was listening to the music, and was killed in action in a sortie from Charleston the following day.

Another story of Banshee music was told me in Oregon by a former

Federal soldier, who was in the temporary employ of an apple merchant in Jackson County. His name was O'Hagan, and he was born in County Clare.

"I emigrated from Ireland with my parents when I was only a few weeks old," he said, "and we settled in New York, where I was working as a porter on the quays when the Civil War broke out. I enlisted in the Marines, and eventually was transferred to a gunboat that patrolled the Carolina coast on the lookout for Confederate blockade runners.

"One night, shortly after I had turned in and was lying in my hammock trying to get to sleep (which was none too easy, for one of my mates, an ex-actor, was snoring loud enough to wake the whole ship), I suddenly heard a tapping on the porthole close beside me. Just a seabird, I thought, but I lay and listened. The sound went on, but it had none of the hardness and sharpness of a bird's beak striking the glass, it was softer and more lingering, more like the tapping of fingers. Every now and then it left off, then started up again, tap, tap, tap, until it unnerved me to such an extent that I jumped out of my hammock and had a peep to see what it was. To my surprise I saw a white face pressed against the porthole looking in at me. It was the face of a woman with black hair that fell in ringlets about her neck and shoulders. She had big golden rings in her ears, and her teeth were the loveliest bits of ivory I've ever seen, absolutely even and without the slightest mar.

"But it was her eyes that fascinated me most. They were large, a beautiful blue or grey, and looked so sad. As I drew nearer she shrank back and pointed with a white hand at a spot on the sea, and then I suddenly heard music, the faraway sound of a harp, coming from about the place she had indicated. It was a still night, and the sounds came to me very distinctly above the soft lapping of the water against the ship's side, and the mechanical squish, squish made by the bows each time they rose and fell, as the ship ploughed slowly onwards. I was so intent on listening that I forgot about the woman with the beautiful face and when I turned back to look at her again, she'd gone and there was nothing there but the moonlit water. Then the music stopped too, and all was quiet.

"For some reason I was left feeling very sad and lonely. I had taken a great fancy to that woman's face, the only really lovely woman's face that had ever looked kindly at me. But I got back again into my hammock and eventually went off to sleep.

"The first letter I received from home, on touching port, informed me of the death of my father, who had died the same night and at just about the same time I had seen that fairy vision and heard that fairy music. When I told my mother about it, some long time afterwards, she said it was the Banshee, and that it had haunted the O'Hagan family for hundreds of years."

There it is, merely a trooper's story, unconfirmed by anyone else's evidence. Yet I believe it was related to me in perfect sincerity, and the narrator had nothing whatever to gain through making it up. I did not even offer him a chew of tobacco, for at that time I was pretty nearly, if not indeed quite as hard up as he was himself.

" IT HAPPENED TO ME "

COUNTLESS GHOSTLY experiences are never recorded, even when they come to the notice of a reputable investigator. This is chiefly because many are isolated " single-sightings ", or phenomena seen only briefly by one or two persons, and therefore deemed unworthy of further inquiry. Perhaps too great a time has elapsed since the ghostly visitation, or as happens in so many instances, the fleeting event is completely unresolved, the ghost unidentified, and all parties at a loss to find any reasonable explanation for the haunting.

It is my belief that if more attention were paid to these fragmentary episodes, and more notice taken of the statements of honest witnesses, research into the subject would proceed much faster. As for judging whether a witness is honest, all I can say is that the practised investigator *knows* when a person has actually seen a ghost, for there is no other emotional experience to compare with it, and it cannot truly be feigned. Also, the most conclusive evidence can emerge from what seems to be simply trivial and tedious detail, and it is these small things attached to the genuine haunting that an impostor finds himself totally unable to invent.

From time to time, efforts are made to gather together the ghostly experiences of ordinary people which otherwise would go no further than the family circle. They range from appeals to readers by responsible magazines, to frivolously sensational articles in the national Press. Even in the latter category, however, some good and worthwhile results can be achieved.

One of the most successful ventures of this kind was launched in the early 1920s by a very popular daily newspaper, now defunct. Its encouragement to readers to tell it frankly—" in the interests of sober truth "—their true ghost stories, no matter how extraordinary, brought an outstanding response. Some three thousand people in all circumstances and all walks of life sent in their stories of how " It happened to me."

I have selected, with permission, a number of these widely varied experiences, and give them here as an illustration of the singular hauntings which occur among us, and go on occurring every week of the year, every year. They offer a measure of comfort to other people who may find themselves caught up in similar unlooked for, upsetting dramas.

ON A Sunday night in early September, a few years ago, my husband and I went for a walk before turning in to bed (we retire early). It had been a particularly good mushroom year and as we came to the field where the mushrooms grew, my husband remarked there would be some as it had been a very close day. We walked down the field, and nearly to the end of the field, which adjoins a wood on two sides, we both stood aghast. One did not warn the other, we both saw the thing at the same time. There was a tree in front of us and we could see quite clearly a man's body dangling from a protruding branch at the end of a cart rope. My husband was going forward to cut the body down, but I pleaded with him, saying that whoever had hung the man there would still be near. As I was in a delicate state of health, and knowing I had had a bad shock, he left the man hanging. We went home and it was the one topic between us—who was it? Who could have done it? We should know in the morning, someone would have found him.

When morning came I thought I must know the worst, so I went to the field, and there stood the tree perfectly straight, no branch protruding as we had seen it the previous night. I never like to look back on that experience, I feel afraid now when I think of it.

A FEW years ago I spent an evening with friends in an East Anglian village. It was late before I set off to cycle back to my lodging in town. Climbing a stiffish hill, with a wood to the right and a path, with hedgerow, to the left, I noticed ahead of me the forms of two women. It was a cloudy, moonlight night and I could see clearly their heavy flowing gowns, and when abreast, the white borders of the hoods these women wore, revealed two nuns.

I am a clergyman, and it was on my lips to speak a word of greeting but the white faces were so set away from me and so oblivious of my presence that I changed my mind and pedalled on.

Before I had covered more than a few yards I took another look at them, but to my amazement the women were not there. It was a great shock. I searched the grey path for many moments, then with an uncanny sense of the proximity of the supernatural, something of fear troubling me, I bent to the task of climbing the hill and leaving that wood behind.

Here is the sequel. Far away from East Anglia I told the story by the fire at Christmas time, and evidently it was kept in mind. These friends from Norfolk, visiting a northern watering place, called on my parents. In the course of conversation my mother laughingly asked if I had ever spoken of my encounter with the two nuns near their home. As we had not met since that night the answer was no; but they begged for the story, and it was told. Smiles died away when the visitors grew solemn, one stating in quiet tones : " It is indeed possible. The ruins of a nunnery stand in that wood, and the old folk of the village claim that the hill is haunted by two nuns, though no one in the locality has seen them."

Strange, for I did not know of the one-time existence of the convent, and was not aware that the path was supposed to be the scene of ghostly visitation.

WE WERE living in an Elizabethan house in Essex, and I had occasion to go into the dining-room for a cigarette case left on the table. The room was well lit up. On reaching over the table for the case I held on to a chair at the head of the table. Immediately my hand touched the chair it was fastened to it; I could not move an inch, and experienced a horrible sensation that something was happening quite near. There was a large mirror at the other end of the room facing me. Looking into this mirror I saw my face reflected as white as a sheet and my hair standing upright. For some seconds I stood like this, unable to move—it seemed hours to me. Suddenly I heard a clashing of steel at the mirror end of the room. Directly the clashing stopped I was released from the spell and I can assure you I removed myself from the room pretty quick. I was eighteen at the time, and I had no thoughts whatever of anything appertaining to the supernatural and had never before, nor have I since, experienced anything out of the common.

FIVE YEARS ago my occupation took me to an island in North Scotland. Most afternoons, with the aid of one of the fishermen's boats, I went deep-sea fishing. On this particular afternoon, not finding an anchor, I took a large piece of rock and length of rope with me.

I had dropped this improvised anchor and had been fishing for about two hours, when either the sudden commotion in the stern of the boat, caused by a plaice making a last bid for freedom, or a premonition, caused me to look round. Unobserved, a thick mist had come up behind me, and in the dense gloom, about ten or fifteen yards away, I saw an apparition, or ghostly object—I can describe it as nothing else. The lower part of the body was shapeless and seemed to be enveloped in white smoke that was rising from the spot over which it was hovering. The arms, which seemed to take shape in a vague, undefined sort of way, were uplifted as if urging me away from the spot, while the face—the only part of the body that had no vapoury substance around it, and was therefore clearly distinguishable—was recognizable as that of a young woman.

Was I dreaming? I rubbed my eyes to see if I was awake. When I looked again the figure had vanished. Then I discovered that my anchor had become disconnected, and that I was steadily drifting towards a small bay, enclosed by rocks. It was low tide at the time, and but for that timely warning, I should have dashed against the rocks with disastrous results.

I told no one of my experience, knowing that I should be ridiculed. Then a few weeks later, a valet expressed the desire to go to this bay for a swim. Waiting for high tide, so that the rocks which formed the entrance to the bay would be submerged, we found on arrival the water like a sheet of glass, with objects at the bottom clearly distinguishable. While he was undressing I took the opportunity of collecting a bucket of winkles, but, suddenly looking up, I saw him poised on a piece of jutting rock with his arms above his head preparatory to plunging in. Then he suddenly drew back. He hesitated for a moment, as if considering, then in a state of obvious agitation, came back to the boat and dressed.

We rowed best part of the way home in complete silence, I pondering on his sudden inexplicable fear of entering the water. I knew he was a very strong swimmer, so I couldn't account for it. Then, as if reading my thoughts, he said, "Don't laugh, but do you believe in ghosts?"

I said "Yes," and told him of my experience of a few weeks previous.

His experience was very similar. According to his description it was the same apparition. She had stood on the water's edge with arms outstretched, warning him not to enter.

We related our joint experiences to the fishermen. One pulled his beard and said: "My bonny boys, you must take more water with it." The other said he'd heard something about it, but didn't believe it, and the third said; "Sure, 'tis Molly Machay from o'er the bay you saw."

We learned afterwards that a lady's maid had been drowned in the bay several years previously under peculiar circumstances.

MY SISTER was a very strong-minded woman and scorned the idea of ghosts, and would not listen to any story of " such rubbish ". But she altered her mind later, and became a firm believer in ghosts. A few months after our father died, she was in bed and sound asleep, with her left arm outside the bed cover, when she was quite suddenly awakened and felt someone stroking her arm. She opened her eyes and there was father, by her bedside. For the moment she forgot he was dead and spoke to him, saying, " Yes, father, what do you want?" But then the vision passed from her. She was so frightened that she went into mother's room and said, " Are you awake, mother?" " Yes, my dear, I have seen your father pass outside my door," came the answer. After that, my sister was a believer that there are ghosts and haunted houses.

As MY parents and I were having breakfast, the maid, who was bringing in some hot water, was seen by my mother to be quietly weeping. " What is the matter, Lucy?" she asked. " Have you a toothache or something." " No, no, ma'am," sobbed the poor girl, " my father is drowned." " But, Lucy, how do you know? The postman has not been yet, and you cannot have had a telegram so early in the morning." Then the maid went on to say that as she came along the hall, she saw her father (who was a fisherman at Grimsby) standing there dripping with water, but smiling at her, and she knew he was drowned.

It came out in due course that the girl was right; but his death had occurred two days before she saw, or fancied she saw, the apparition, when he had been lost from his fishing smack of which he was the skipper. I cannot account for the incident unless it be some form of telepathy, the girl being an only child and much attached to her father.

SOME YEARS ago my sister died suddenly as a result of an accident. Previously she had lived with me and helped in the care of my two children. After her sad death I changed my residence and went to live in a large old house in Lupus Street, Pimlico.

Within a few weeks of being in our new home my little daughter, aged two-and-a-half, was taken ill, and to comfort her I took her into my bed and nursed her in my arms. About midnight I was awakened by her clinging frantically to me and calling out : " Look ! There's auntie." To my amazement I saw a filmy, phosphorescent form up against the wooden window shutters. The room was in total darkness as the nightlight had burnt out, and no ray of light could possibly penetrate when the shutters were closed. The apparition took the form of my dead sister in her nightclothes. Myself and child were so terrified that we buried our heads under the bedclothes, and remained so until morning.

Just four weeks later, my little daughter died. Did my sister's spirit come as a warning?

IN 1915 a young friend of my family, who had joined up at the beginning of the Great War, was sent out to Gallipoli on board the ill-fated *Royal Edward,* and when that vessel was torpedoed in the Aegean Sea, and sank three minutes after being struck, this merry handsome laddie, who had set out so bravely and eagerly to defend his home and country, was reported among the missing.

His parents and sister, though stricken with grief (the mother lost her speech) clung to a persistent hope that, in some way, he might have survived and been marooned on one of the islands. This hope was buoyed up by the fact that at the time the vessel sank, the boy, equipped exactly as he would have been when he left the ship, appeared to his sister, laughing gaily, and said : "Tell Mums not to worry, Mabs, I'm all right." The next night he came again, this time with a gash across his forehead, yet with the same buoyant smile; and later, she saw him again, also a log of wood which seemed to move towards her until she could discern some writing on it, but which she was too excited to decipher. During the same period my mother also received a visit from him, when he just bent over her and smiled sweetly as he used to do.

I made every possible inquiry, and at last got in touch with one of the survivors of the *Royal Edward,* who had trained with our friend, named Howard. He told me that while he was clinging to an upturned boat with several others he saw Howard clinging to a log of wood, and that he had a nasty cut on his forehead. That was the last seen or heard of him.

For years, Howard's mother, to whom he was passionately attached, clung to a forlorn hope that some day he would return, but we all now believe that his visitations were made at the time he passed over, and were actuated by his keen desire to cheer his sorrowing mother, and assure her that in spirit he was still as much alive as ever, and was near her and thinking of her.

SHORTLY AFTER my husband left the Army after the war we rented a small cottage bungalow overlooking the Kentish marshes. Despite the housing shortage it had been standing empty for many years.

I was sitting one evening alone, expecting my husband to return any minute. I heard, as I thought, his footsteps down the side of the house, and went to the back door to welcome him. To my surprise no one was there. A few evenings afterwards the same thing happened again. I was rather alarmed this time and made a thorough search, but could find no traces of footsteps in the mud, nor anyone lurking about. Several times after that, always at dusk or after dark, I heard the same thing, and sometimes my husband was present and heard them too. When we heard the footsteps together we used to go, one to the front door and one to the back, but never found an explanation.

We moved up to Oxfordshire after two years of it, and I am glad to say that this house is not so mysterious.

ONE NIGHT, just as I was ready for bed, a friend of mine who had always professed the utmost contempt for ghosts and ghostly super-stitions, came to my house. He seemed very surprised to see me, but said nothing until we were both seated before the fire.

Then he asked, quite suddenly; "Who was being buried at Crwys cemetery tonight, John?" "Tonight?" I answered in amazement. "Yes," he said. "The funeral passed me at the corner of this street when I was on my way home, about twenty minutes ago. You were there among the mourners, so I came to see what was wrong."

"But I haven't been out," I said. "What!" he said doubtfully. "But I saw you walking with Mrs. Jones, your sister-in-law. You nodded to me as you passed." At this I laughed, and tried to persuade him that his imagination had run away with him, but he remained adamant, and soon he left for home in a rather unfriendly frame of mind.

Next morning I had a telegram informing me of the death of my brother Tom.

A FEW years before the war I lived with my parents and sister in an old house in North London. The house was said to be haunted. Late one evening my sister and I were busy talking, when suddenly we heard the garden gate open and footsteps coming up the steps to the front door. Then there was the sound of feet stopping, and finally the knocker went rat-a-tat-tat. I said to my sister : "Who can it be? Wait, I'll go and see." I went, opened the door, and found no one there.

Another night I was alone and coming downstairs when I distinctly heard the sound of weeping. I put my ear to the wall and listened, and sure enough I could hear weeping and sobbing as of a woman in great distress. Yet the staircase wall was the outside wall of the house.

I AM just an ordinary woman without much time to fancy things. A couple of years ago my husband, who is interested in music, bought an old dulcimer, which he hoped to repair so that he could play it. He put it on the dressing table in the bedroom, much to my annoyance, but I left it there. One night I found myself sitting up in bed wide awake looking towards the dressing table, where in the dim light I saw the figure of a man bending over the dulcimer with his back towards me, showing his long hair glossy on his neck and his shoulders partly bare. Then he disappeared, and I saw the figures of men and women dancing; then it grew dark again.

Strange to say I did not feel afraid until afterwards. Then I wondered if anything was going to happen, but as nothing serious has come about yet, I conclude that I saw the man who once owned the dulcimer, and it stands just as it was, but I always feel when I dust it a sort of reverence for the man who played the dulcimer.

SEVERAL YEARS before the war I and my son were employed on redecorating part of the inside of a six-roomed villa which lay on the outskirts of town. The house had been previously tenanted by a widowed lady and her daughter. The daughter died, the lady sold everything and gave up possession, and went away to America, so I was told, about two or three weeks before we began work.

One day we were just starting our work after the dinner hour when a knock came to the front door. The door was opened by a tall lady dressed in deep black, with a thick crepe veil covering her face. In a distinct voice, with a sob in it, she said to me: " Excuse me, but may I go up into the room where my dear daughter died?" "Yes, madam, certainly," I said. Without another word she turned to the staircase and walked up as any ordinary person would, and, on the landing turned to the right, entered a bedroom and shut the door. I furtively watched her by going half up the stairs, and saw her enter the room.

We then went on with our work, I at the foot of the main staircase in the front part of the little hall, and my son about ten or twelve feet away at the back of the hall. We talked of the strangeness of the affair, as we had thought the former tenant to be in America. We could hear her walking about the room and wondered what she could be doing. She had been there three-quarters of an hour when the moving ceased, and there was perfect quiet. After another quarter of an hour passed we began to get uneasy. We were just contemplating whether we should go and see if all was well, when suddenly there was a thud, as if a heavy body had fallen on the floor above. We looked at one another for a second or two, my son turned pale and I said: " She's fainted, or perhaps it's a case for the coroner." We both hurried up to the room. We listened, no sound. I spoke, no answer. Then I rapped on the door panel, no answer.

Cautiously I turned the door knob and peeped in, but saw nothing. Both of us entered, to find the room quite empty. There were two windows, but neither had been opened, and both the sashes were fastened. We went into all the other rooms and hunted every corner, but found nothing. It made such an impression on us that we were very glad when our work was finished and we got away. The house became uncanny to us.

We have often spoken about it since, but have never heard any more of the " Lady in Black ", as my son calls her. He can substantiate all I have said; it's a simple account of what happened, and perfectly true in every detail, as God is my witness. But what I, or we, would like to know is : Was it a real woman or a wraith—or what? Also, how did she leave that room?

IN MY childhood we lived in Deptford in a house that dated from Elizabethan times, with oak-panelled rooms and huge tiled fireplaces. My sister and I were sleeping in a room at the top of the house. One summer evening, after laughing and talking, as we usually did, we were settling down to sleep, just as it was getting dusk, when suddenly I looked up and saw the door opening noiselessly. Thinking it might be my father, I was about to call out to him, but the figure that came into the room was that of a very tall man wearing a soft felt hat, turned up at one side. He had a big moustache and short, pointed beard. He came and stood at the foot of the bedstead, leaning his arms on the rail.

Too terrified to scream, I touched my sister and whispered : " Can you see that man?" Evidently she had seen him, for she was crying and shivering under the bedclothes. After looking at us for what seemed a very long time, he slowly turned and withdrew as quietly as he had come, closing the door, which was painted white and clearly visible, behind him. With his departure our paralysed nerves—and tongues—regained their power, and the shrieks we gave vent to soon brought mother up to see what was wrong. Of course she laughed at our fears, but got my father and some neighbours to search the premises from attic to cellar. No trace of the intruder could be found, but my mother had us transferred to another room and we never saw our visitor again.

Now comes the curious sequel to the story. Years afterwards, when we were all grown up, I was telling a friend of this experience. I had just started to describe the man, when one of my brothers who was present exclaimed : " I know the chap—he wore a big slouch hat, didn't he? I used to dream about him when I was a little kid—and he always seemed to be climbing in at the window, resting one knee on the sill to threaten me."

This brother was younger than I and my sister, and we had been strictly forbidden to mention the matter to him at the time. It is perhaps worthy of note that his room was at the back of the house, on the same floor as the one where we saw our ghost.

WHEN I was a little girl we lived in a cottage in Cheshire and the greatest bother of our lives was the kitchen fire. Whatever the weather or direction of the wind, it would never burn beyond a dull, smoky red, and when it was very cold or there was much cooking to be done, we always had to use the sitting-room grate.

In the course of time the property was acquired for the erection of an engineering works, and the old cottage was pulled down. It was then that the mystery of the bad fire was, we think, explained. Under the hearth were found the skeletons of two tiny children.

MY UNCLE was in great trouble owing to his wife having left him and their two children. He deserted the house, placing the children with relatives and taking rooms for himself. One night he called at my home (I was then thirteen years old) and said he wanted a particularly beautiful plant from his deserted home, as he had promised it to a friend. I volunteered to go with him and bring the plant, as he would have other things to carry. We got to the house, which was, of course, quite in darkness. While uncle fumbled taking the key out of the lock, I walked forward into an inner room, and to my extreme astonishment found a lady there with her back to me, apparently lighting something at the fireplace. The room was lit with an unearthly brilliance and I could see plainly everything in it. I called to my uncle, saying: "Have you a housekeeper, uncle?" He heard me talking and came into the room. The lady by this time had turned towards me, and I can still see her now, after a lapse of some forty years, almost as clearly as I saw her then. She was of medium build with grey hair parted down the middle and rolled over her ears. She had on a black silk dress of the kind of silk old-fashioned umbrellas used to be covered with, very fine and closewoven. On this was worn a small black apron. She also had on paramatta boots, and carried a lighted candle in a silver candlestick.

She looked hard at me, and then turned to my uncle, at whom she seemed to gaze lovingly and ardently. He rapped on a table several times and called to her to go. She went, and at once we were in utter darkness. My uncle then struck a match and lit the gas.

The whole incident had been so real and so like an ordinary scene that I was quite unafraid when I was left for a few minutes while uncle collected what he wanted. Neither he nor I said anything to each other about the episode. I started off home alone with the plant, and on arrival, burst into the house exclaiming: "I have seen a most brilliant light and a lady in my uncle's house." My mother listened to my description and recognized my grandmother who had died thirteen years before, when I was not quite a year old. She got me quietly to bed, but before I was downstairs the next morning, uncle was in the house corroborating my description and assuring my parents it was his and my father's own mother he had seen, every detail of her dress and features perfect.

I have often wondered if she had a message for him in his trouble; also whether his hostility caused her to leave again without saying a word.

SOME YEARS ago my husband and I visited a friend and her husband every Saturday evening. One evening while there, I came over faint and, during the short attack, I saw quite plainly a tall young woman in a hat and short cape standing on the bank of a river. She was crying and clasping her hands, and seemed very distressed. I told the others what I had seen, and my friend asked me if I could recognize the cape and hat. I said I could, and she went into her bedroom and brought to me a cape and hat exactly as I had seen them. She then told me that her sister's body had been found in the river a long way from her home, and the hat and cape were found further up the river bank. I described as near as possible the scene of my vision and it was all verified. I knew nothing of their families and did not even know she had a sister. Why did she appear to me?

ALTHOUGH I am a middle-aged woman, and the following incident occurred when I was only five years old, it is as plain to me today as when it happened.

We lived in the country, and an epidemic of diphtheria swept through the village. My parents had four children, and each child became a victim of the disease. Two of the children died and were buried on the same day. I am aged between the two. Of course, I knew nothing about death at that age; I knew these children had gone away, but thought that we would see them again soon. I never thought they had gone away for ever. I don't know how long it was after my brother and sister died, but I was getting better, when I saw my sister in the spirit. I say spirit now, but then, being only a child, I thought she was in the body. I was sleeping in bed with my mother and the bed was in a corner. I was next to the wall, and the bedroom door was on the same side wall. I was awake in the night when I saw my sister come through the wall at the foot of the bed and trip round the room sideways, close to the walls, past the windows, back of the bed and round to my side. She then embraced me round the neck.

I asked her not to squeeze me so tight as my throat was not quite better yet. She released her hold, but did not speak. Then she tripped on past the door to the wall through which she had entered, and stood still and began to flicker and fade like a light going out. I said to her: "Don't go yet, Edith," and I shook my mother's arm to awake her, as I wanted her to see too, but she did not wake up till my sister had gone. It did not seem strange to me at the time that she came and went through the wall. What impressed me as strange was that her feet made no noise and she did not speak. She looked happy and shining all about her like a sunbeam.

Years after, my mother told me how I startled her in the night by telling her Edith had just been and gone through the wall. I am sure you will agree that it was a very extraordinary experience for a child.

WE WENT to live at an old manor house. Directly we entered the large, square hall, I said: "There is a genial spirit in this house."

I entered our bedroom one day and saw, sitting on a chair by the bedside, one of the dearest old men imaginable. It was difficult to realize that he was not of flesh and blood, for intelligence beamed in his eyes, and joy sparkled on his lip. I was sorry when he vanished, particularly as he seemed to desire urgently to tell me something. I saw him several times, but only in the one room, and only when alone. Some time after, a number of friends were visiting us, and one of them asked of another: "Who used to live here, Tom?"

"Why, Mr. So-and-So," said Tom. "Don't you remember him? Oh no, I suppose he died before your time."

"What was he like?"

Tom began to describe him, but I interrupted and said: "Wait a minute. I'll tell you what he's like." I then described very minutely my ghostly visitor.

"How in the world do you know him so well?" said Tom. "He died long before you came here."

"Yes," I said, "and I have never heard of him till today. Yet I have seen him many times, and hope to do so again." I then told them how he had visited me, and there was a rare outcry.

TWENTY YEARS ago my mother kept a boarding house in this historic city of Bath. Among the furniture was a massive mahogany bedstead which had been bought from the previous owner of the house. This bedstead was used in the best bedroom. Imagine my mother's astonishment when on three different occasions visitors declared they had the bedclothes stripped from the bed at midnight. Each visitor came from a different county and had no knowledge of the previous happening. One gentleman was quite indignant, saying the next morning: "You might tell your visitors to make sure of their room number, as it is not pleasant to have an intruder taking the clothes off your bed!"

After this my mother sold the bedstead to a dealer for a mere song, and who knows, maybe the ghost is even now disturbing somebody's sweet slumber.

SOME YEARS ago I was asked to take my sister's place in service in a large house in Wiltshire on account of her illness. One day, when there, I was going upstairs with some linen, when I met and passed a very pale-faced lady with lovely black hair and dark rings round her eyes. She wore a very shiny dress. On asking the housekeeper who this lady was, I was told not to be afraid, as she was the master's late wife, who was seen very often about the house and had also been seen in the garden under the trees. The housekeeper impressed upon me that the lady would not hurt me in any way, but she had said she would worry the master if it were possible as they had not lived very happily together. She left a baby boy when she died and, when the child died, several years later, she could be plainly seen waiting with outstretched arms. After this she had been only rarely seen about the house.

My sister told me afterwards that she was quite used to seeing the ghost woman and took no notice.

I WRITE on behalf of my father who, up till the incident which I now recount, was a scoffer at any stories of the supernatural. His story of the "Flying Dutchman" is as follows:

I was second mate on the large whaling steamer *Orkney Belle* on a whaling cruise. When about five miles from Reykjavik, Iceland, on an evening in January 1911, the captain and I were on the bridge and a thin mist swirled over everything. Suddenly the mist thinned out, leaving visibility easy. To our mutual horror and surprise, a sailing vessel loomed practically head-on. I rammed the helm hard-a-port and seemed to escape collision by a hair's breadth. Meanwhile the captain had signalled "Dead slow" to the engineroom.

Then, with startling suddenness, old Anderson, the carpenter, bawled: "The Flying Dutchman!" The captain and I scoffed at him, for we thought that that oft-fabled ship existed only in the minds of superstitious sailors. As the strange vessel slowly slid alongside, within a stone's throw, we noticed to our amazement that her sails were billowing, yet there was no wind at all. She was a replica of a barque I had once seen in a naval museum—high poop and carved stern—but we could not observe her name. Meanwhile practically all the crew had rushed to the side, some in terror, but unable to resist their curiosity. Not a soul was to be seen aboard this strange vessel, not a ripple did her bows make. Then, like a silver bell, for so sweet was the tone, three bells sounded as from the bowels of the phantom vessel.

Suddenly, as if in answer to a signal, the strange craft heeled starboard and disappeared into the fog which seemed to be returning.

I sailed with the old *Orkney Belle* several times, but never saw the queer ship again. If any of my old shipmates on the *Orkney Belle* are still alive, I am sure they would corroborate my statement.

ONE WINTER's evening three years ago we were all sitting round the fireside, my father, mother and we six children, older girls and school-boys, talking, laughing and generally making as much noise as a happy family can. I mention this to show that my mind was in a normal state and not morbid.

I was sewing and found I needed another reel of cotton which was in my bedroom, and ran upstairs whistling or humming. I reached the top of the first flight and was turning round to go up the next three stairs which led to my room when I met coming down them my brother, who had been killed in the war early in 1915. He was in Scottish uniform, but I could see through him. We looked at one another and I moved to one side to let him pass, but was too overcome to speak. I got my cotton and went downstairs again, but did not mention anything to the others, nor have I done to this day; but I like to think he had come to have a look round the old home, and wonder, has he been since, as shortly afterwards I left to start a home of my own in an adjoining county.

SOME YEARS ago we were living in a flat off the Edgware Road. My little boy, aged six, and myself were the only occupants of the bedroom, my boy sleeping in a bed beside my own.

I woke up one night and saw my mother, who had been dead twenty years, standing at the foot of my bed, dressed as I had last seen her. She did not speak to me, but looked at me very hard and then slowly moved backwards through the folding doors, still keeping her eyes fixed on mine. I saw her close the door.

Immediately my son, who was asleep, sat up in bed and said: " Grandma's gone, Mamma," and lay back on his pillow.

My child's words astonished me more than my mother's apparition. It has always been a mystery to me how he knew it was his grand-mother I had seen.

THE FOLLOWING incident is strictly true and I tell it just as it occurred. In the village of Cowpen, near Blyth, where I lived for seventeen years, my friend Mr. J. T. Furnass, an evangelist connected with the London Evangelisation Society, was at the time the incident occurred, conducting revival services in the mission hall in Cowpen village. At the close of each evening service it was customary for Mr. Furnass and I to go for a long walk before retiring.

One lovely bright moonlight night, when returning from our usual stroll and near to a Roman Catholic cemetery (time 11.30 p.m.) a large black dog appeared at our side. From whence it came we knew not. It had the appearance of having travelled a long distance, judging by its lolling tongue, and its tired and jaded look. It stood for half a minute or so and we both spoke to it and remarked that it must be lost, and we were about to walk on when to our great surprise the dog seemed to pull itself together and rising before our eyes, gradually spread itself out to about the size of an ordinary bed quilt, then it sailed away from whence we stood, leaving us standing spellbound. We watched it drift away over the tops of trees and finally disappear from our view travelling skyward. During Mr. Furnass's short stay at Cowpen he and I went to the same spot two or three times at the same hour, but we never again saw the dog or anything unusual.

THE CURSING PSALM

IN SOME parts of the country, especially in Cornwall, there is a general belief that if a greatly injured person, the last thing before death, reads or recites the 109th Psalm, usually called the " Cursing Psalm ", applying its threats of divine wrath to the injurer, the dying invocation is sure to take effect ("He clothed himself with cursing, like as with raiment : and it shall come into his bowels like water, and like oil into his bones. . . .").

A daunting example of the working of the Cursing Psalm comes from West Cornwall.

Many years ago in the village of Gwinear, near Redruth, there lived a young man called Thomas Thomas, who for years courted his cousin, Elizabeth Thomas, of the same village. She was very much attached to Thomas and showed the utmost trust in him, but after a small disagreement he slighted her and proposed to another girl living in Gwinear. Not content with that, he seems to have taken a peculiar delight in flaunting his new betrothal before his old love.

One Sunday afternoon Thomas took his new fiancée for a walk, passing by his old sweetheart's door deliberately to spite her. Soon after they had gone, the betrayed and wretched Elizabeth, who was known to have a quick, impulsive temper, took a rope and a Prayer Book, went into a roadway field and hanged herself near the path by which her faithless lover and his partner had passed, and would probably return.

In the event, however, the couple came home by another road. On their arrival back in the village someone asked if they had seen Elizabeth, as she could not be found anywhere. At that, Thomas wondered if he had gone too far. "Good God!" he exclaimed, "has she made away with herself? More than once she threatened she would if I slighted her." Then, as if drawn there by her spirit, he went, followed by others, directly to the tree from which they found the distraught girl hanging. On the ground at her feet was her open Prayer Book. Thomas picked it up and found a leaf turned down at the Cursing Psalm. On the leaf, too, he read her name, followed by the note : " When this you see, remember me."

Thomas knew then how she had doomed him. He said bitterly for all to hear : " I'm ruined, I'm ruined, for ever and ever."

For a long time the cheating lover wandered about like one distracted, working in various parts of the country, sometimes at mining, other times at farming, and never once returning to Gwinear. Little was seen of him by anyone who knew him until after some years, when he went south to live at Marazion, on Mount's Bay. Even then he would never venture into church for fear of hearing the 109th Psalm read, and for the same reason he dreaded to pass too close to a school.

Several times, Thomas was hurt in the mines in which he worked, and he attributed all his misfortune and bad luck to the curse of Elizabeth, whose avenging ghost, he claimed, often appeared to him, by night and day, with an open Prayer Book in her hand. He could never sleep without a friend in the room for company, and seldom even then. Although dog-tired from his labours he would often start up in bed in the small hours, crying out in agony : " Oh, dear Betsy, shut the book—do shut the book!"

The terror of his haunting apart, Thomas remained a fine, strong man and his friends advised him to get married, saying there was nothing like having a living wife to drive away the spirit of a dead sweetheart. Taking their advice he paid court to several young women of the neighbourhood and others far afield, but none would have anything to do with him. They treated him with scorn, for the story of his unfortunate first love had become well known. If he persisted, a girl would ask whether he wished to bring all the ill-wishes of the Cursing Psalm down upon her head, too.

At length, however, a widow in Marazion took pity on Thomas and consented to throw in her lot with him, after which Elizabeth's ghost apparently left him in peace for a time. But on the road to St. Hilary Church, where Thomas and the widow went to marry, the weather suddenly changed. From a calm and sunshine it became a heavy storm with thunder and lightning, and a cloud, black as night, hung over them while rain poured along the churchway path.

Thomas, trembling with fear, then saw Elizabeth's ghost with her open Prayer Book standing menacingly in the path before him. He would have turned back, had the widow not urged him on, saying she saw no ghost and had no fear of it, either. And so they were married.

They lived peaceably for a few years and Thomas's wife bore him two children. Then he was again disturbed by visits from Elizabeth's avenging phantom, and some misfortune always closely followed its appearance.

Finally Thomas, worn out in body and mind, died and was buried at St. Hilary.

Another story of the Cursing Psalm comes from the Isles of Scilly. This concerns the disastrous shipwreck of Admiral Sir Cloudesley Shovell, in 1707.

On October 21 of that year Sir Cloudesley's fleet of fifteen sailing ships were returning from the siege of Toulon, where eight French ships had been sacked and gold taken from them as they sank. The loot was considerable, the Admiral having aboard HMS *Association*, his flagship, fourteen chests of personal treasure. In fact, there was so much treasure that in a celebration party at Toulon, before sailing, he had given away presents of it to guests.

When the Admiral's fleet was nearing home, but rather off course, one of the crew of HMS *Association* who was a native of Scilly and well acquainted with the channel grew very worried, and petitioned Sir Cloudesley that the course the ship was taking would bring her on to the Scilly rocks. Sir Cloudesley and his officers were much incensed at the man's presumption, but he still boldly insisted in saying that the ship's way was wrong, and would bring them to destruction. The Admiral thereupon condemned him to be hanged for insubordination and endeavouring to excite mutiny.

When the poor seaman was tied to the mast, preparatory to his being suspended by his neck from the yardarm, he begged as a last favour, that a Psalm might be read before his execution. His request was granted and he choose the 109th, and repeated certain imprecatory portions of it after the reader. The last words he uttered were to the effect that Sir Cloudesley Shovell and those who saw him hanged should never reach the land alive.

Little heed was paid to him, and his body, shrouded in a hammock with a shot to sink it, was cast into the sea.

Hours later the weather changed for the worse and the fleet was in real trouble. Some of the more superstitious members of the crew now recalled the dying man's curse, which seemed all the more awful when, in the gale, the dead man's corpse, divested of its rude winding sheet, was thrown up by the sea to float near the *Association*. The body followed the doomed ship with its face turned towards her, until she struck on the Gilstone Rock, a few miles out from St. Agnes, Scilly. She went down in minutes.

Two other warships were wrecked and sank with the *Association*, with the loss of nearly two thousand officers and men. The flagship suffered the worst disaster, only one man from her living to tell the tale. This was a seaman who saved himself by floating on a piece of timber to Hellweathers reef, some three miles from Gilstone, where he was marooned for some days before the weather permitted any boat to approach and take him off to St. Agnes.

Sir Cloudesley Shovell perished along with his two sons, his naked body being washed ashore at Port Hellick, St. Mary's, about eight miles from the Gilstone. He was found lying on a hatch of the ship on which he had tried to save himself, and a little dog lay dead beside him.

At least, Sir Cloudesley was believed to have been dead when washed ashore, but thirty years later the truth came out. A woman who was the first to find his body, coveting an emerald ring on one of the fingers, saw that he was still breathing, and callously extinguished the flickering life. She confessed to the crime on her deathbed, when she produced the ring to the clergyman attending her to administer the last rites.

Such had been the sweet revenge of the hanged seaman.

THE MASTER OF THE SARAH EMMA

SOME years ago I stayed a night in an hotel close to the North Road Station, Plymouth. Among the few guests there was a gentleman named Grant. He got to know of my interest in the supernatural and, seeking me out, told me the following story, which, he said, was his one experience with the unknown and one he had not felt able to relate to anyone at length before, for fear of scepticism. Yet all the facts of the story could be verified.

Grant said it happened in Liverpool when he was a boy. He was living with an uncle in Duke Street, and his chief delight at the time was wandering about the docks looking at the ships. One day a young friend of his came along in great glee to say that his dad had bought an old ship lying in one of the small docks for timber. The men had not yet started demolishing her and if they went to look her over one of the men would row them across to the vessel.

The two boys went off at once.

They learned that the ship, a small brig, had not been to sea for more than twenty years. She had been built at the beginning of the last century and employed for the greater part of her career in the fruit trade with Barcelona and other eastern Spanish seaports. As they were rowed out towards her they had never seen a more dreary or dilapidated looking hulk.

Once on board her there was little to see, only a couple of bare masts and a wheel, and an equally forlorn looking deck-house. Yards, canvas, ropes, were all absent. The spirit of adventure, however, was on both boys, and making their way rather gingerly over the slippery deck to the main hatchway, they descended the companion ladder to the passage leading to the cabins and forecastle. They found the whole place swimming in water, while occasional loud splashes and quick scampering announced the presence of rats.

They had finished exploring all they dared, and were retracing their steps along the passage leading to the companion ladder, when Grant's friend suddenly gasped with surprise and gripped him by the arm, asking sharply, "Whatever was that?"

Grant looked up and there before them in the act of coming down the ladder was a tall man clad in the sort of costume sailors used to wear in the early part of the nineteenth century. The light from above deck falling directly on his face threw it into strong relief. It was that of a middle-aged man with very pronounced features, black curly hair, beard and whiskers, though his cheeks were absolutely colourless.

He came slowly and leisurely down, and advanced straight towards the two boys. As he drew near they instinctively shrank against the wall. He did not seem to notice them, however, but walking on past them, still with the same slow, leisurely tread, he entered one of the cabins they had just explored.

Grant's friend, looking very pale and scared, caught hold of Grant's arm and half dragged him up the companion ladder and on to the deck.

"Did you notice anything peculiar about that man apart from his clothes?" he said, as they stood waiting for the boat which was to bring them to shore.

"I thought it odd that he never once looked at us," Grant replied.

"That's true," his friend observed, "but there was something else besides. His feet *made no sound*. He walked absolutely noiselessly."

"What do you think then?" Grant said, an uncomfortable feeling stealing over him.

"What do I think?" whispered the other boy, casting a terrified glance in the direction of the companion hatchway. "I don't think at all, I'm certain. What we saw was no man at all but a ghost. This old hulk is *haunted*."

The rowboat could not arrive too soon for them.

The day after their strange adventure Grant's friend came running to see him in a rare state of excitement.

"What I told you yesterday," he said, "is perfectly true. That old hulk *is* haunted, and if you will come with me to the man who sold it to my dad he will tell us all about it."

Grant went with him to a house close to the Victoria Dock where this man lived. He was a very old man, near ninety, but he still retained that kind of breeziness which long association with the sea almost invariably breeds.

The boys then learned from him that he had in fact once sailed in the old ship—he had served his apprenticeship aboard her. He was not at all surprised to hear about the ghost and, in a clear steady voice, told this story to the two boys, which I put down in his own words as Grant described them for me.

"It was a hot, sultry night in the summer of 1825 (*the old man began*). I had been at sea then just over two years, and we were lying at anchor in a small bay a little to the south of Barcelona. The captain and the first mate had gone ashore early in the morning to arrange for a cargo of fruit being shipped on board the following day. When I went below deck at the end of the second dog watch they had not returned, and speculations were rife as to what could have detained them so long. There was another apprentice on board, and we shared a small cabin next to the captain's.

"Well, it didn't take me long to slip off my clothes and tumble into my bunk, for I was very tired, and in a few minutes I was fast asleep. I awoke with a start, to hear in the distance a wild, prolonged scream. It seemed to come from the shore. There was something so harrowing about it that the blood in my veins froze.

"I sat up and called out 'Jack! Did you hear that?'

"'Yes,' my companion, whose name was Jack Weston (he is still alive and director of a big shipping firm) replied. 'I did. It was probably someone being done in by one of those dagos. Murders are as plentiful as blackberries in and around Barcelona, you know. I wonder if the old man and Masters (he was the first mate) are back yet?'

"'I wonder too,' I said, and lying down again I tried to go to sleep. It was a vain effort, however. My thoughts kept going back to that cry and I became full of a strong sense of foreboding. Could it have had anything to do with our captain?

"I got up and going to the porthole looked out. The night was superb. Overhead an ultramarine sky, a full silvery moon and myriads of bright stars; below and on either side, perfectly calm water, glittering and shining like the scales on a fish's back, while in front was a long strip of silver sand bordered by the dark forms of gently nodding firs and beeches, with away in the far distance the dark outlines of heavily wooded mountains. It was the sort of thing one sees in picture postcards and seems too good to be true.

"Well, I stood and gazed at the scene for a long time, and all the while I could hear nothing but the lap, lap of the water against the ship's sides and the creaking and groaning of the idle rudder. Finally, the impulse seizing me to go on deck I yielded to it, and left the cabin as noiselessly as possible.

"I was in the act of ascending the companion ladder when Captain Gale—that was the name of our skipper—suddenly appeared at the head of the steps and began to descend."

"What did the captain look like?" Grant timidly interrupted to ask the old man.

"What was Captain Gale like? Why, he was a tall man with rather marked features and black hair, beard and whiskers. On this day, however, he looked ghastly pale.

"He came down and when he was close to me, I touched my cap and said, 'Good evening, sir. I am. . . .'

"I was about to add something else but he did not give me time. Without apparently seeing me he walked past and went straight into his cabin, slamming the door to behind him.

"I can hear that slam now.

"Thinking this rather odd but supposing he was vexed about something, I went on deck and going up to the second mate, who was on duty, I said, 'I see the captain's back!'

"The mate stared at me. 'What do you mean?' he said.

" 'The captain's back,' I repeated. 'When did he come aboard?'

"The mate's face hardened. 'He hasn't come aboard,' he growled. 'Are you trying to have me on?'

" 'No, mister,' I said, and I explained to him how I had just met the captain on the companion ladder.

"I never saw a man look queerer—plainly wondering what I was up to. He stuck out that neither the captain nor the first mate had returned yet, and it ended in our going below deck and knocking at the captain's cabin. There was no reply. We knocked again, and as there was still no response we opened the door and looked in. Not a sign of the captain was to be seen anywhere.

" 'You've been fooling me,' the second mate said grimly, and I could see I was for it if I continued to argue. So I went back to my cabin while he resumed duty on deck.

"Next morning there was still no sign of the two missing officers and in the end we were obliged to return to Liverpool without them.

"Their fate was an absolute mystery. The ship, however, was haunted. A ghostly figure, the exact counterpart of Captain Gale, was constantly seen descending the companion ladder and going into the captain's cabin. The crew in consequence were much demoralised and on our reaching port they left in a body. That was how the Sarah Emma first got the reputation for being haunted."

"The Sarah Emma?" Grant exclaimed. "You can't see any name on her now."

"I suppose not," said the old man. "She hasn't had a coat of paint on her for five and twenty years, but that was the name by which she was known when first I sailed in her. She subsequently changed it, not once but many times. And all owing to the ghost.

"Although I stuck to the Sarah Emma, I didn't go to that part of Spain again for several years, not indeed until I was second mate. It then so happened that we came to an anchorage one day in the same bay and pretty well the same spot, and as there was every prospect of our remaining there for some time I obtained leave to spend a day or two ashore.

"When I landed I had no idea where to go or what to do, but after wandering about for some time I eventually decided to penetrate inland and see a little of the scenery that had so captivated me from the ship. After strolling along for some distance I came to a spot where several paths met, and was debating which of them to take when I suddenly saw before me a figure that seemed strangely familiar. It was that of a tall man in sailor's rig. As his back was towards me I could not see his face but from his general appearance I gathered that he was English. Cheered at the sight of a fellow countryman I followed him, and in a few minutes arrived in sight of a small inn.

"He went right up to the front door of it, and then halting, turned slowly round and looked at me. To my amazement it was Captain Gale—and what clinched matters was that he smiled at me.

"Before I could do or say anything, however, he had turned the handle of the door and entered the building.

"Trembling all over with excitement I at once approached the door and knocked. No one came at first, but on my knocking again a woman emerged, and in broken English enquired what I wanted. I told her a night's lodging, adding that I had just seen an old friend of mine enter the house.

"'An old friend of yours?' she replied. 'That is impossible—there is no friend of yours here. There is no one in the house at all but myself.'

"I told her she was mistaken and that I was quite positive Captain Gale was in the building, as I had just seen him pass through the doorway. She looked a little uneasy, I fancied, at the mention of Captain Gale, but she still emphatically denied there was anyone in the house saving herself.

"Seeing it was useless to argue I changed the subject and asked her to let me have the best room she could, and ordered a meal.

"Well, nothing of any moment happened till the night. I had gone to my room, but not liking the appearance of the bed, which was a huge fourposter, made use of an armchair instead. I had been in it for perhaps an hour or so, trying to sleep, when I heard footsteps very softly approach my door, and after an interval of several minutes, during which I felt someone was listening, the bed gave a loud creak.

"I at once looked at it and in the moonlight saw to my horror the big canopy on the top slowly commencing to descend. It did not, however, get far, for more footsteps came along the passage outside and it at once stopped. There was then an altercation carried on in low voices, a sudden scuffle, a sharp cry of pain, and a loud thud. Leaping to my feet I rushed to the door and threw it open. Lying on the floor outside was a man whom I recognised at once. It was Masters, the first mate of the Sarah Emma, the man who had so mysteriously disappeared along with the captain several years before.

"He recognised me too, and bidding me kneel down and listen, he made an extraordinary confession.

"Masters said that he and Captain Gale had come to that house, that they had both had the room that had been given to me, that Captain Gale had been murdered, and that he owed his preservation to the fact that not liking the appearance of the bed he had slept in consequence on the floor. He said he was so infuriated with the murderess that he would have killed her offhand, had she not gone on her knees and implored pity.

"This moved him so he had spared her, and in the end she inveigled him into staying with her, and they married. He declared he had been very unhappy, however, as she had the most ungovernable and cruel temper. He said he often had to be away from the house for nights together and he had on more than one occasion suspected her of enticing people into the inn during his absence and murdering them.

"He said on this particular night, returning unexpectedly, he had surprised her in the act and on his remonstrating with her, she had stabbed him.

"This was Masters' tale, and when he had finished it I carried him at his request into the parlour downstairs, and then left him.

"Hurrying to the shore I got into a boat and rowed right away to the Sarah Emma. Nothing was done that night but in the morning the captain, myself and several others of the crew rowed in to Barcelona and reported the matter to the British Consul there.

He at once communicated with the local police, with the result that about a dozen of them accompanied us to the inn, only to find it deserted. The wounded man and the woman had both disappeared, and what subsequently became of them I was never able to find out.

"As for the Sarah Emma, she still continued to be haunted by the ghost of Captain Gale, and from what you boys have told me she still is."

So ended the old seaman's story in this account told me by Mr. Grant at the Plymouth hotel, a strangely involved tale which he assured me could be verified from many sources including his boyhood friend in Liverpool; descendants of the old man, who had heard the same story from his lips; and more particularly from the actual records of the ill-starred Sarah Emma and from others who had sailed in her.

THE POOL OF HORRORS

THERE is no pool of water in England which has been the scene of more suicides and murders, and consequently, which is more sinister in reputation, than that known as the Suicide Pool in Epping Forest. Among the many weird things that are said to occur at this pool every now and then is the ghostly rehearsal of any impending tragedy, and it was a rumour such as this that prompted me to spend a night by the pool.

When I arrived at the scene of my vigil, the rich autumn moonlight gilded the surface of the water where, in places, it was free from the shadows of the neighbouring trees. If only those trees could speak, I thought, what dark secrets they could tell.

I was thinking then of the mystery concerning Emma Morgan, a pretty young servant who was last seen alive walking through Woodford, Essex, in the direction of Epping Forest with a baby in her arms.

Emma had been in the service of a wealthy Tottenham tradesman who had dismissed her because, although a married woman, she had encouraged numerous lovers, and by one of them had had the child. Being homeless, for her husband would not take her back, no enquiries were made about her, and probably never would have been, had not her body and that of the child been found not, strange to say, in the pool, but close to it.

Both Emma and her baby had been most horribly murdered, and their fiendish assailant was never brought to book.

I thought of this and other tragedies as I stood on the edge of the pool, peering into its dark, still water and listening to the rustling of the wind through the half naked branches of the neighbouring trees.

Every now and then a dog from afar off howled and a night bird wailed, and once, from close behind me, came a noise so like a cough that I swung round fully expecting to see someone, but although in the moonlight everything around me stood out clearly and distinctly no one was to be seen.

Soon after this I heard a faint, feeble cry, like that of a child in pain. Again I swung round, and again I saw nothing. Then, from a distance, came the sound of a strange tramping, the steady march of a host of people. On and on towards the pool came this tramping, solemn and in step, but although I heard it distinctly I could see no one.

Then, within a few feet of me, the tramping suddenly ceased, and I visualised very clearly a number of black-robed figures standing with bowed heads, supporting in their midst a coffin, and apparently waiting for something to happen. A noise from near at hand made me look round, and though I still saw no physical presence, my mental vision brought to me the image of a young man with a white, evil face. He was dressed in a grey suit and he was bending over the body of a woman.

Picking up the body, he came staggering with it to the pool and threw the body into the still, gleaming water. For some seconds he stood scowling at the body as it floated on the surface. Then, muttering angrily to himself, he walked away.

Directly he was out of sight, I again heard the slow, measured tramping and sensed that the procession of black-robed figures had moved on.

I waited till all was silent again and then came away.

The experience of the night was so vivid and puzzling that I described it to an old inhabitant of Epping. In my description of the woman he was particularly interested, and told me that, according to newspaper cuttings he had, my account of her tallied exactly with that of a woman who had been murdered and thrown into the pool by an unknown person in the summer of 1887.

The same man then told me of a strange experience of his own.

He said that early one morning, shortly before the first world war, when taking a walk in the neighbourhood of the Suicide Pool, he had been horrified to see the body of a man lying face downwards in a ditch, and standing by it a stout, stockily built, shabbily dressed man with a gun.

He was still more horrified when, just as he was about to approach and question the man, both he and the body in the ditch disappeared.

The incident, however, was more or less explained, he thought, by the fact that two days later, the body of an ex-N.C.O. was actually found lying face downwards in the same ditch. The circumstances plainly pointed to murder, but no one was ever apprehended and the man's death remains one of the many unsolved mysteries of Epping Forest.

THE WEEPING TOMB OF KILMALLOCK

In the south-west of Ireland, in County Limerick, lie the ruins of what was once the imposing Abbey of Kilmallock. At the end of one of the ruined aisles is a heap of stones, all that is left of the tomb of Sir Maurice Fitzgerald, better known as the White Knight.

They are called the Weeping Stones, and there is a remarkable story associated with them, one embracing both tradition and fact.

Fitzgerald, a fierce warrior figure of the Middle Ages, lived in the grim Castle of Michelstown, in County Cork, and earned the title of the White Knight from the suit of very light armour that he wore. He was not of ancient Irish descent and in fact his connection with Ireland was of short duration, but he had a great reputation as a soldier and much of the land in the south belonged either to him or to his numerous relatives.

Although a generally hard man he had one soft spot, and that was for his son Edmund, a tall, handsome youth.

Fitzgerald had great aims for Edmund, whom he wanted to marry either the daughter of a powerful English nobleman, or the daughter of one of the famous Irish chieftains of the north. He was most anxious for his son not only to live up to the fighting reputation of the family but to increase it.

Edmund, however, had little ambition along these lines. He was of a dreamy, sensitive, retiring nature, and would far sooner have been a monk or hermit than a soldier.

One fine summer evening Edmund mounted his chestnut charger and rode off, as usual, in the direction of the Kilworth Mountains, which were one of his favourite haunts. Lost in reverie he rode slowly on, plunging deeper and deeper into a region which at last became totally unknown to him.

Suddenly his horse shied and all but unseated him. When he had calmed the animal Edmund saw that he had been riding along a narrow path through a dense and gloomy wood. Standing under the wide-spreading branches of a giant elm tree was the figure of a woman. She was short and bent, and clothed from head to foot in black.

She laughed, and, thrusting her head forward, said in a harsh, man-like voice, "Do you not know me? They call me the Witch of Kilworth, and I am on my way to the Hole in the Rocks to see how the Blue Lights burn. Do you want to know your fate and how long you have to live, Edmund Fitzgerald?"

"How do you know my name, old woman?" he asked.

"I am in league with the Powers that rule man's future," the hag replied, "and if you will come with me I will show you yours."

Edmund hesitated. The Church forbade him to have anything to do with superstition and magic, but his love of adventure was strong. The hag laughed again at his indecision.

"Fear not," she said, "I have nought toward you—at least as yet —but friendly feelings. Follow where I lead and no harm will befall you."

Stepping out from under the tree she set off along a path that ran at right angles to the one he had been following. Crossing himself several times in rapid succession, Edmund turned his horse's head and followed closely at her heels.

On and on she led him, over hill, across torrents and through rock-strewn defiles, until at length they emerged into a small, grassy open space confronting a high, gaunt cliff, in the face of which was a black cavern.

"See!" she cried, waving a skinny hand in the direction of the cave. "The lights—the Candles of Fate. Come and look—yours is among them."

She advanced again as she spoke, and Edmund now saw a number of mysterious blue lights, like great candle flames, flickering in the mouth of the cavern. Keeping close behind his guide he followed her to the entrance to the grotto, and then descending from his horse he went into the cave after her.

He could feel presences all round him. Instinct told him that the candles he saw floating apparently in mid-air and emitting the bluish-green flames were, in reality, supported by phantoms. They—the candles—surrounded him on all sides, some being quite tall and seemingly just lighted, and others, very, very short; in fact, almost burned out.

"There is one for every person in this country," the hag said, "and the height of them denotes the number of years each man, woman and child has still to live. That is yours!"

She pointed to a candle that was only about a quarter burned.

"You see, you have many years to live yet. Satisfactory, is it not? But crow not, fair gentleman, for sorrow will come to you before long, to such an extent that, times without number, you will wish that candle but a guttering wick. Now look!"

Turning round, she pointed towards the mouth of the grotto. Edmund obeyed, and drew back in wonder, for gone was the scenery he had last looked on before entering the cavern. Facing him now and sweeping horizonward was a great drift of solemn pines, the like of which for size he had never seen either in County Cork or in County Limerick. Or so, at least, it seemed to him in that hour of mystery.

Far behind the trees the evening sky had chilled to a deep wash of blood red, across which lay a long bar of black cloud. Under the trees was a high grey-stone wall, in the centre of which was a wooden door studded with brass-headed nails.

As Edmund stared at this door it opened, and a young girl in a loose flowing garment of white appeared. Stepping forward she advanced towards the grotto, the moonbeams throwing into strongest relief her face and figure. She was tall and slim, and the extraordinary beauty of her features was enhanced by a mass of bright gold hair that fell about her neck and shoulders.

But it was her eyes that took his attention most. They were wide and blue, blue as the waters of Killarney, and in the moonlight they shone with a starlike lustre. She smiled as he looked at her— then shuddered, and gazing piteously up at him from under the long lashes which had lain momentarily upon her pale cheeks, held out her hands, as if inviting him to take hold of them.

Edmund sprang forward and was about to reach out to her when the hag behind gave a harsh cry, and the girl and all the tableau in the background at once vanished.

"Son of the Knight of Michelstown," she said, "she whom you saw is your fate, and you will find her within the grey walls of Kilmallock Abbey."

"Her name, old woman? How is she called?" Edmund demanded.

There was no response, only a blinding flash. He staggered forward and, when his vision cleared, found himself standing outside the grotto by the side of his horse. He peered into the cavern, which was now in total darkness, and shouted to the old woman. There was no reply, and yielding to a sudden terror,

Edmund vaulted into his saddle and rode off.

For the next two or three days he had constant mental pictures of the beautiful girl in white, and his desire to put his experience to the test and see if it was only a dream at length became so great that he decided to visit the Abbey of Kilmallock. At first he thought of making the trip alone, but the distance being rather far, and the roads infested with enemies of his clan, he eventually took with him one of his father's retainers, a man he believed he could trust to hold his tongue.

They made the journey without mishap, and when he arrived at a bend in the road that led right to Kilmallock, Edmund saw confronting him, almost within a stone's throw, a great sweep of giant pines, and in the front of them a long grey wall with a big nail-studded door in the centre of it.

He recognised the tableau in an instant; it was the exact counterpart of what he had seen in the old hag's cave. While he was staring at it, the door in the wall suddenly opened and a procession of girls, all in white, began slowly to approach the spot where he and his henchman were stationed. As they drew nearer he eagerly scanned each face, and to his great joy saw in one of the girls who walked in the very last row of all, the living likeness of his vision-girl of the golden locks.

Not daring to reveal himself, for several nuns accompanied the procession, he waited with his retainer till the girls had all returned to the seclusion of the abbey. He then gave thought as to how he could discover who the fair girl was, and exchange word with her. For hours he lingered in sight of the building but could devise no feasible scheme, and he was beginning to give way to despair when the door opened again and an old crone came out, carrying an earthenware pitcher.

He approached her, and the gift of a little silver brought him the necessary information. The crone told him that the girl with the golden locks was Elgiva O'Rourke, daughter of the Prince of Brefni.

This was dismaying news, for of all the enemies of the Fitzgeralds of Michelstown, the O'Rourkes were by far the most formidable, and there was none his father hated with a fiercer bitterness. Indeed, Edmund feared for the girl's safety should his father discover where she was, and he warned his retainer that on no account must he repeat a word of what had been said.

Thinking now only of the girl's welfare, Edmund resolved to return home and visit the spot again in the near future, but alone. Accordingly, the two men rode off.

All might have gone well had it not been for the frailty of the retainer. One day, when under the influence of some of the good vintage of the White Knight's cellars, he allowed his tongue to wag a little too freely and disclosed the secret of Elgiva O'Rourke's whereabouts.

A meanly disposed page, eager for a reward, reported what he had heard to the White Knight, and, full of wrath at discovering one of the tribe he hated being so close as within a score or so miles of him, Maurice Fitzgerald rode for Kilmallock and demanded that Elgiva be handed over to him.

The Abbess yielded; unless she wanted the whole place pulled down about her ears she could scarcely have done otherwise, for Maurice had a considerable force at his back.

Surprisingly, however, when once he had Elgiva in his power he did not treat her badly, at least not then. He took her back with him to the Castle of Michelstown and entrusted her to the keeping of certain of his female retainers.

Elgiva's presence there soon became known to Edmund, who, waiting his opportunity, at length made himself known to her and passionately declared his love. Thereafter the lovers used to meet clandestinely in a wood adjoining the castle.

The White Knight inevitably got to know of this and was secretly making arrangements to have Elgiva sent away when Edmund forestalled him by eloping with Elgiva. He rode with her, accompanied by one faithful retainer, to the Abbey of Kilmallock, and on arriving there, implored the Abbess to secure the services of a priest, so that they could be married at once. The Abbess, though she feared the anger of the White Knight, was overcome by Edmund's entreaties and sent a messenger for a cleric.

They were actually in the middle of the marriage ceremony when into the abbey, sword in hand, burst the infuriated Maurice Fitzgerald. A spy had informed him of his son's flight.

Shouting out his hatred of the O'Rourkes, Fitzgerald rushed at the terrified girl and, before she had time to avoid him, stabbed her in the breast. She sank to the floor and, fixing her eyes on her murderer, gasped, "For this cruel deed of yours, Heaven will punish you! Your doom will be to weep, to weep and weep—*even after you are dead!*"

She said no more, but, with a tender glance at Edmund, expired.

The anger of the White Knight did not, however, end there. He sent the sorrow-stricken Edmund, under strong escort, to a remote spot on his lands and kept him there for years, while he had the faithful retainer put in a small chasm or cleft between two rocks and left there to starve to death.

Only in recent times, when the foundations of the castle of the late Earl of Kingston were being laid, the skeleton of this wretched man was found in the exact position tradition had described. He had died, so it was affirmed, in the most dreadful agony.

But the malicious acts of the White Knight were not to pass unchallenged. As soon as the O'Rourkes heard of Elgiva's murder, they gathered and rode against Maurice Fitzgerald, and though they themselves were almost entirely destroyed, they inflicted terrible losses on the White Knight's followers.

Other misfortunes came in their wake, and to the day of his death the White Knight knew no peace. He was buried in a splendid tomb in Kilmallock Abbey, and the very next day the doom pronounced by the dying Elgiva was found to be at work. A kinsman of the White Knight visiting the tomb found on its surface many spots of what, apparently, was water, and the same thing happening the following day he mentioned the occurrence to the then Abbess, and very soon the whole county got to hear of it.

The phenomenon continued. No matter how fine or dry the day, there was always moisture on the White Knight's marble effigy, and there was no accounting for its presence there, saving on the basis of the supernatural.

Unquestionably, those who witnessed the phenomenon argued, and they were many, Elgiva's word had come true—the White Knight, even though dead, was still lamenting, with bitter tears, his foul crime.

The phenomenon went on through long centuries, until some years ago, when the tomb was broken open and practically demolished by an avaricious soldier, who dreamed several times in succession that it contained a treasure. As a matter of fact, it contained only some bones, a sword, spurs, and some broken pieces of armour.

But still the heap of stones that was once the White Knight's tomb continued to weep its strange tears.